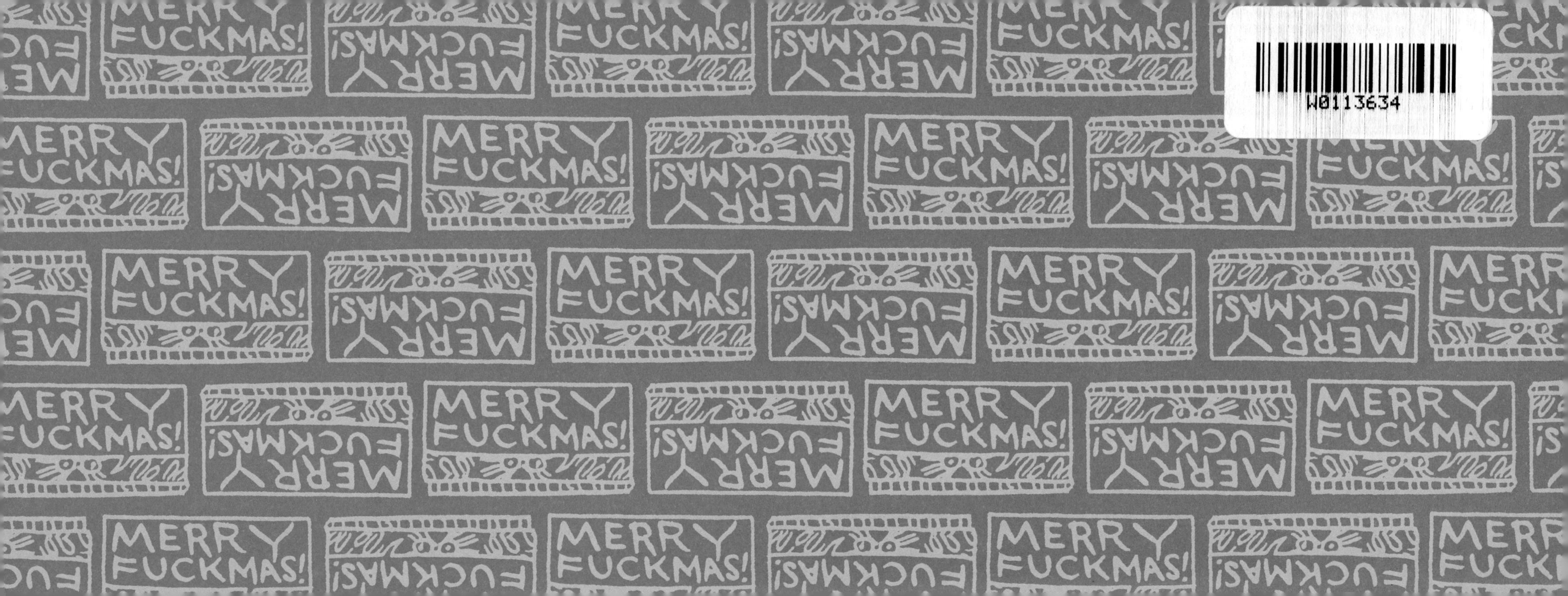
MERRY FUCKMAS!

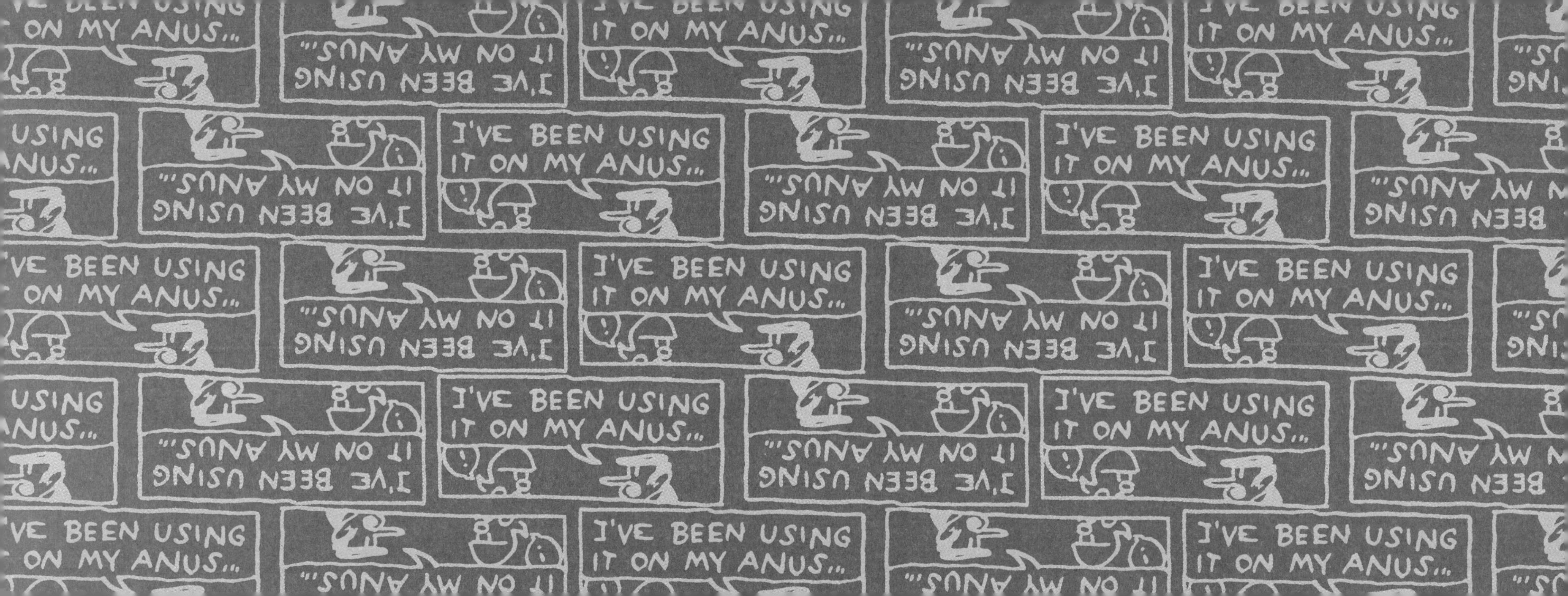
I'VE BEEN USING IT ON MY ANUS...

LITTLE MAAKI

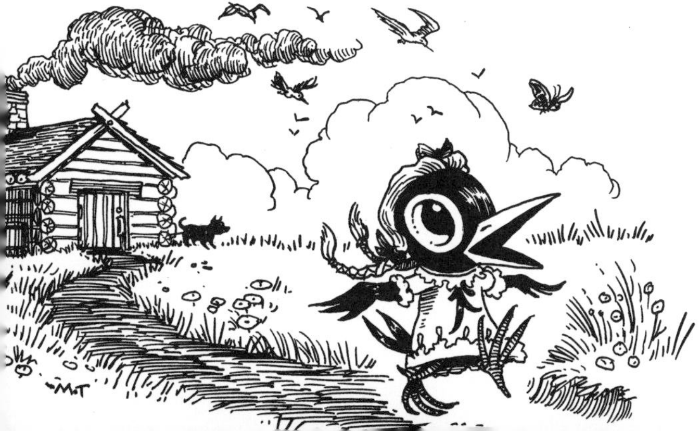

ON THE PRAIRIE

OTHER BOOKS BY TONY MILLIONAIRE

Maakies collections from Fantagraphics

* *Maakies* (out of print)
* *The House at Maakies Corner* (out of print)
* *When We Were Very Maakies* (out of print)
Der Struwwelmaakies
Premillennial Maakies (reprints *Maakies*)
The Maakies With the Wrinkled Knees
Drinky Crow's Maakies Treasury (collects * above)

also from Fantagraphics

Billy Hazelnuts
Billy Hazelnuts and the Crazy Bird
Mighty Mite: The Earmite

also from Dark Horse Books

The Art of Tony Millionaire

"Sock Monkey" graphic novels rom Dark Horse Books

The Adventures of Tony Millionaire's Sock Monkey
The Collected Works of Tony Millionaire's Sock Monkey
Sock Monkey: Uncle Gabby
Sock Monkey: The Inches Incident

childrens' books from Dark Horse Books

Sock Monkey: A Children's Book (out of print)
Sock Monkey: The Glass Doorknob
Little and Large
That Darn Yarn

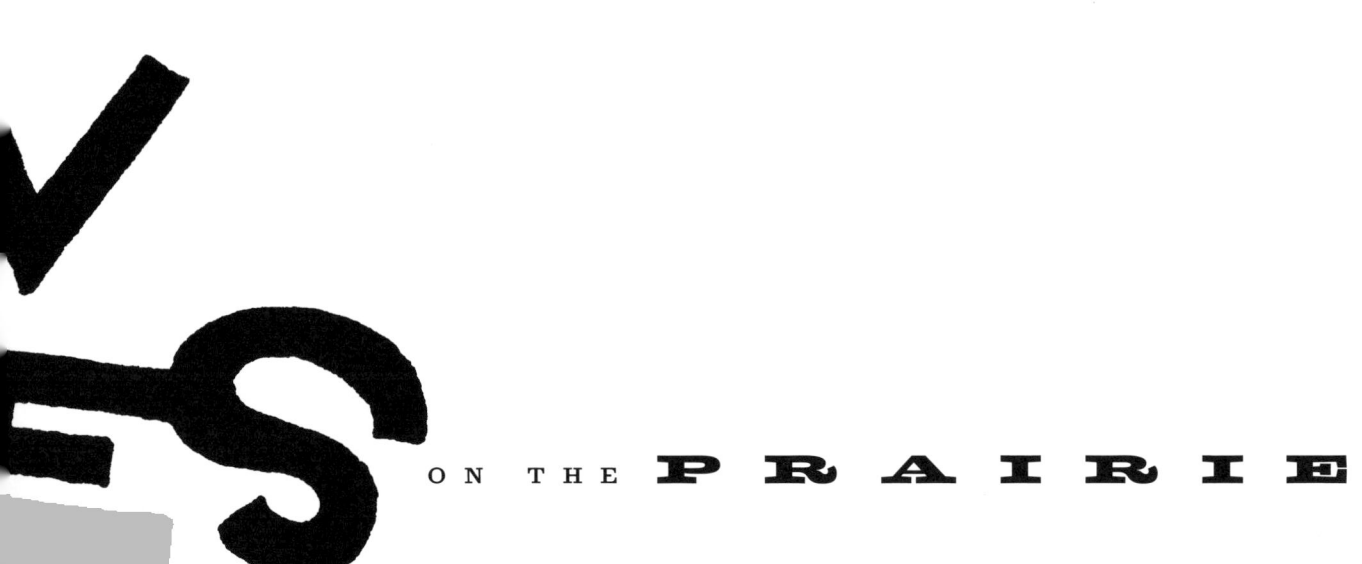

FANTAGRAPHICS BOOKS
7563 Lake City Way NE
Seattle WA 98115

Edited by Kim Thompson
Designed by Chip Kidd
Production by Paul Baresh
Associate Editor: Eric Reynolds
Published by Gary Groth and Kim Thompson

To receive a free catalog of comics, call 1-800-657-1100 or write us at Fantagraphics Books, 7563 Lake City Way NE, Seattle, WA 98115.

Distributed in the U.S. by W.W. Norton and Company, Inc. (212-354-5500)
Distributed in Canada by Canadian Manda Group (416-516-0911)
Distributed in the United Kingdom by Turnaround Distribution (208-829-3009)

Visit the Maakies website at www.maakies.com
Visit the Fantagraphics website at www.fantagraphics.com

First printing: September, 2010

ISBN-13: 978-1-60699-392-7

Printed in China

FOR LENNY RICHARDSON

TONY MILLIONAIRE

BY BOOK KIDD

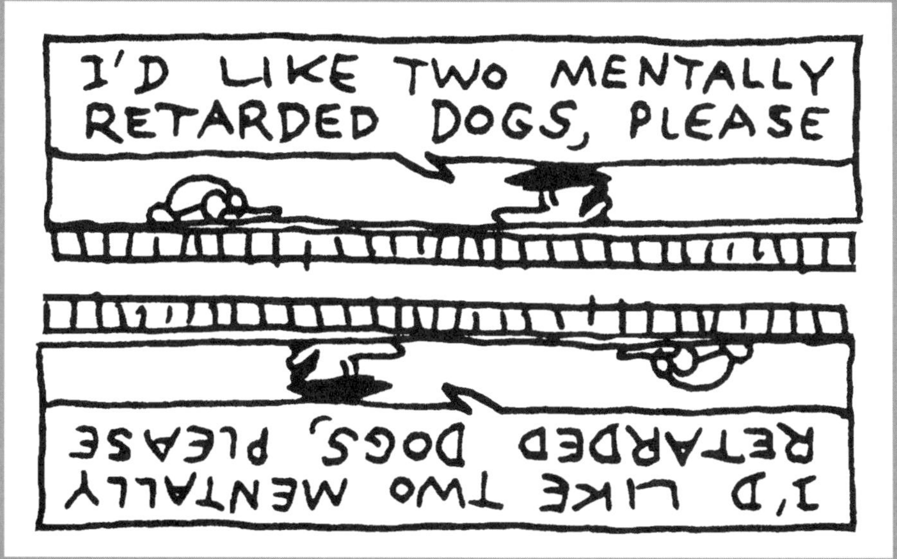
I'D LIKE TWO MENTALLY RETARDED DOGS, PLEASE

CHIP DESIGN

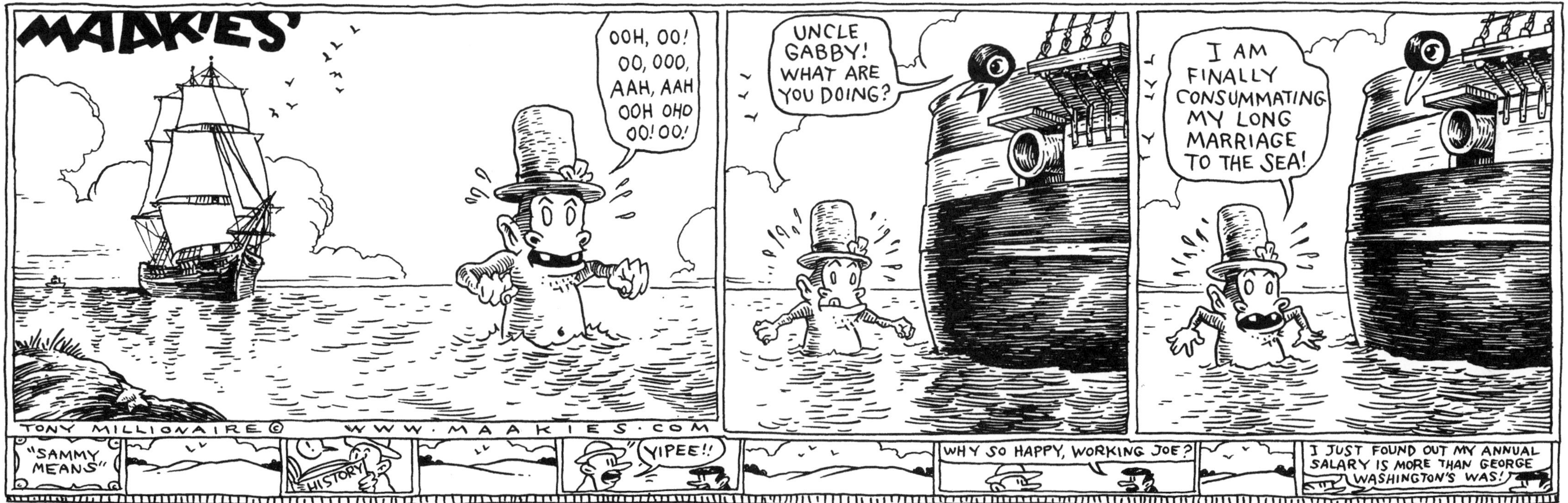
MAAKIES
OOH, OO! OO, OOO, AAH, AAH OOH OHO OO! OO!
TONY MILLIONAIRE ©
WWW.MAAKIES.COM
UNCLE GABBY! WHAT ARE YOU DOING?
I AM FINALLY CONSUMMATING MY LONG MARRIAGE TO THE SEA!
"SAMMY MEANS"
HISTORY
YIPEE!!
WHY SO HAPPY, WORKING JOE?
I JUST FOUND OUT MY ANNUAL SALARY IS MORE THAN GEORGE WASHINGTON'S WAS!

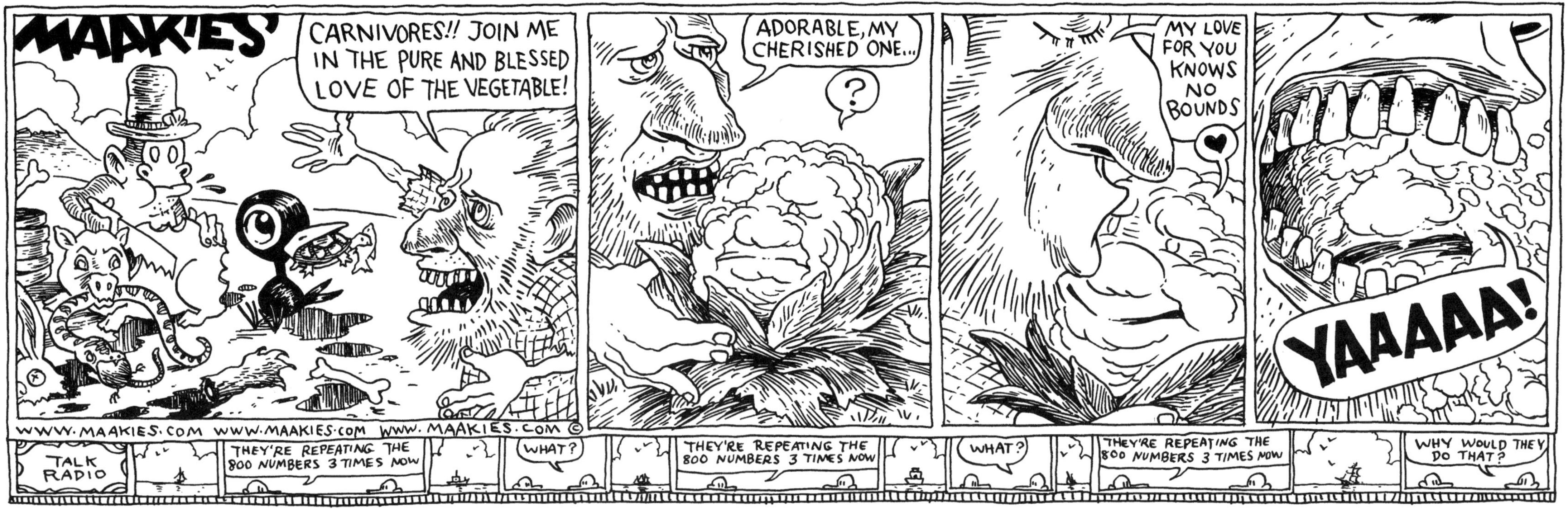
MAAKIES
CARNIVORES!! JOIN ME IN THE PURE AND BLESSED LOVE OF THE VEGETABLE!
ADORABLE, MY CHERISHED ONE...
?
MY LOVE FOR YOU KNOWS NO BOUNDS
YAAAAA!
WWW.MAAKIES.COM WWW.MAAKIES.COM WWW.MAAKIES.COM ©
TALK RADIO
THEY'RE REPEATING THE 800 NUMBERS 3 TIMES NOW
WHAT?
THEY'RE REPEATING THE 800 NUMBERS 3 TIMES NOW
WHAT?
THEY'RE REPEATING THE 800 NUMBERS 3 TIMES NOW
WHY WOULD THEY DO THAT?

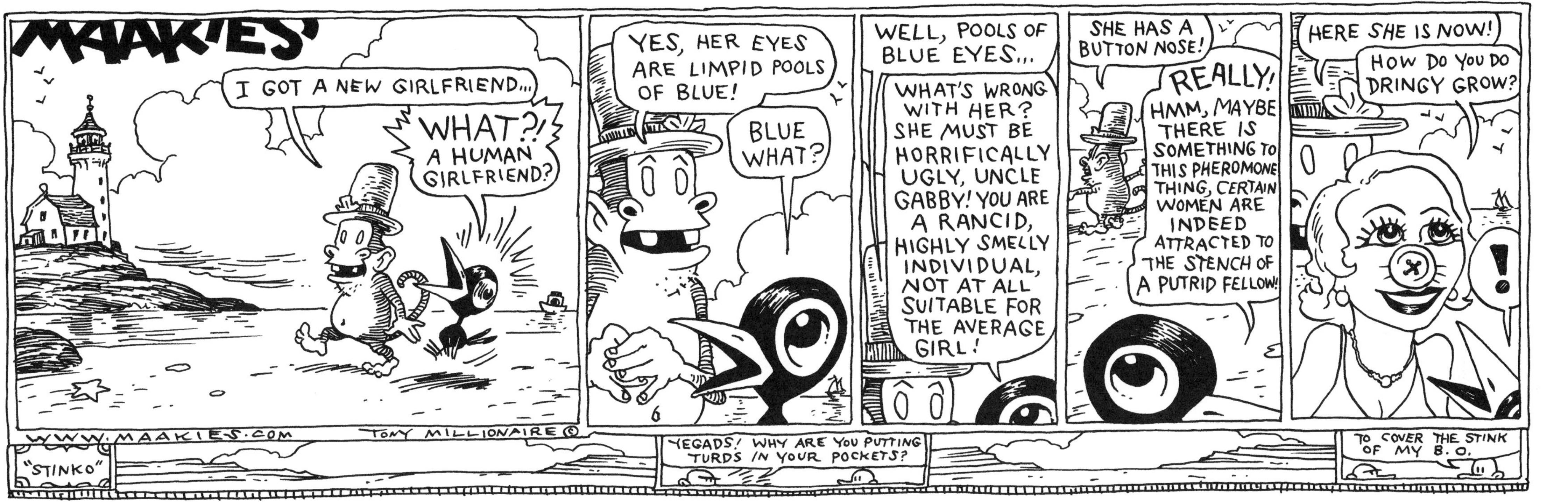

MAAKIES
I GOT A NEW GIRLFRIEND...
WHAT?! A HUMAN GIRLFRIEND?
YES, HER EYES ARE LIMPID POOLS OF BLUE!
BLUE WHAT?
WELL, POOLS OF BLUE EYES...
WHAT'S WRONG WITH HER? SHE MUST BE HORRIFICALLY UGLY, UNCLE GABBY! YOU ARE A RANCID, HIGHLY SMELLY INDIVIDUAL, NOT AT ALL SUITABLE FOR THE AVERAGE GIRL!
SHE HAS A BUTTON NOSE!
REALLY! HMM, MAYBE THERE IS SOMETHING TO THIS PHEROMONE THING, CERTAIN WOMEN ARE INDEED ATTRACTED TO THE STENCH OF A PUTRID FELLOW!
HERE SHE IS NOW!
HOW DO YOU DO DRINGY GROW?
!
WWW.MAAKIES.COM
TONY MILLIONAIRE ©
"STINKO"
YEGADS! WHY ARE YOU PUTTING TURDS IN YOUR POCKETS?
TO COVER THE STINK OF MY B.O.

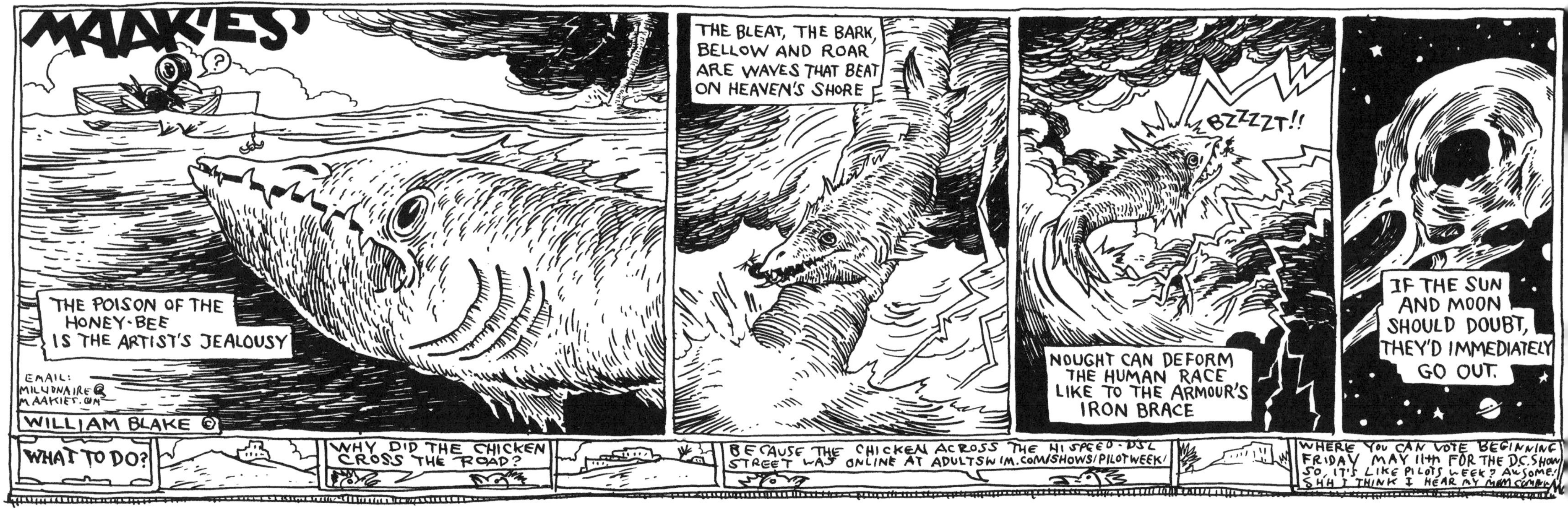

MAAKIES
?
EMAIL: MILLIONAIRE@MAAKIES.COM
WILLIAM BLAKE ©
THE POISON OF THE HONEY-BEE IS THE ARTIST'S JEALOUSY
THE BLEAT, THE BARK, BELLOW AND ROAR ARE WAVES THAT BEAT ON HEAVEN'S SHORE
BZZZZT!!
NOUGHT CAN DEFORM THE HUMAN RACE LIKE TO THE ARMOUR'S IRON BRACE
IF THE SUN AND MOON SHOULD DOUBT, THEY'D IMMEDIATELY GO OUT.
WHAT TO DO?
WHY DID THE CHICKEN CROSS THE ROAD?
BECAUSE THE CHICKEN ACROSS THE HI SPEED-DSL STREET WAS ONLINE AT ADULTSWIM.COM/SHOWS/PILOTWEEK/
WHERE YOU CAN VOTE BEGINNING FRIDAY MAY 11th FOR THE D.C. SHOW SO, IT'S LIKE PILOTS WEEK? AWSOME! SHH I THINK I HEAR MY MOM COMING

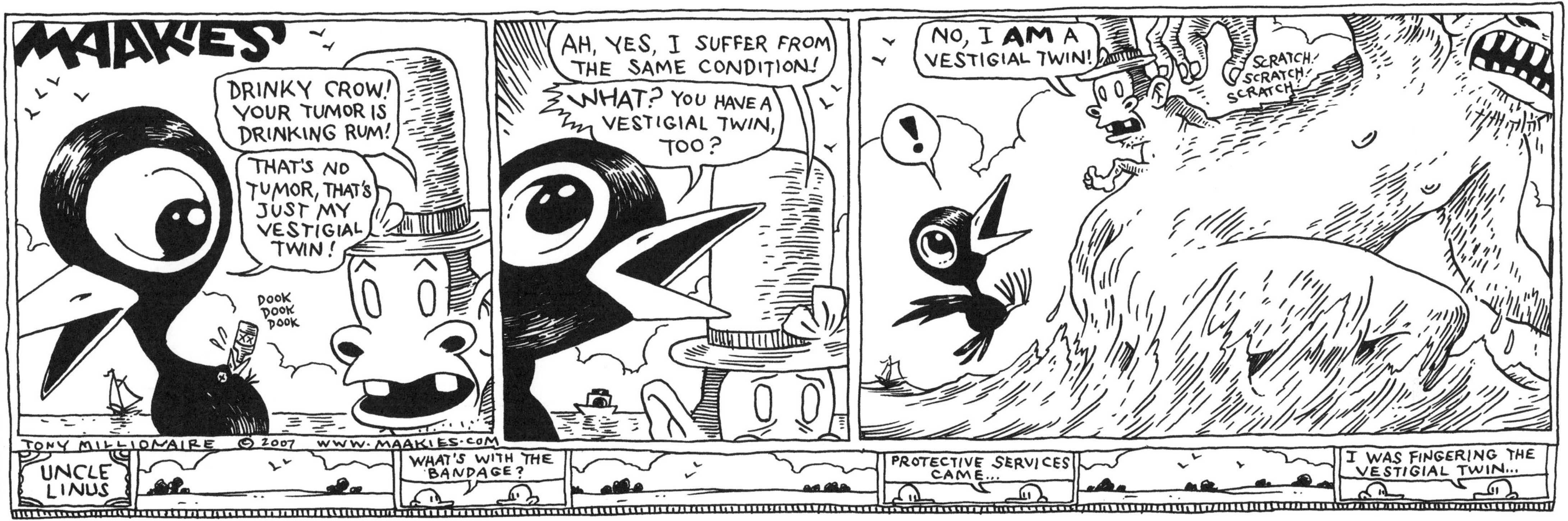
MAAKIES
DRINKY CROW! YOUR TUMOR IS DRINKING RUM!
THAT'S NO TUMOR, THAT'S JUST MY VESTIGIAL TWIN!
DOOK DOOK DOOK
AH, YES, I SUFFER FROM THE SAME CONDITION!
WHAT? YOU HAVE A VESTIGIAL TWIN, TOO?
NO, I AM A VESTIGIAL TWIN!
!
SCRATCH! SCRATCH! SCRATCH!
TONY MILLIONAIRE © 2007 WWW.MAAKIES.COM
UNCLE LINUS
WHAT'S WITH THE BANDAGE?
PROTECTIVE SERVICES CAME...
I WAS FINGERING THE VESTIGIAL TWIN...

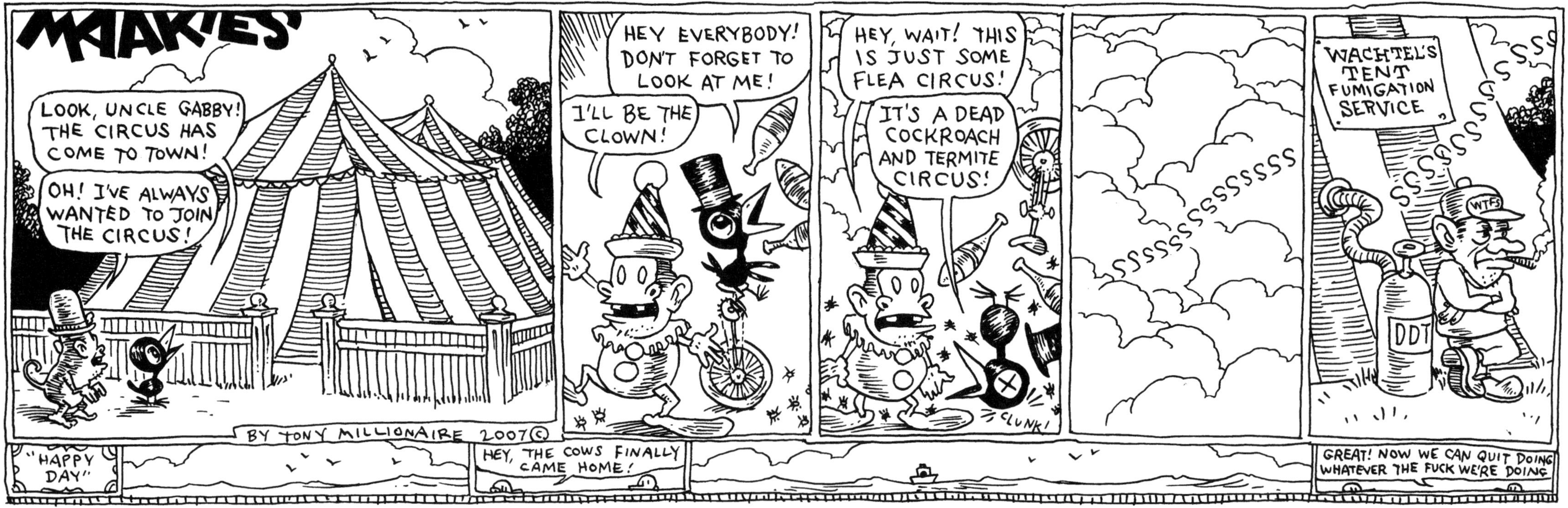
MAAKIES
LOOK, UNCLE GABBY! THE CIRCUS HAS COME TO TOWN!
OH! I'VE ALWAYS WANTED TO JOIN THE CIRCUS!
BY TONY MILLIONAIRE 2007©
HEY EVERYBODY! DON'T FORGET TO LOOK AT ME!
I'LL BE THE CLOWN!
HEY, WAIT! THIS IS JUST SOME FLEA CIRCUS!
IT'S A DEAD COCKROACH AND TERMITE CIRCUS!
CLUNK!
SSSSSSSSSSSSSSSSSSS
WACHTEL'S TENT FUMIGATION SERVICE
SSSSSSSSSSSS
WTFS
DDT
"HAPPY DAY"
HEY, THE COWS FINALLY CAME HOME!
GREAT! NOW WE CAN QUIT DOING WHATEVER THE FUCK WE'RE DOING

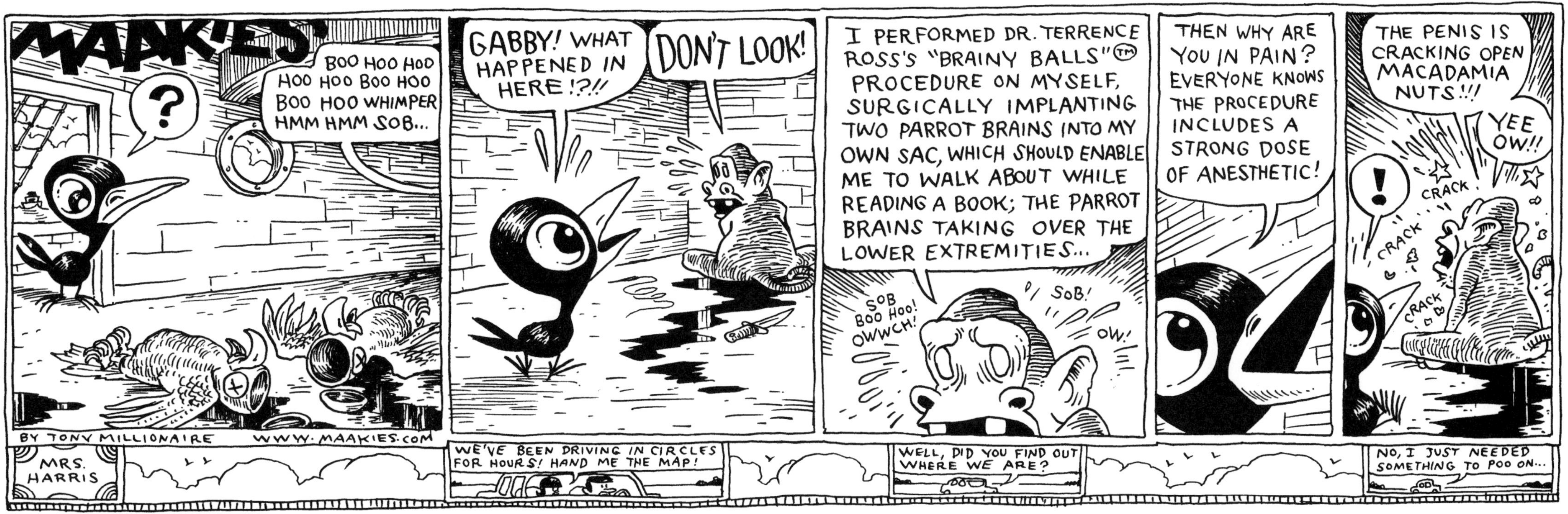
MAAKIES
?
BOO HOO HOO HOO HOO BOO HOO BOO HOO WHIMPER HMM HMM SOB...
BY TONY MILLIONAIRE
WWW.MAAKIES.COM
GABBY! WHAT HAPPENED IN HERE!?!!
DON'T LOOK!
I PERFORMED DR. TERRENCE ROSS'S "BRAINY BALLS"™ PROCEDURE ON MYSELF, SURGICALLY IMPLANTING TWO PARROT BRAINS INTO MY OWN SAC, WHICH SHOULD ENABLE ME TO WALK ABOUT WHILE READING A BOOK; THE PARROT BRAINS TAKING OVER THE LOWER EXTREMITIES...
SOB BOO HOO! OWWCH!
SOB!
OW!
THEN WHY ARE YOU IN PAIN? EVERYONE KNOWS THE PROCEDURE INCLUDES A STRONG DOSE OF ANESTHETIC!
THE PENIS IS CRACKING OPEN MACADAMIA NUTS!!!
YEE OW!!
!
CRACK
CRACK
CRACK
MRS. HARRIS
WE'VE BEEN DRIVING IN CIRCLES FOR HOURS! HAND ME THE MAP!
WELL, DID YOU FIND OUT WHERE WE ARE?
NO, I JUST NEEDED SOMETHING TO POO ON...

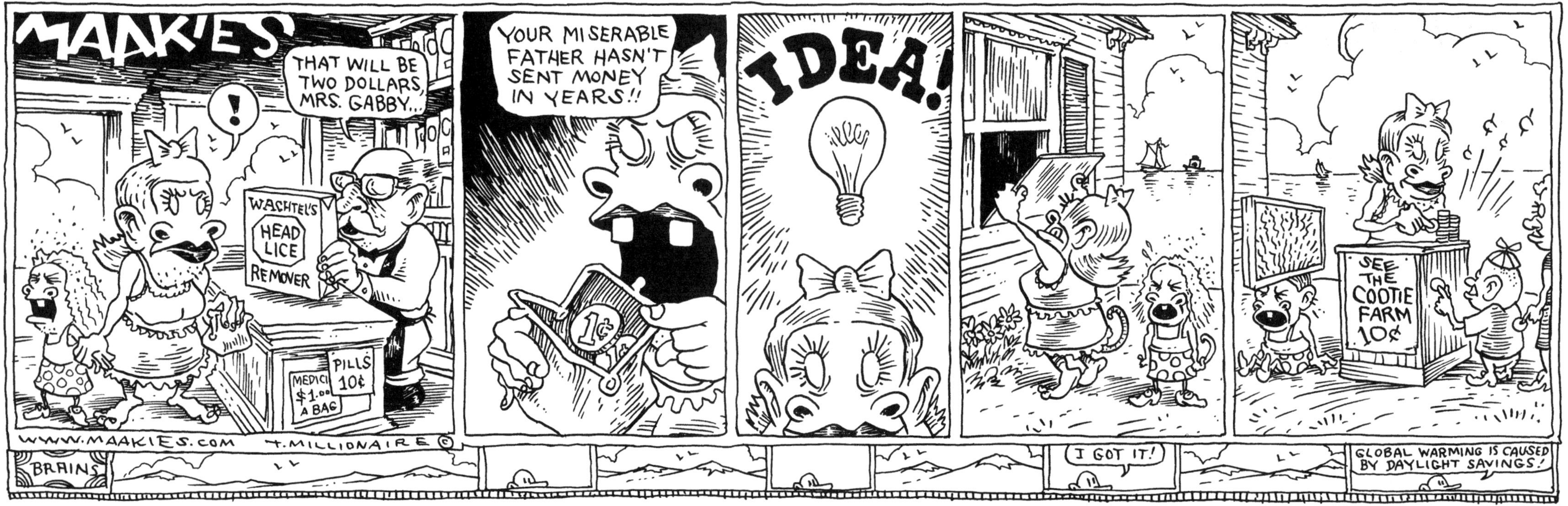
MAAKIES
!
THAT WILL BE TWO DOLLARS, MRS. GABBY...
WACHTEL'S HEAD LICE REMOVER
PILLS 10¢
$1.00 A BAG
YOUR MISERABLE FATHER HASN'T SENT MONEY IN YEARS!!
1¢
IDEA!
SEE THE COOTIE FARM 10¢
WWW.MAAKIES.COM
T. MILLIONAIRE ©
BRAINS
I GOT IT!
GLOBAL WARMING IS CAUSED BY DAYLIGHT SAVINGS!

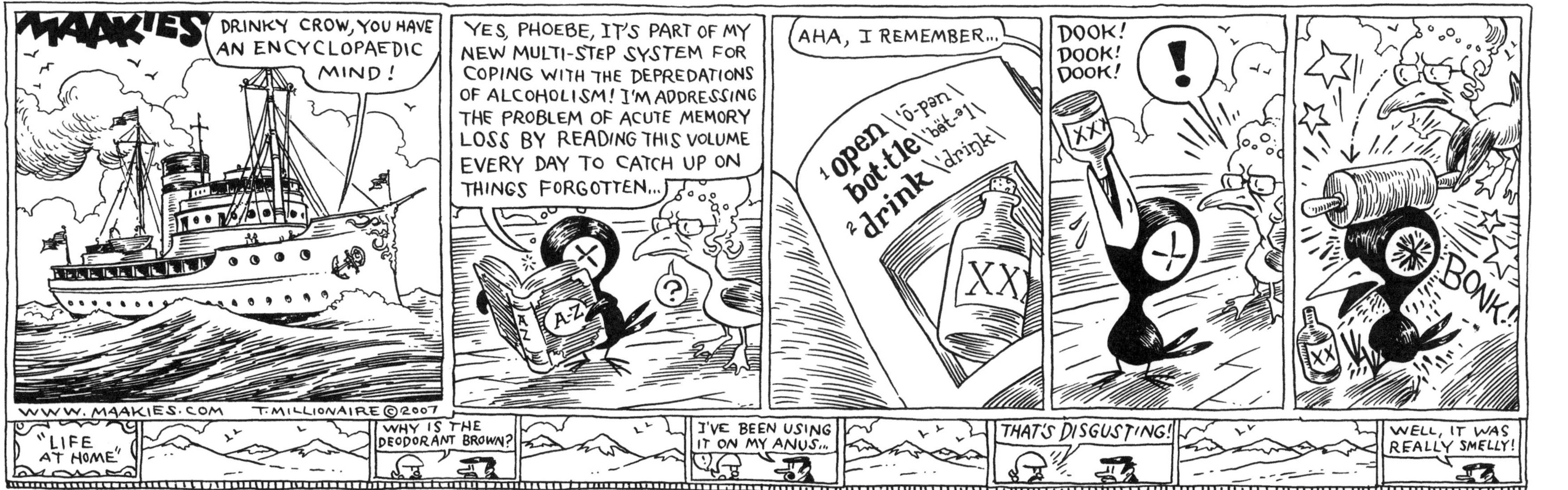
MAAKIES
DRINKY CROW, YOU HAVE AN ENCYCLOPAEDIC MIND!
WWW.MAAKIES.COM
T. MILLIONAIRE © 2007
YES, PHOEBE, IT'S PART OF MY NEW MULTI-STEP SYSTEM FOR COPING WITH THE DEPREDATIONS OF ALCOHOLISM! I'M ADDRESSING THE PROBLEM OF ACUTE MEMORY LOSS BY READING THIS VOLUME EVERY DAY TO CATCH UP ON THINGS FORGOTTEN...
A-Z
?
AHA, I REMEMBER...
1 open \ˈō-pən\
bot·tle \ˈbät-əl\
2 drink \ˈdriŋk\
XXX
DOOK! DOOK! DOOK!
!
XXX
BONK!!
XX
"LIFE AT HOME"
WHY IS THE DEODORANT BROWN?
I'VE BEEN USING IT ON MY ANUS...
THAT'S DISGUSTING!
WELL, IT WAS REALLY SMELLY!

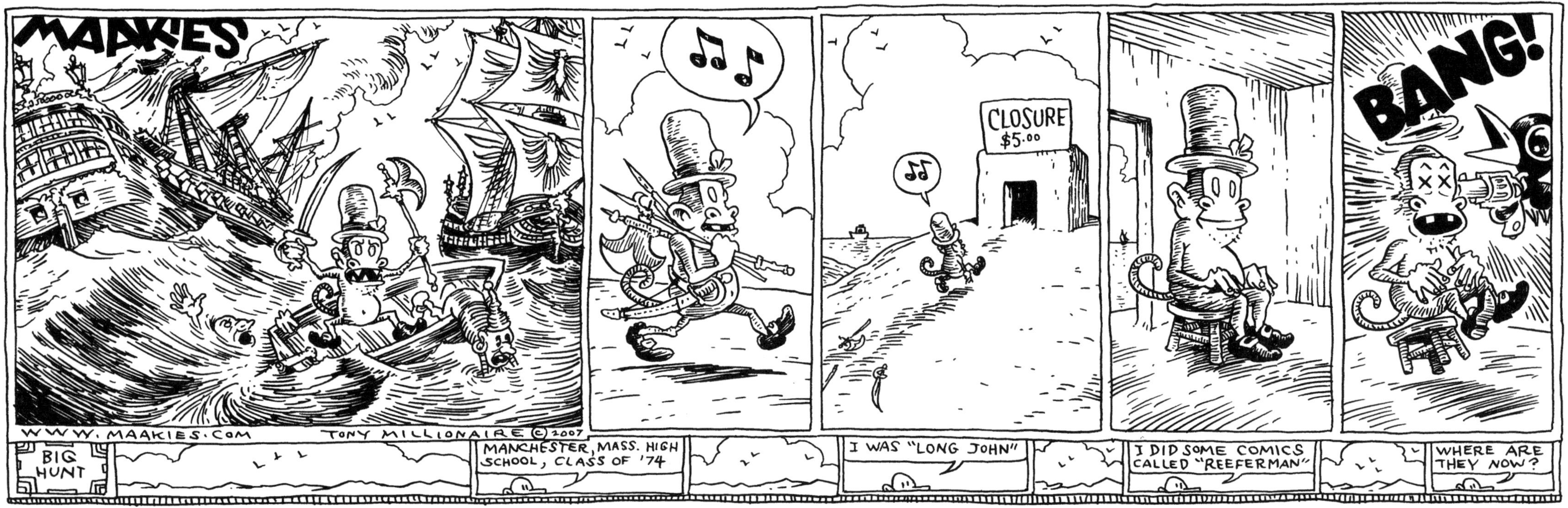
MAAKIES
WWW.MAAKIES.COM
TONY MILLIONAIRE © 2007
CLOSURE $5.00
BANG!
BIG HUNT
MANCHESTER, MASS. HIGH SCHOOL, CLASS OF '74
I WAS "LONG JOHN"
I DID SOME COMICS CALLED "REEFERMAN"
WHERE ARE THEY NOW?

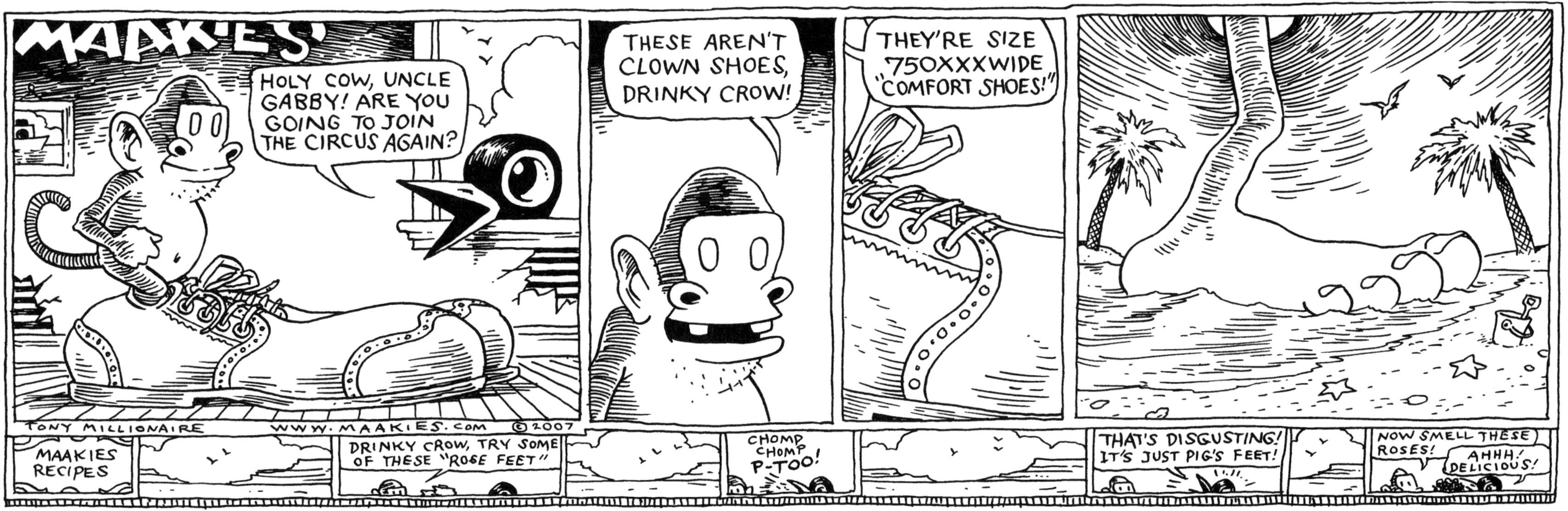
MAAKIES
HOLY COW, UNCLE GABBY! ARE YOU GOING TO JOIN THE CIRCUS AGAIN?
THESE AREN'T CLOWN SHOES, DRINKY CROW!
THEY'RE SIZE 750XXXWIDE "COMFORT SHOES!"
TONY MILLIONAIRE
WWW.MAAKIES.COM
© 2007
MAAKIES RECIPES
DRINKY CROW, TRY SOME OF THESE "ROSE FEET"
CHOMP CHOMP
P-TOO!
THAT'S DISGUSTING! IT'S JUST PIG'S FEET!
NOW SMELL THESE ROSES!
AHHH! DELICIOUS!

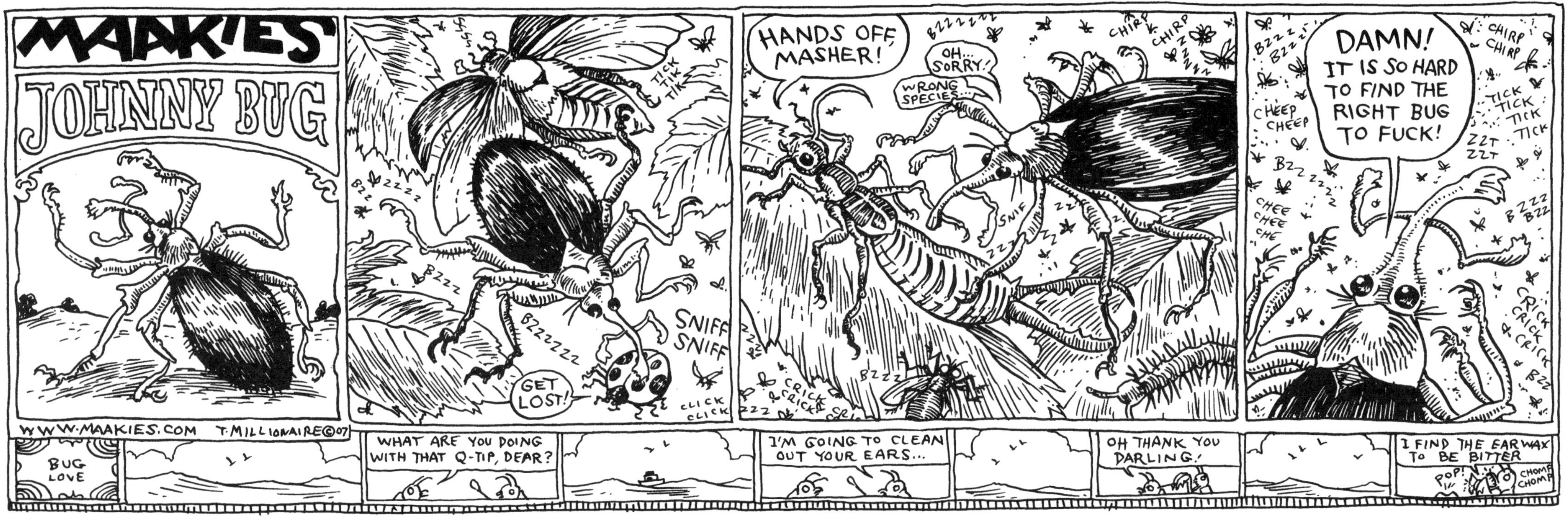
MAAKIES
JOHNNY BUG
WWW.MAAKIES.COM
T. MILLIONAIRE ©07
SSS
TICK TIK TIK
BZZZZZ
BZZZ
BZZZZZZZ
GET LOST!
SNIFF SNIFF
CLICK CLICK
HANDS OFF, MASHER!
OH... SORRY!
WRONG SPECIES...
BZZZZZZ
CHIRP CHIRP
SNIF
BZZZ
CRICK CRICK
DAMN! IT IS SO HARD TO FIND THE RIGHT BUG TO FUCK!
CHIRP CHIRP
BZZZ BZZZ
CHEEP CHEEP
TICK TICK TICK TICK
ZZT ZZT
CHEE CHEE CHE
BZZZZ BZZ
CRICK CRICK & CRICK
BUG LOVE
WHAT ARE YOU DOING WITH THAT Q-TIP, DEAR?
I'M GOING TO CLEAN OUT YOUR EARS...
OH THANK YOU DARLING!
I FIND THE EARWAX TO BE BITTER
POP!
CHOMP CHOMP

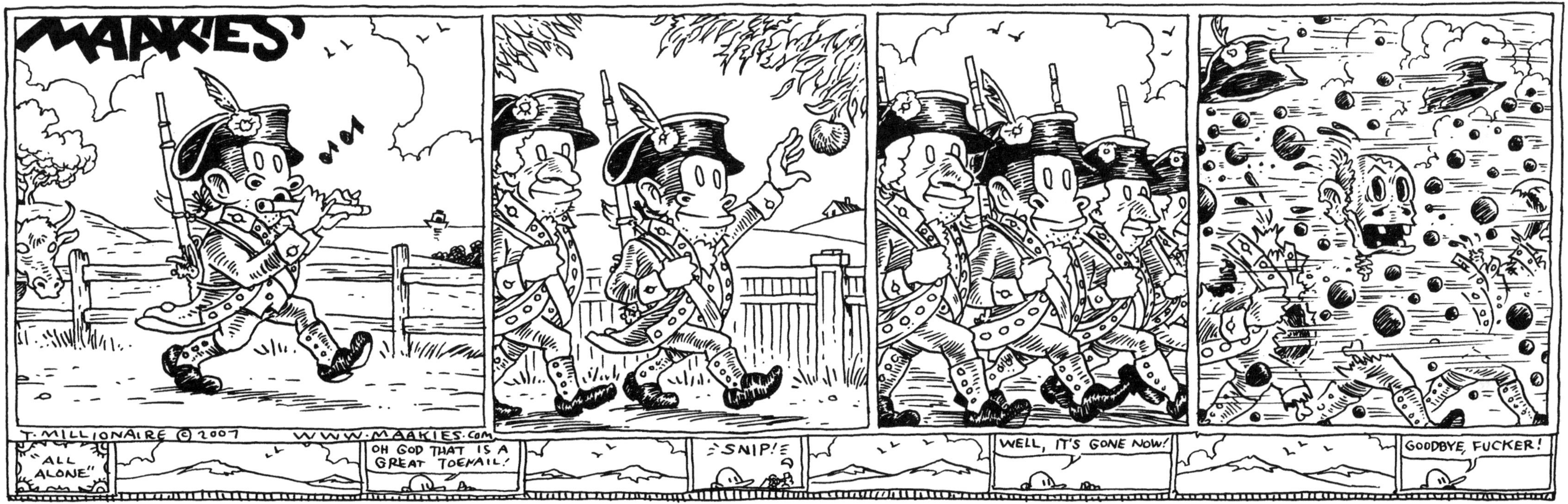
MAAKIES
T. MILLIONAIRE © 2007
WWW.MAAKIES.COM
"ALL ALONE"
OH GOD THAT IS A GREAT TOENAIL!
"SNIP!"
WELL, IT'S GONE NOW!
GOODBYE, FUCKER!

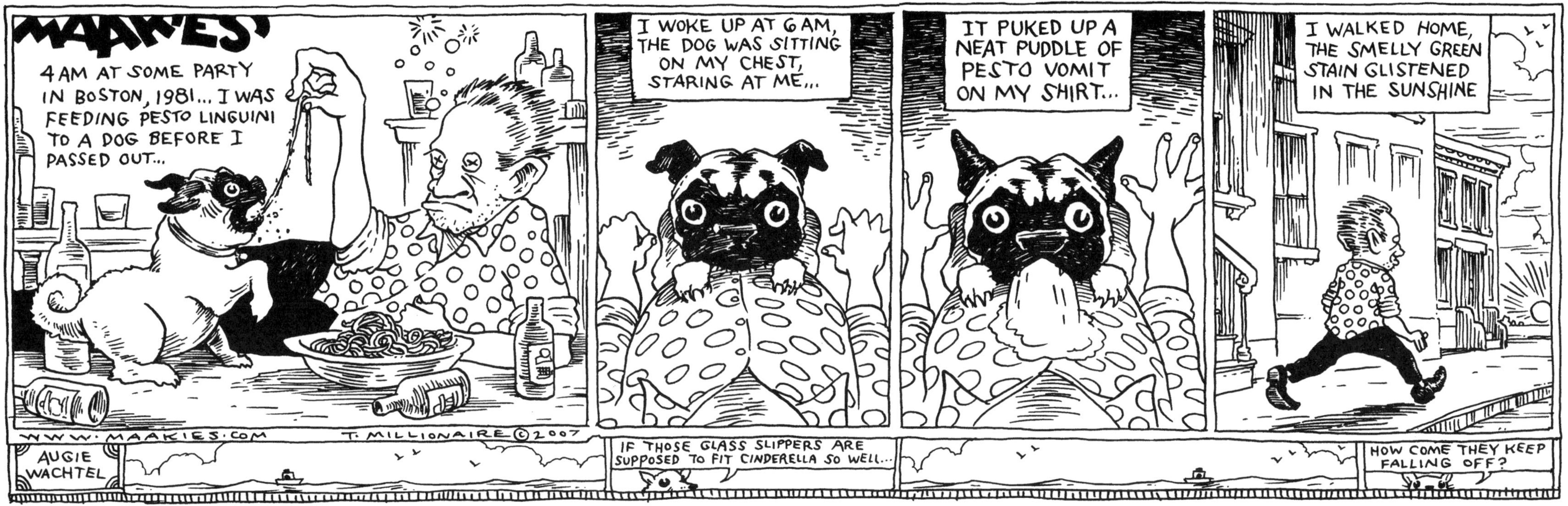
MAAKIES
4 AM AT SOME PARTY IN BOSTON, 1981... I WAS FEEDING PESTO LINGUINI TO A DOG BEFORE I PASSED OUT...
I WOKE UP AT 6 AM, THE DOG WAS SITTING ON MY CHEST, STARING AT ME...
IT PUKED UP A NEAT PUDDLE OF PESTO VOMIT ON MY SHIRT...
I WALKED HOME, THE SMELLY GREEN STAIN GLISTENED IN THE SUNSHINE
WWW.MAAKIES.COM
T. MILLIONAIRE © 2007
AUGIE WACHTEL
IF THOSE GLASS SLIPPERS ARE SUPPOSED TO FIT CINDERELLA SO WELL...
HOW COME THEY KEEP FALLING OFF?

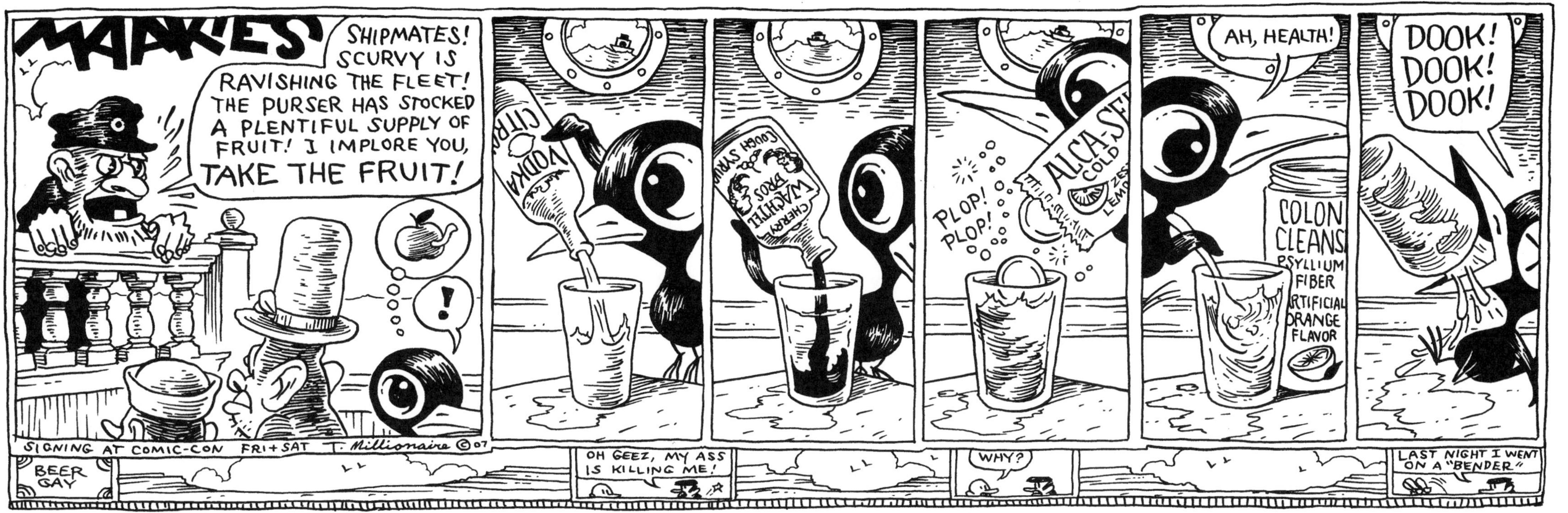
MAAKIES
SHIPMATES! SCURVY IS RAVISHING THE FLEET! THE PURSER HAS STOCKED A PLENTIFUL SUPPLY OF FRUIT! I IMPLORE YOU, TAKE THE FRUIT!
!
VODKA CITR
CHERRY WACHTEL BROS COUGH SYRUP
PLOP! PLOP!
ALCA-SE COLD LEMO ZES
AH, HEALTH!
COLON CLEANS PSYLLIUM FIBER ARTIFICIAL ORANGE FLAVOR
DOOK! DOOK! DOOK!
SIGNING AT COMIC-CON FRI+SAT
T. Millionaire ©07
BEER GAY
OH GEEZ, MY ASS IS KILLING ME!
WHY?
LAST NIGHT I WENT ON A "BENDER"

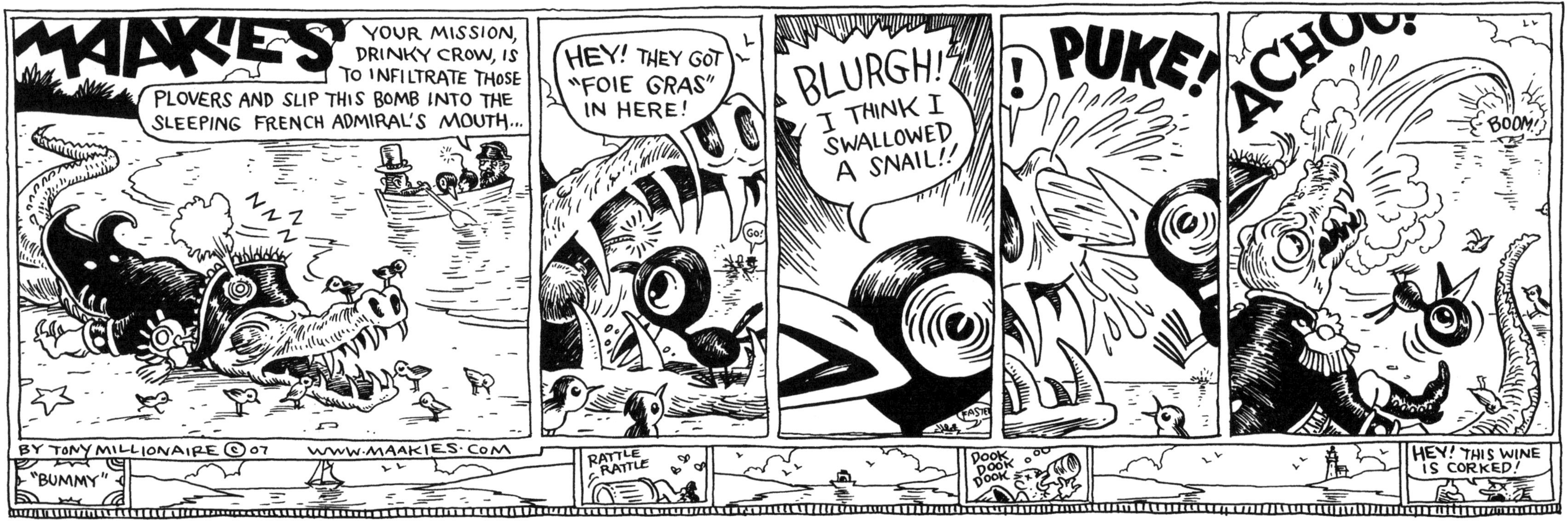
MAAKIES
YOUR MISSION, DRINKY CROW, IS TO INFILTRATE THOSE PLOVERS AND SLIP THIS BOMB INTO THE SLEEPING FRENCH ADMIRAL'S MOUTH...
Z Z Z
HEY! THEY GOT "FOIE GRAS" IN HERE!
GO!
BLURGH! I THINK I SWALLOWED A SNAIL!!
FASTER
!
PUKE!
ACHOO!
BOOM!
BY TONY MILLIONAIRE © 07
WWW.MAAKIES.COM
"BUMMY"
RATTLE RATTLE
DOOK DOOK DOOK
HEY! THIS WINE IS CORKED!

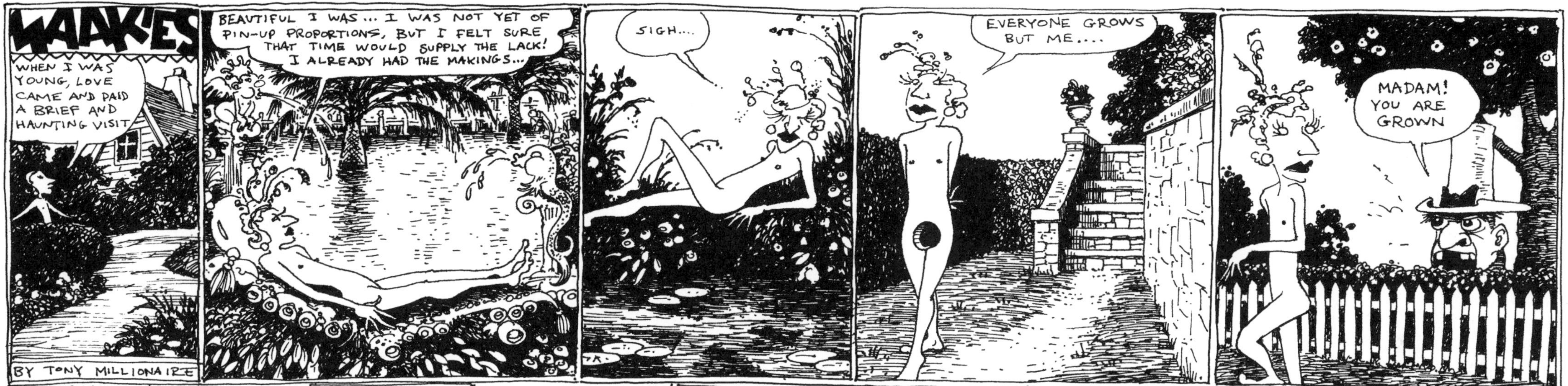
MAAKIES
WHEN I WAS YOUNG, LOVE CAME AND PAID A BRIEF AND HAUNTING VISIT
BY TONY MILLIONAIRE
BEAUTIFUL I WAS... I WAS NOT YET OF PIN-UP PROPORTIONS, BUT I FELT SURE THAT TIME WOULD SUPPLY THE LACK! I ALREADY HAD THE MAKINGS...
SIGH...
EVERYONE GROWS BUT ME....
MADAM! YOU ARE GROWN

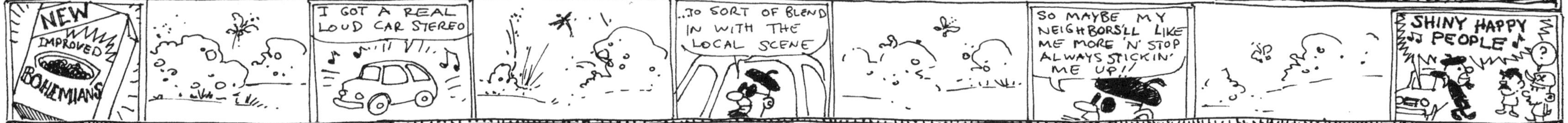
NEW IMPROVED BOHEMIANS
I GOT A REAL LOUD CAR STEREO
..TO SORT OF BLEND IN WITH THE LOCAL SCENE
SO MAYBE MY NEIGHBORS'LL LIKE ME MORE 'N' STOP ALWAYS STICKIN' ME UP!!
SHINY HAPPY PEOPLE

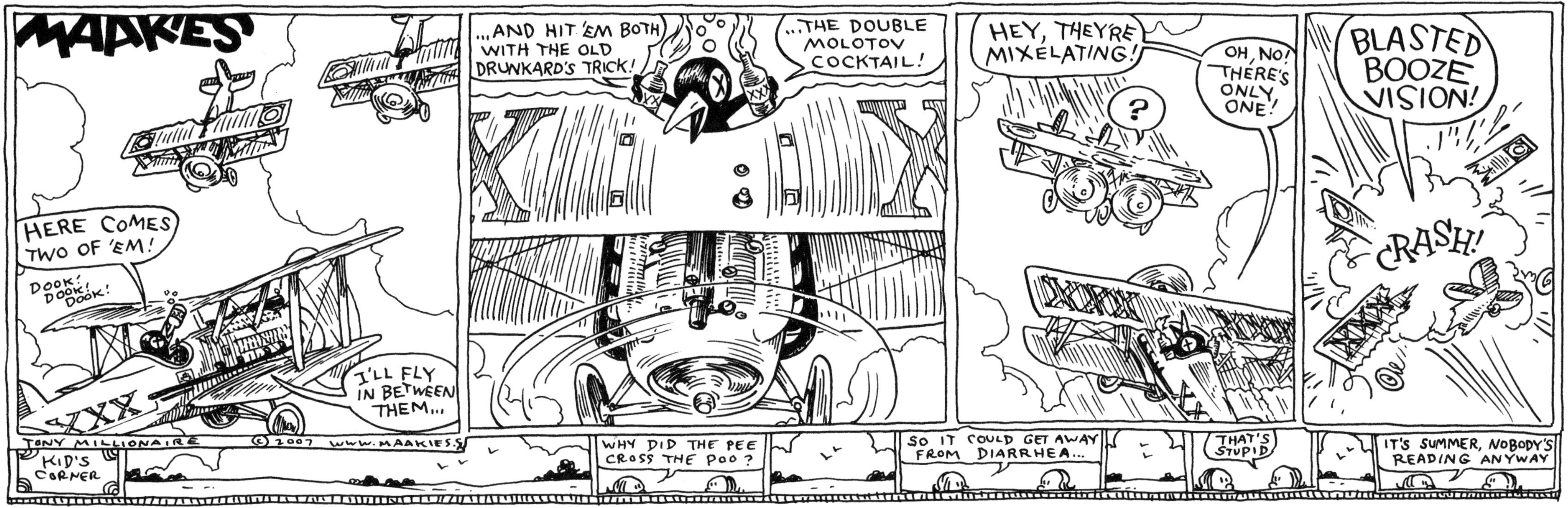
MAAKIES
HERE COMES TWO OF 'EM!
DOOK! DOOK! DOOK!
I'LL FLY IN BETWEEN THEM...
...AND HIT 'EM BOTH WITH THE OLD DRUNKARD'S TRICK!
...THE DOUBLE MOLOTOV COCKTAIL!
HEY, THEY'RE MIXELATING!
OH, NO! THERE'S ONLY ONE!
?
BLASTED BOOZE VISION!
CRASH!
TONY MILLIONAIRE © 2007 WWW.MAAKIES.
KID'S CORNER
WHY DID THE PEE CROSS THE POO?
SO IT COULD GET AWAY FROM DIARRHEA...
THAT'S STUPID
IT'S SUMMER, NOBODY'S READING ANYWAY

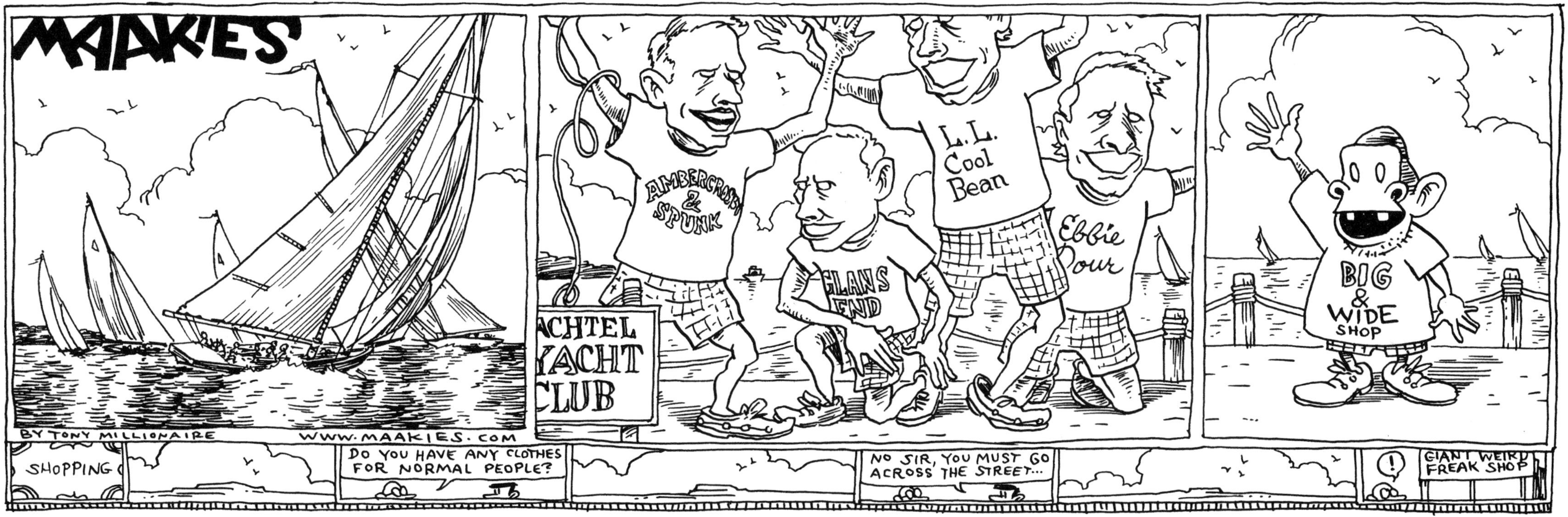

MAAKIES
BY TONY MILLIONAIRE
WWW.MAAKIES.COM
ACHTEL YACHT CLUB
AMBERCROSBY & SPUNK
GLANS END
L.L. Cool Bean
Ebbie Dour
BIG & WIDE SHOP
SHOPPING
DO YOU HAVE ANY CLOTHES FOR NORMAL PEOPLE?
NO SIR, YOU MUST GO ACROSS THE STREET...
!
GIANT WEIRD FREAK SHOP

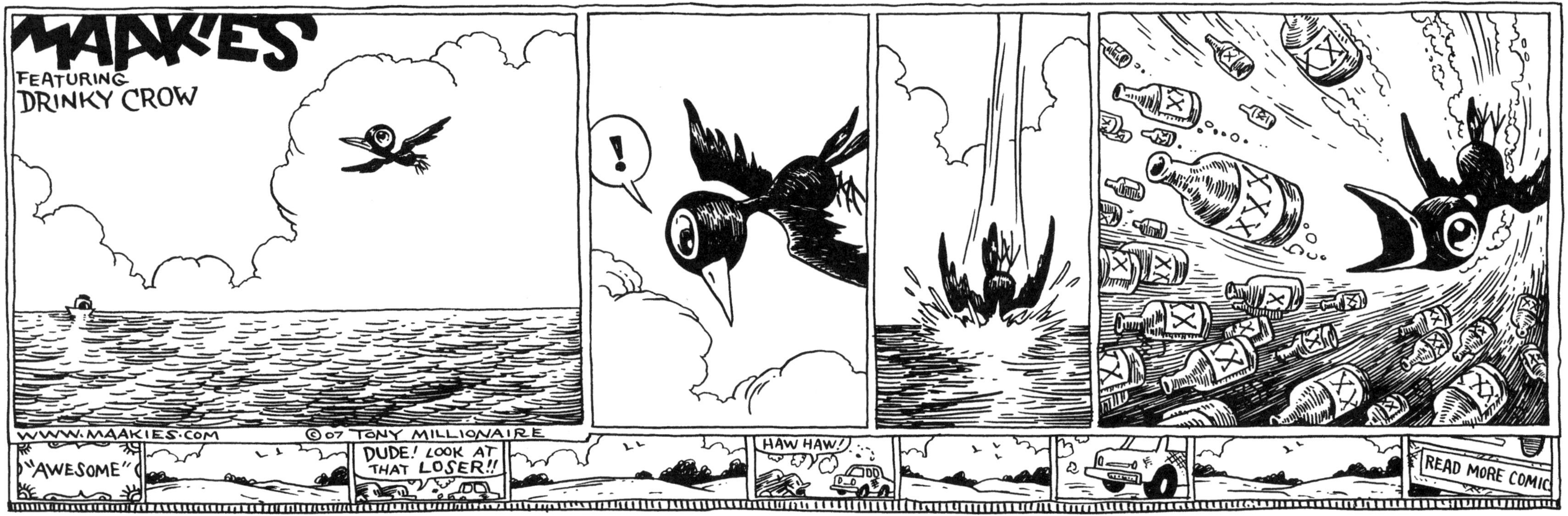
MAAKIES
FEATURING
DRINKY CROW
!
WWW.MAAKIES.COM
©07 TONY MILLIONAIRE
"AWESOME"
DUDE! LOOK AT THAT LOSER!!
HAW HAW!
READ MORE COMIC

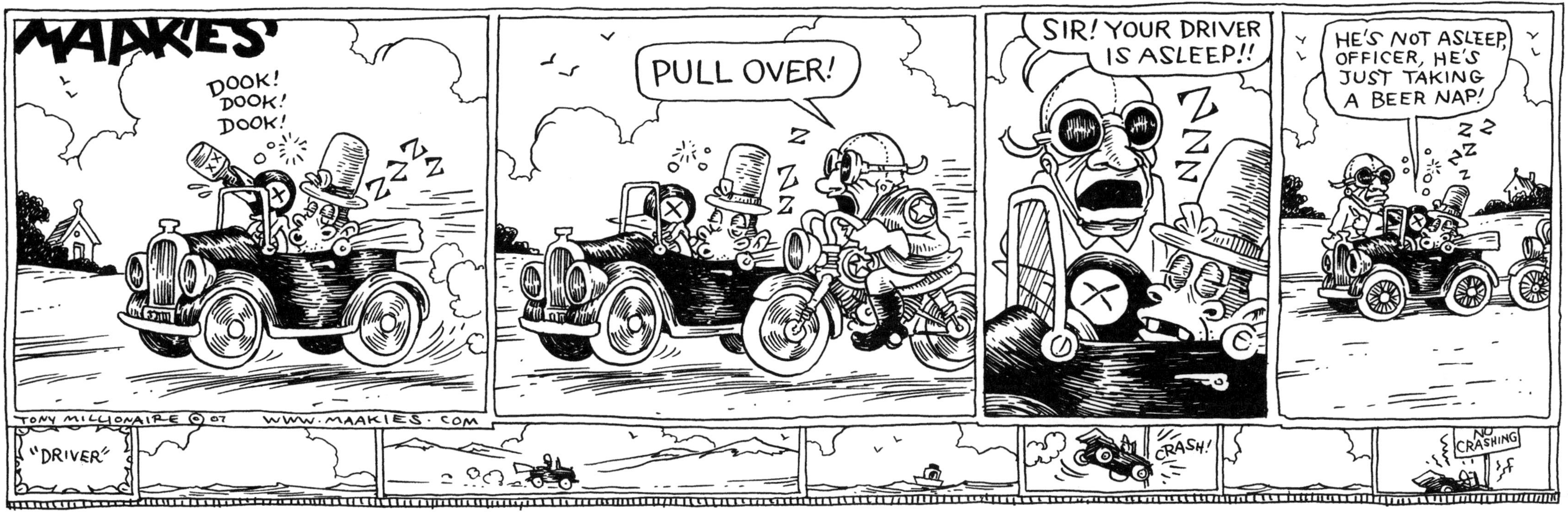
MAAKIES
DOOK! DOOK! DOOK!
TONY MILLIONAIRE © 07
WWW.MAAKIES.COM
PULL OVER!
SIR! YOUR DRIVER IS ASLEEP!!
HE'S NOT ASLEEP, OFFICER, HE'S JUST TAKING A BEER NAP!
"DRIVER"
CRASH!
NO CRASHING

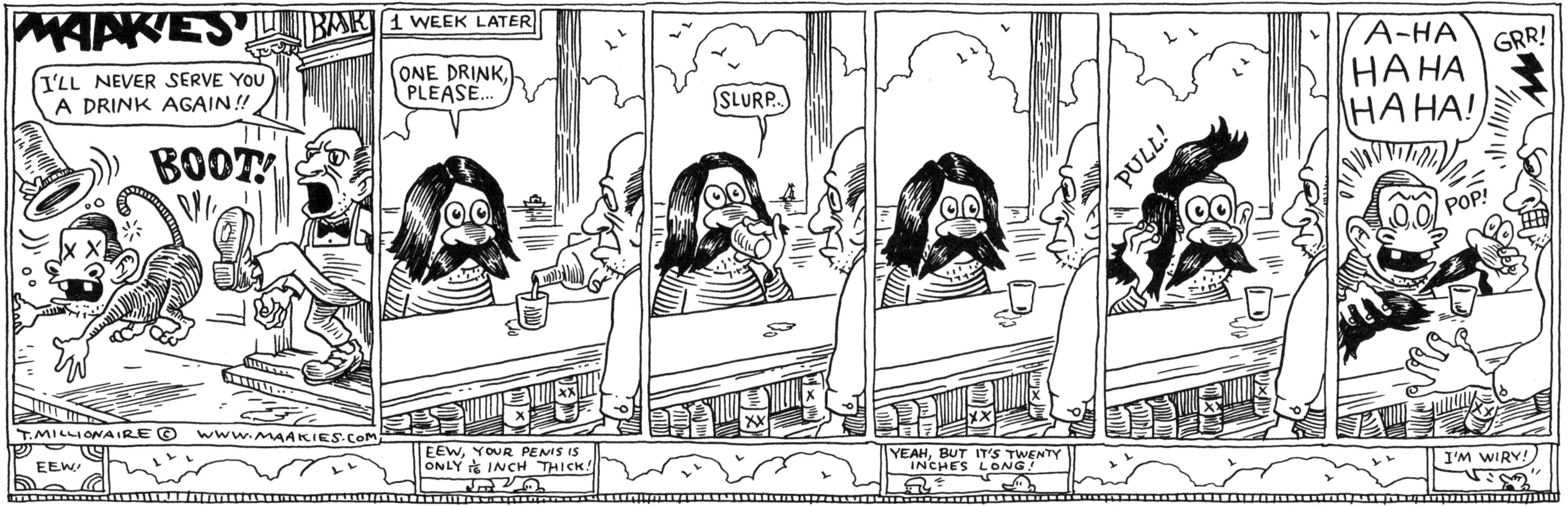
MAAKIES'
BAR
I'LL NEVER SERVE YOU A DRINK AGAIN!!
BOOT!
T. MILLIONAIRE ©
WWW.MAAKIES.COM
1 WEEK LATER
ONE DRINK, PLEASE...
SLURP..
PULL!
A-HA HA HA HA HA!
GRR!
POP!
EEW!
EEW, YOUR PENIS IS ONLY 1/16 INCH THICK!
YEAH, BUT IT'S TWENTY INCHES LONG!
I'M WIRY!

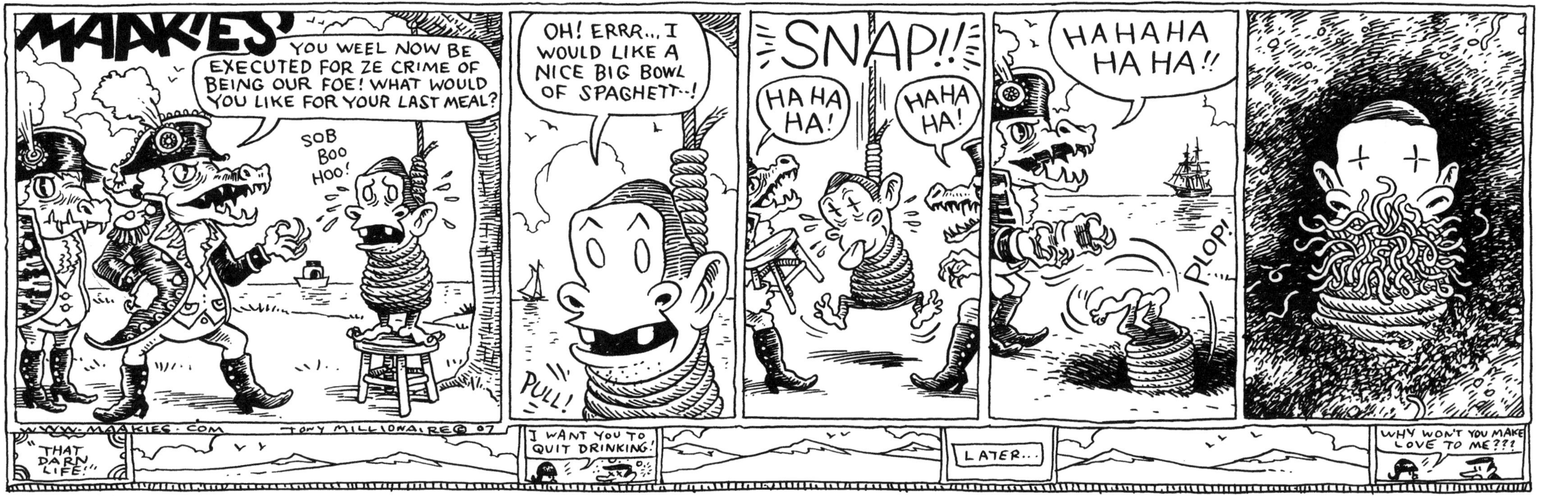
MAAKIES
YOU WEEL NOW BE EXECUTED FOR ZE CRIME OF BEING OUR FOE! WHAT WOULD YOU LIKE FOR YOUR LAST MEAL?
SOB BOO HOO!
OH! ERRR... I WOULD LIKE A NICE BIG BOWL OF SPAGHETT--!
PULL!
SNAP!!
HA HA HA!
HAHA HA!
HAHAHA HA HA!!
PLOP!
WWW.MAAKIES.COM
TONY MILLIONAIRE© 07
"THAT DARN LIFE!"
I WANT YOU TO QUIT DRINKING!
LATER...
WHY WON'T YOU MAKE LOVE TO ME???

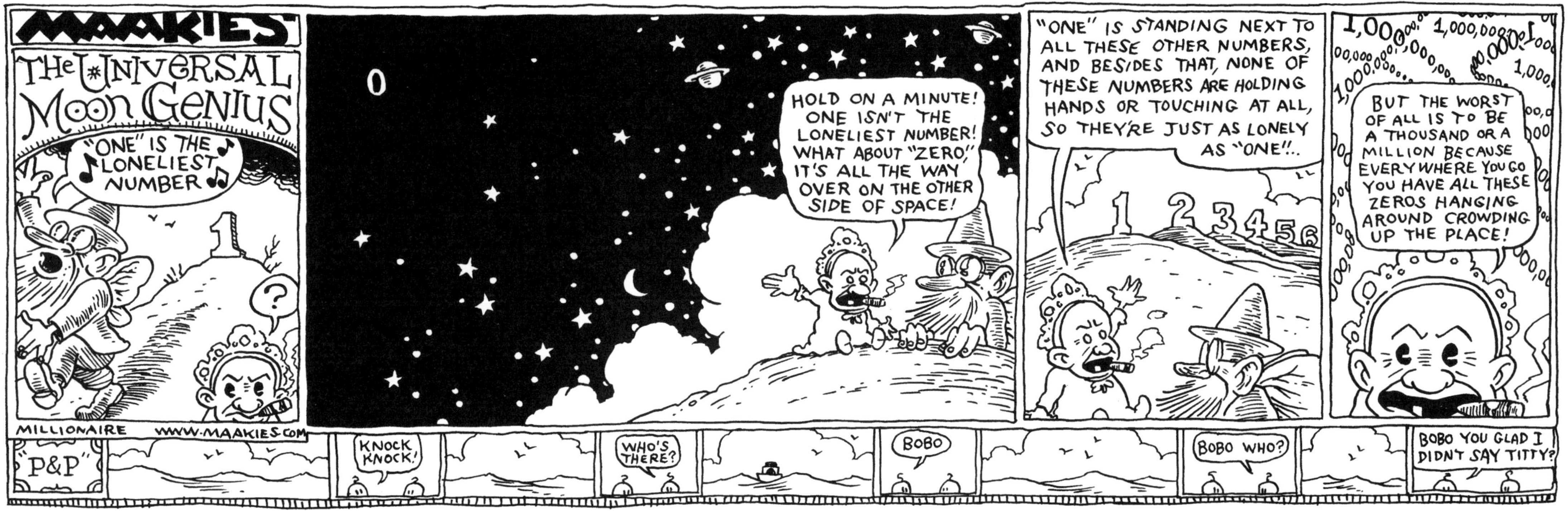
MAAKIES
THE UNIVERSAL MOON GENIUS
"ONE" IS THE LONELIEST NUMBER
?
0
HOLD ON A MINUTE! ONE ISN'T THE LONELIEST NUMBER! WHAT ABOUT "ZERO", IT'S ALL THE WAY OVER ON THE OTHER SIDE OF SPACE!
"ONE" IS STANDING NEXT TO ALL THESE OTHER NUMBERS, AND BESIDES THAT, NONE OF THESE NUMBERS ARE HOLDING HANDS OR TOUCHING AT ALL, SO THEY'RE JUST AS LONELY AS "ONE"!..
1 2 3 4 5 6
BUT THE WORST OF ALL IS TO BE A THOUSAND OR A MILLION BECAUSE EVERYWHERE YOU GO YOU HAVE ALL THESE ZEROS HANGING AROUND CROWDING UP THE PLACE!
MILLIONAIRE
WWW.MAAKIES.COM
"P&P"
KNOCK KNOCK!
WHO'S THERE?
BOBO
BOBO WHO?
BOBO YOU GLAD I DIDN'T SAY TITTY?

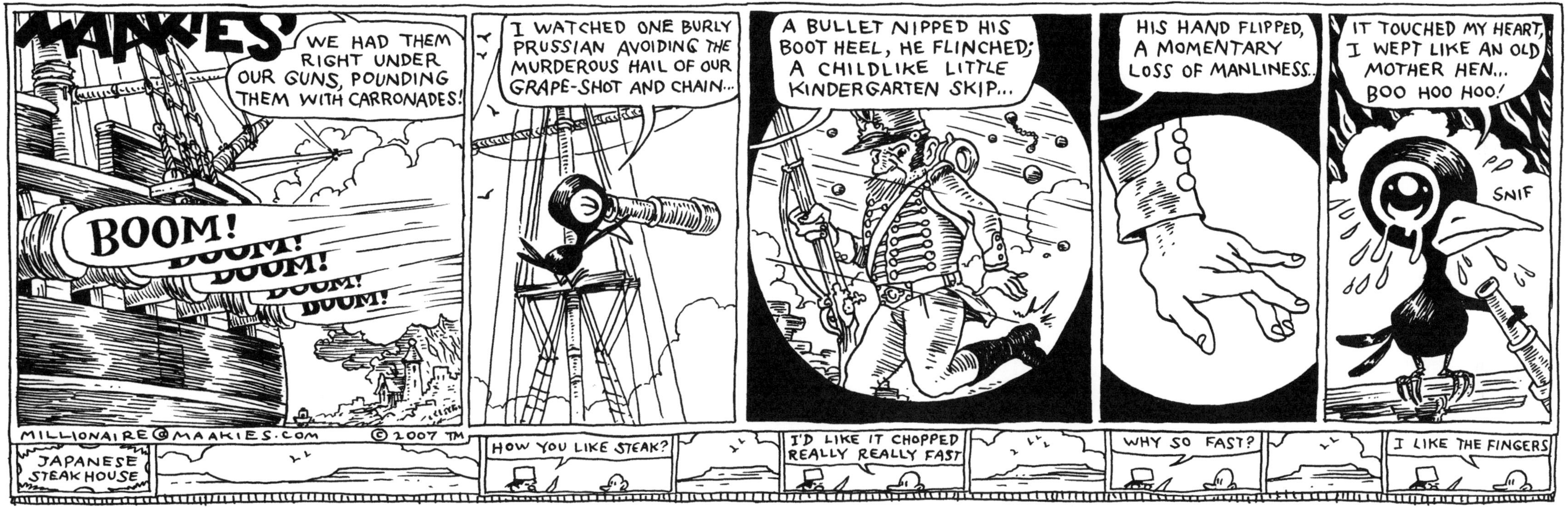
MAAKIES
WE HAD THEM RIGHT UNDER OUR GUNS, POUNDING THEM WITH CARRONADES!
BOOM!
BOOM!
BOOM!
BOOM!
BOOM!
I WATCHED ONE BURLY PRUSSIAN AVOIDING THE MURDEROUS HAIL OF OUR GRAPE-SHOT AND CHAIN...
A BULLET NIPPED HIS BOOT HEEL, HE FLINCHED; A CHILDLIKE LITTLE KINDERGARTEN SKIP...
HIS HAND FLIPPED, A MOMENTARY LOSS OF MANLINESS..
IT TOUCHED MY HEART, I WEPT LIKE AN OLD MOTHER HEN... BOO HOO HOO!
SNIF
MILLIONAIRE@MAAKIES.COM
© 2007 TM
JAPANESE STEAK HOUSE
HOW YOU LIKE STEAK?
I'D LIKE IT CHOPPED REALLY REALLY FAST
WHY SO FAST?
I LIKE THE FINGERS

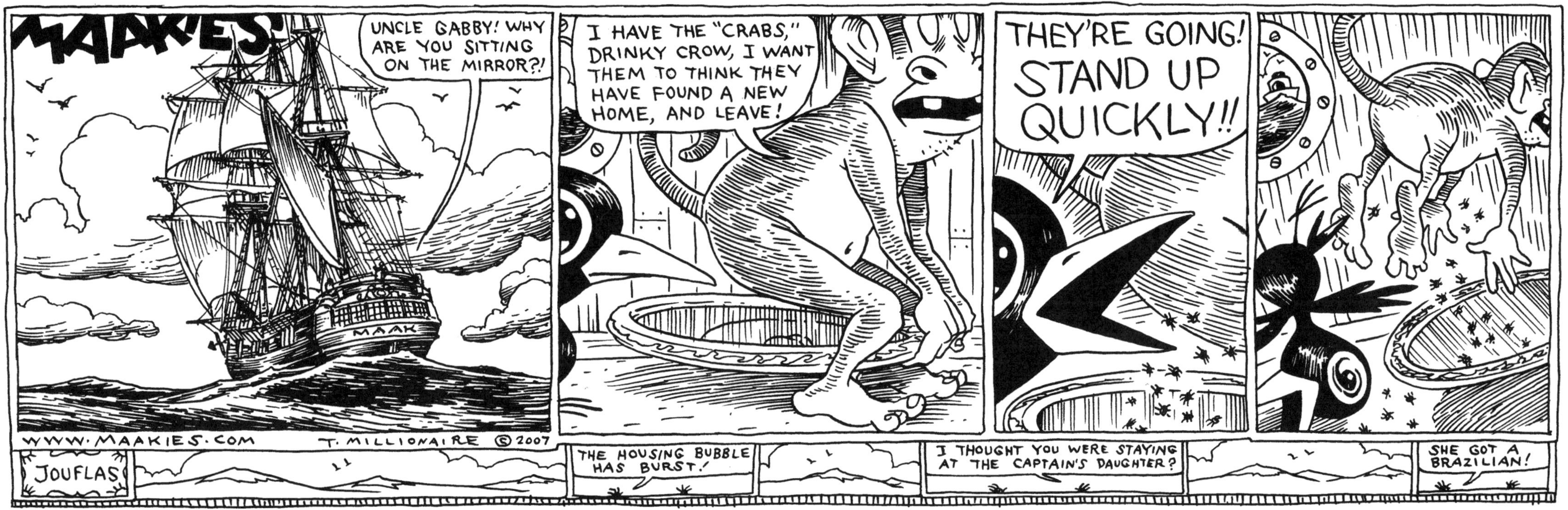
MAAKIES!
UNCLE GABBY! WHY ARE YOU SITTING ON THE MIRROR?!
MAAK
I HAVE THE "CRABS," DRINKY CROW, I WANT THEM TO THINK THEY HAVE FOUND A NEW HOME, AND LEAVE!
THEY'RE GOING! STAND UP QUICKLY!!
WWW.MAAKIES.COM
T. MILLIONAIRE © 2007
JOUFLAS
THE HOUSING BUBBLE HAS BURST!
I THOUGHT YOU WERE STAYING AT THE CAPTAIN'S DAUGHTER?
SHE GOT A BRAZILIAN!

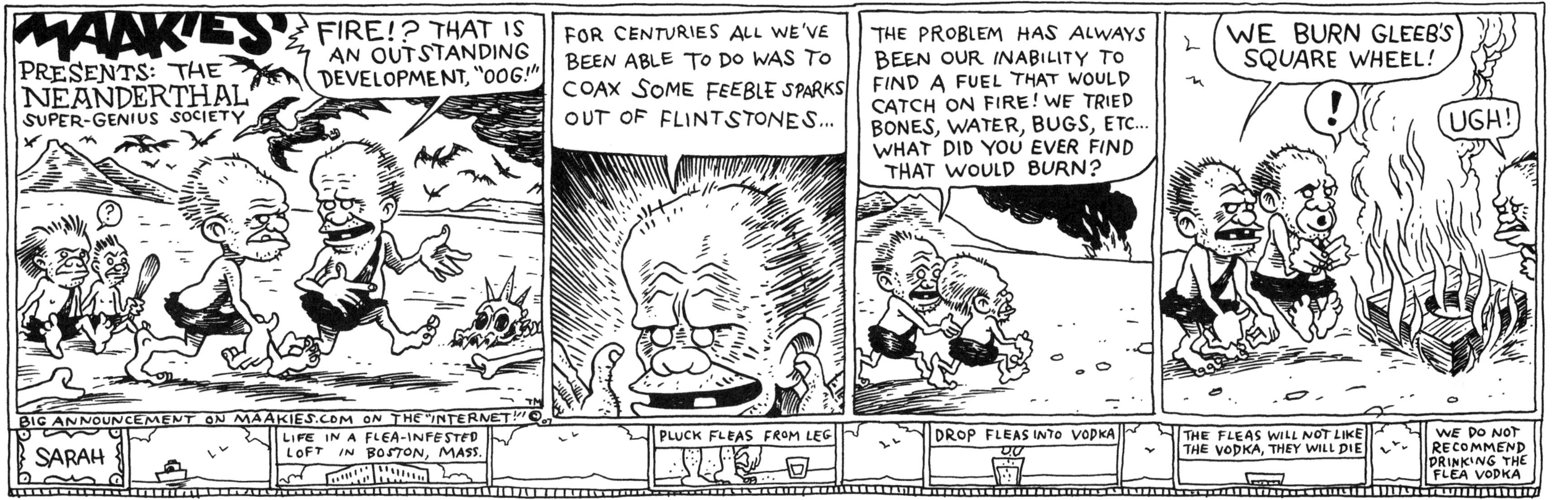

MAAKIES
PRESENTS: THE NEANDERTHAL SUPER-GENIUS SOCIETY
FIRE!? THAT IS AN OUTSTANDING DEVELOPMENT, "OOG!"
?
FOR CENTURIES ALL WE'VE BEEN ABLE TO DO WAS TO COAX SOME FEEBLE SPARKS OUT OF FLINTSTONES...
THE PROBLEM HAS ALWAYS BEEN OUR INABILITY TO FIND A FUEL THAT WOULD CATCH ON FIRE! WE TRIED BONES, WATER, BUGS, ETC... WHAT DID YOU EVER FIND THAT WOULD BURN?
WE BURN GLEEB'S SQUARE WHEEL!
!
UGH!
BIG ANNOUNCEMENT ON MAAKIES.COM ON THE "INTERNET!" ©07
SARAH
LIFE IN A FLEA-INFESTED LOFT IN BOSTON, MASS.
PLUCK FLEAS FROM LEG
DROP FLEAS INTO VODKA
THE FLEAS WILL NOT LIKE THE VODKA, THEY WILL DIE
WE DO NOT RECOMMEND DRINKING THE FLEA VODKA

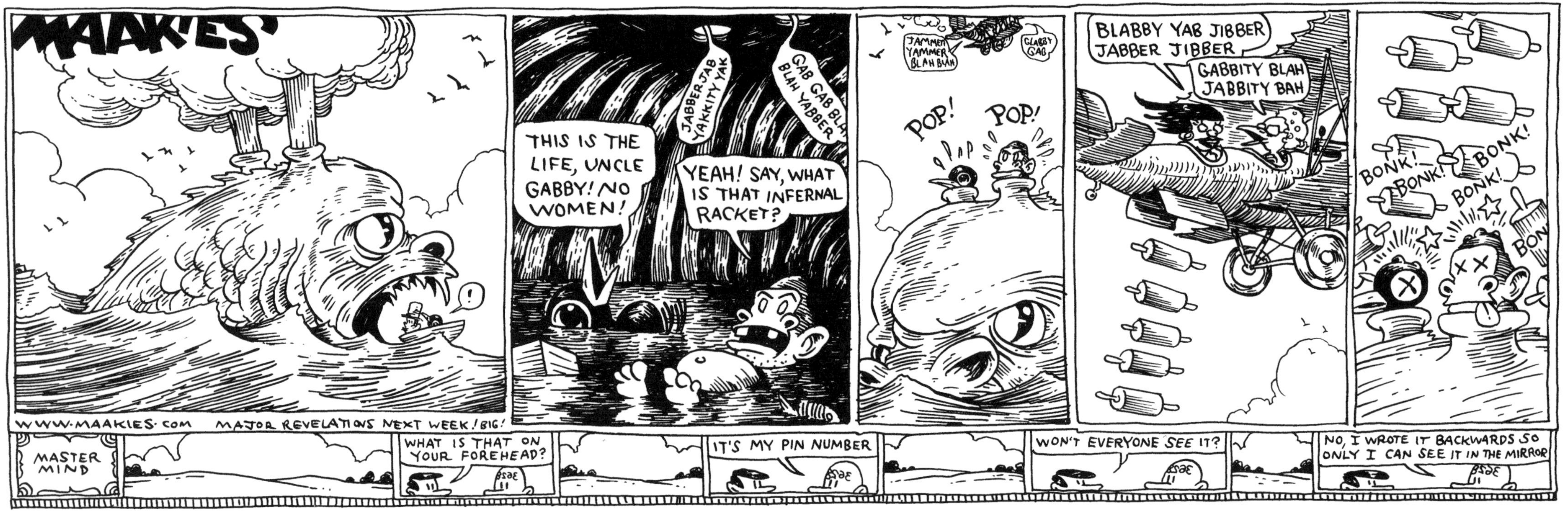
MAAKIES
!
THIS IS THE LIFE, UNCLE GABBY! NO WOMEN!
JABBER JAB YAKKITY YAK
GAB GAB BLAH BLAH YABBER
YEAH! SAY, WHAT IS THAT INFERNAL RACKET?
JAMMER YAMMER BLAH BLAH
GABBY GAB
POP!
POP!
BLABBY YAB JIBBER JABBER JIBBER
GABBITY BLAH JABBITY BAH
BONK!
BONK!
BONK!
BONK!
BON
WWW·MAAKIES·COM
MAJOR REVELATIONS NEXT WEEK!
MASTER MIND
WHAT IS THAT ON YOUR FOREHEAD?
IT'S MY PIN NUMBER
WON'T EVERYONE SEE IT?
NO, I WROTE IT BACKWARDS SO ONLY I CAN SEE IT IN THE MIRROR

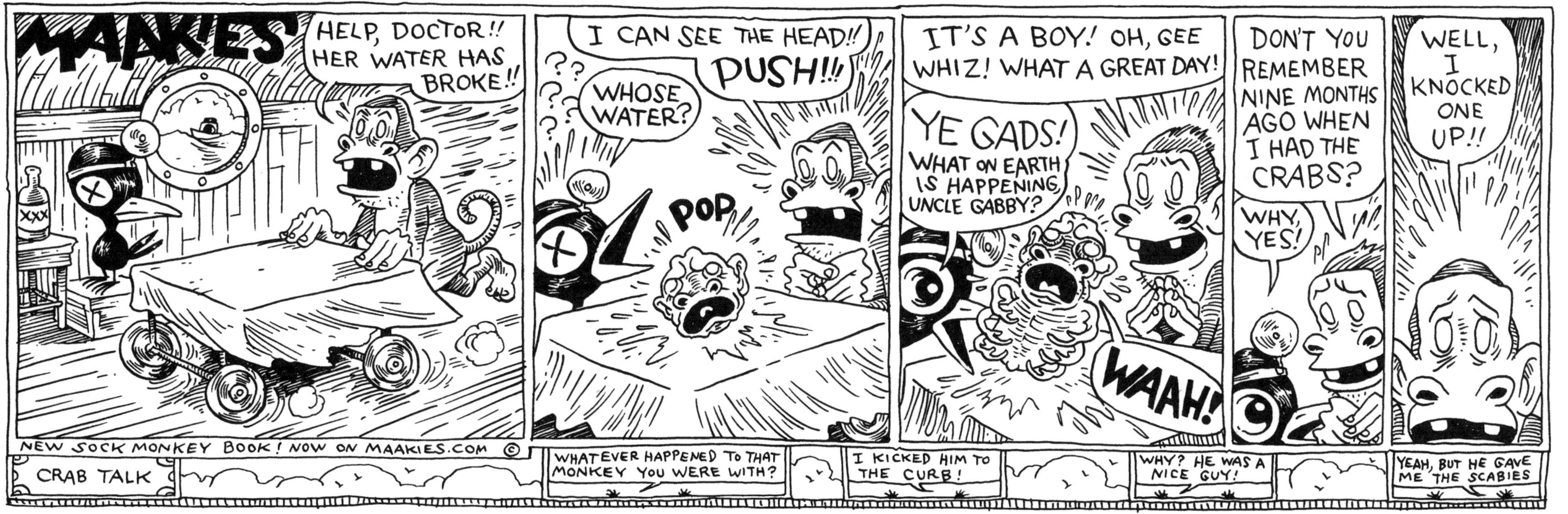
MAAKIES
HELP, DOCTOR!! HER WATER HAS BROKE!!
XXX
I CAN SEE THE HEAD!!
PUSH!!!
WHOSE WATER?
POP
IT'S A BOY! OH, GEE WHIZ! WHAT A GREAT DAY!
YE GADS! WHAT ON EARTH IS HAPPENING, UNCLE GABBY?
WAAH!
DON'T YOU REMEMBER NINE MONTHS AGO WHEN I HAD THE CRABS?
WHY, YES!
WELL, I KNOCKED ONE UP!!
NEW SOCK MONKEY BOOK! NOW ON MAAKIES.COM ©
CRAB TALK
WHATEVER HAPPENED TO THAT MONKEY YOU WERE WITH?
I KICKED HIM TO THE CURB!
WHY? HE WAS A NICE GUY!
YEAH, BUT HE GAVE ME THE SCABIES

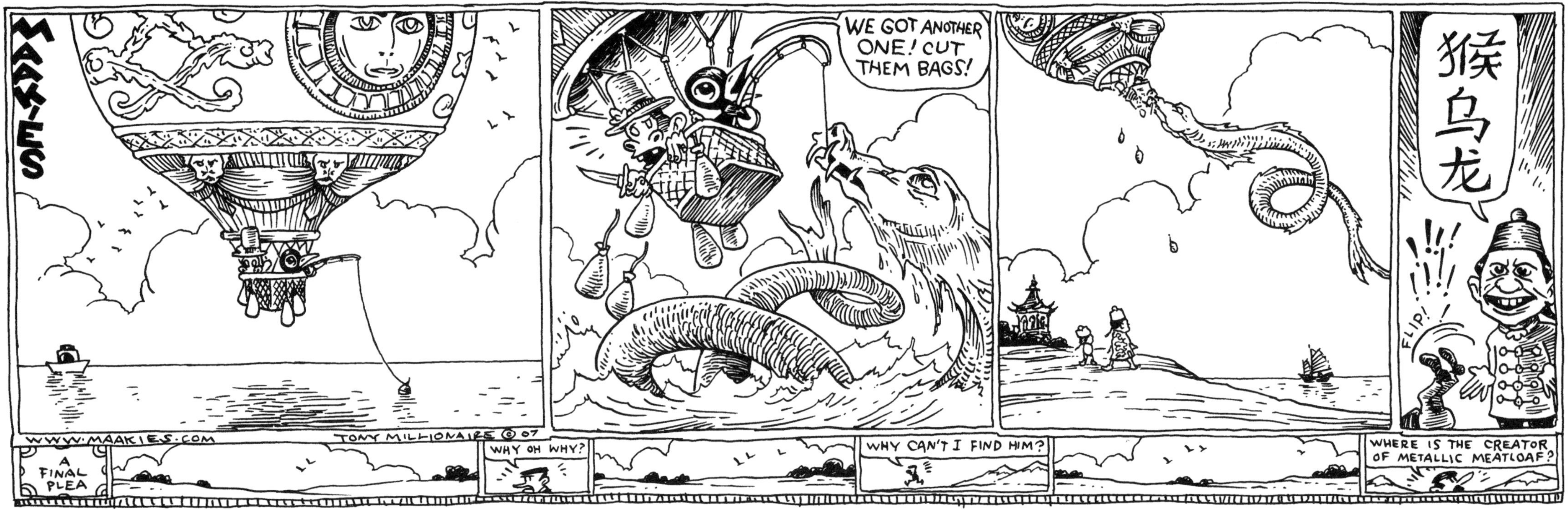
MAAKIES
WE GOT ANOTHER ONE! CUT THEM BAGS!
猴乌龙
FLIP!
WWW.MAAKIES.COM
TONY MILLIONAIRE © 07
A FINAL PLEA
WHY OH WHY?
WHY CAN'T I FIND HIM?
WHERE IS THE CREATOR OF METALLIC MEATLOAF?

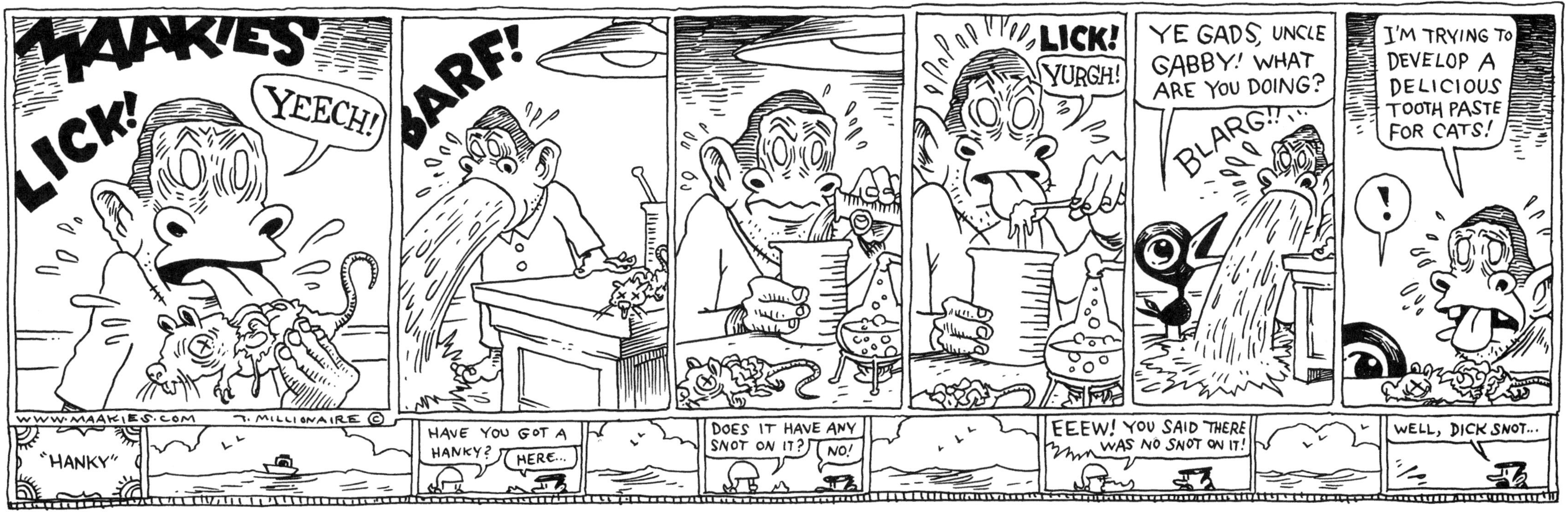
MAAKIES
LICK!
YEECH!
BARF!
LICK!
YURGH!
YE GADS, UNCLE GABBY! WHAT ARE YOU DOING?
BLARG!!
I'M TRYING TO DEVELOP A DELICIOUS TOOTH PASTE FOR CATS!
!
WWW.MAAKIES.COM
T. MILLIONAIRE ©
"HANKY"
HAVE YOU GOT A HANKY?
HERE...
DOES IT HAVE ANY SNOT ON IT?
NO!
EEEW! YOU SAID THERE WAS NO SNOT ON IT!
WELL, DICK SNOT...

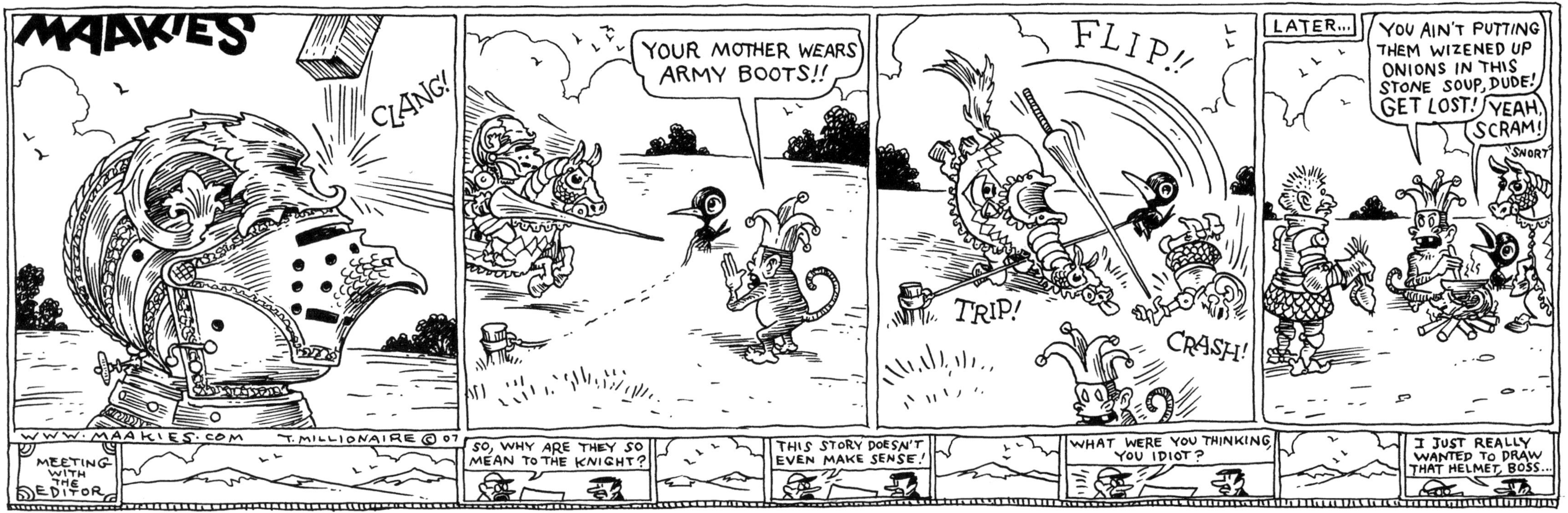

MAAKIES
CLANG!
YOUR MOTHER WEARS ARMY BOOTS!!
FLIP!!
TRIP!
CRASH!
LATER...
YOU AIN'T PUTTING THEM WIZENED UP ONIONS IN THIS STONE SOUP, DUDE! GET LOST!
YEAH, SCRAM!
SNORT
WWW.MAAKIES.COM
T. MILLIONAIRE © 07
MEETING WITH THE EDITOR
SO, WHY ARE THEY SO MEAN TO THE KNIGHT?
THIS STORY DOESN'T EVEN MAKE SENSE!
WHAT WERE YOU THINKING, YOU IDIOT?
I JUST REALLY WANTED TO DRAW THAT HELMET, BOSS...

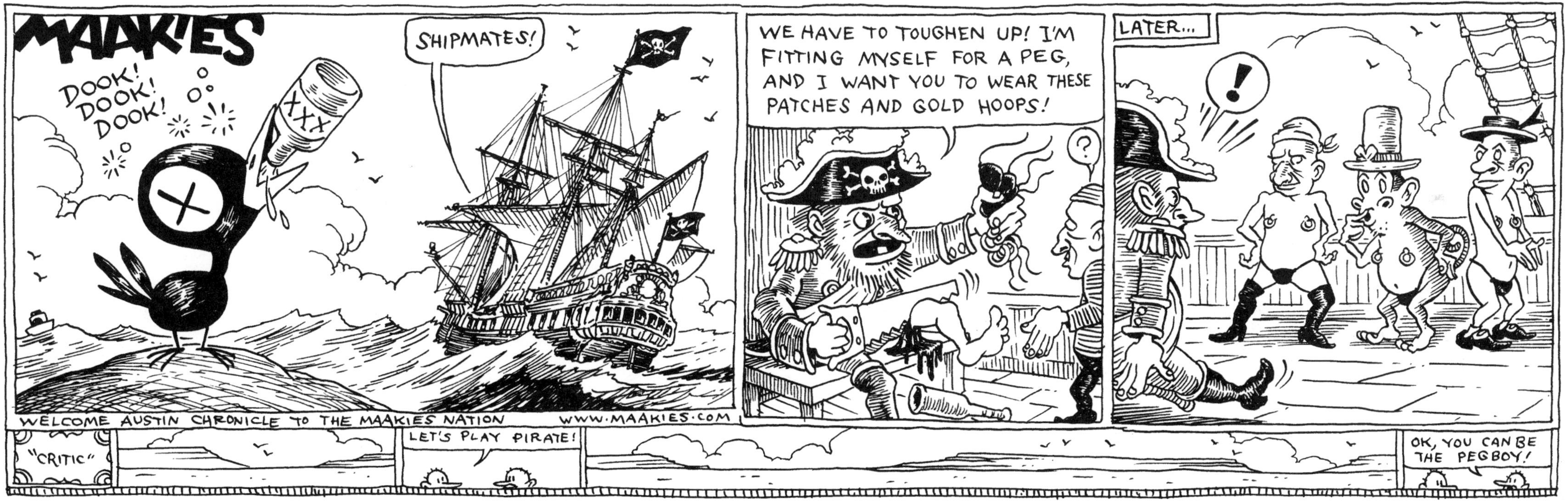
MAAKIES
DOOK! DOOK! DOOK!
XXX
SHIPMATES!
WE HAVE TO TOUGHEN UP! I'M FITTING MYSELF FOR A PEG, AND I WANT YOU TO WEAR THESE PATCHES AND GOLD HOOPS!
?
LATER...
!
WELCOME AUSTIN CHRONICLE TO THE MAAKIES NATION
WWW.MAAKIES.COM
"CRITIC"
LET'S PLAY PIRATE!
OK, YOU CAN BE THE PEGBOY!

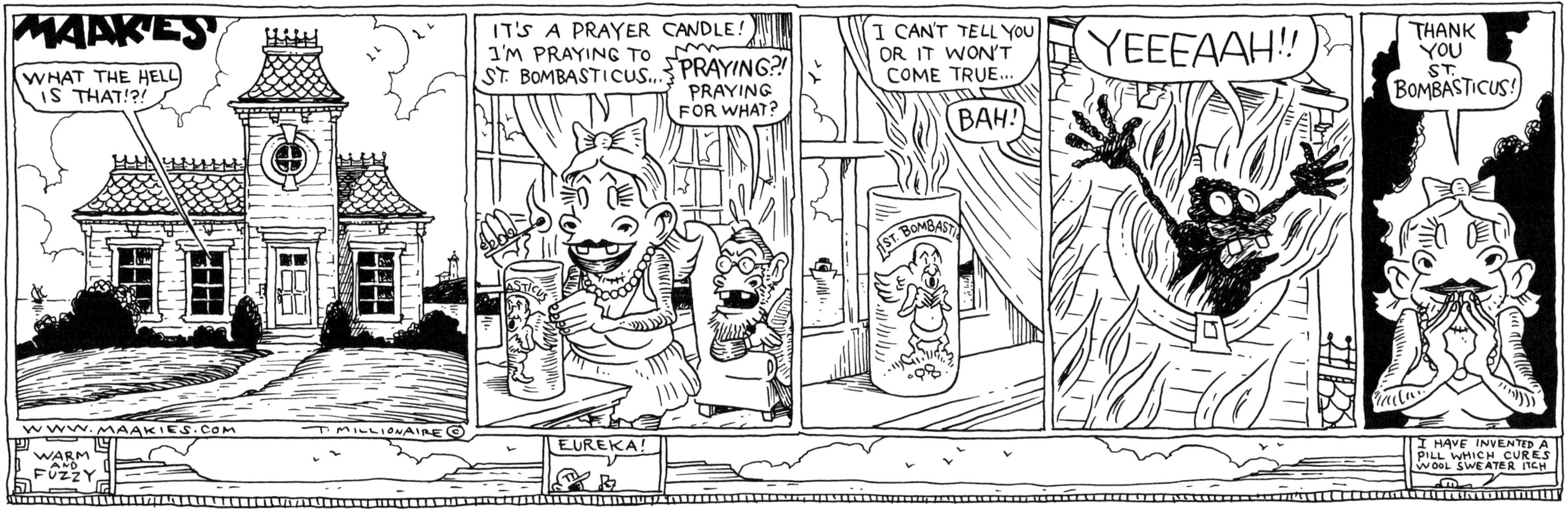
MAAKIES
WHAT THE HELL IS THAT!?!
WWW.MAAKIES.COM
T. MILLIONAIRE ©
IT'S A PRAYER CANDLE! I'M PRAYING TO ST. BOMBASTICUS...
PRAYING?! PRAYING FOR WHAT?
I CAN'T TELL YOU OR IT WON'T COME TRUE...
BAH!
ST. BOMBASTI
YEEEAAH!!
THANK YOU ST. BOMBASTICUS!
WARM AND FUZZY
EUREKA!
I HAVE INVENTED A PILL WHICH CURES WOOL SWEATER ITCH

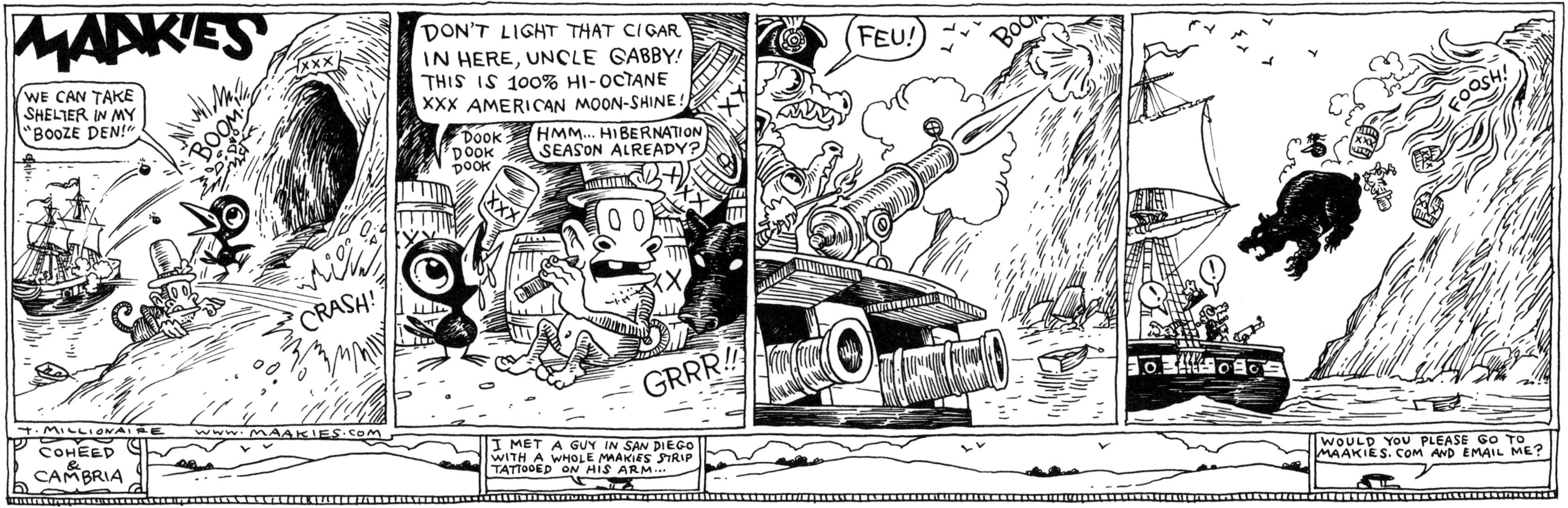
MAAKIES
WE CAN TAKE SHELTER IN MY "BOOZE DEN!"
XXX
BOOM!
CRASH!
DON'T LIGHT THAT CIGAR IN HERE, UNCLE GABBY! THIS IS 100% HI-OCTANE XXX AMERICAN MOON-SHINE!
DOOK DOOK DOOK
HMM... HIBERNATION SEASON ALREADY?
XXX
GRRR!!
FEU!
BOOM
FOOSH!
!
!
T. MILLIONAIRE
WWW.MAAKIES.COM
COHEED & CAMBRIA
I MET A GUY IN SAN DIEGO WITH A WHOLE MAAKIES STRIP TATTOOED ON HIS ARM...
WOULD YOU PLEASE GO TO MAAKIES.COM AND EMAIL ME?

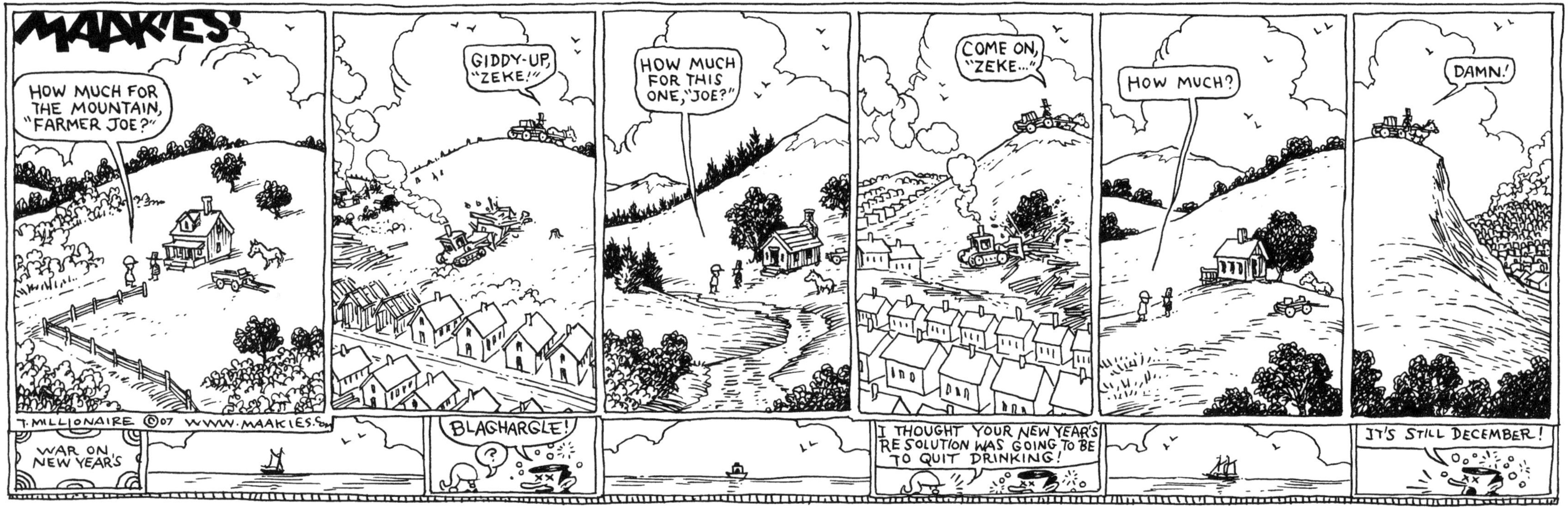
MAAKIES
HOW MUCH FOR THE MOUNTAIN, "FARMER JOE?"
GIDDY-UP, "ZEKE!"
HOW MUCH FOR THIS ONE, "JOE?"
COME ON, "ZEKE..."
HOW MUCH?
DAMN!
T. MILLIONAIRE ©07 WWW.MAAKIES.COM
WAR ON NEW YEAR'S
BLAGHARGLE!
?
I THOUGHT YOUR NEW YEAR'S RESOLUTION WAS GOING TO BE TO QUIT DRINKING!
IT'S STILL DECEMBER!

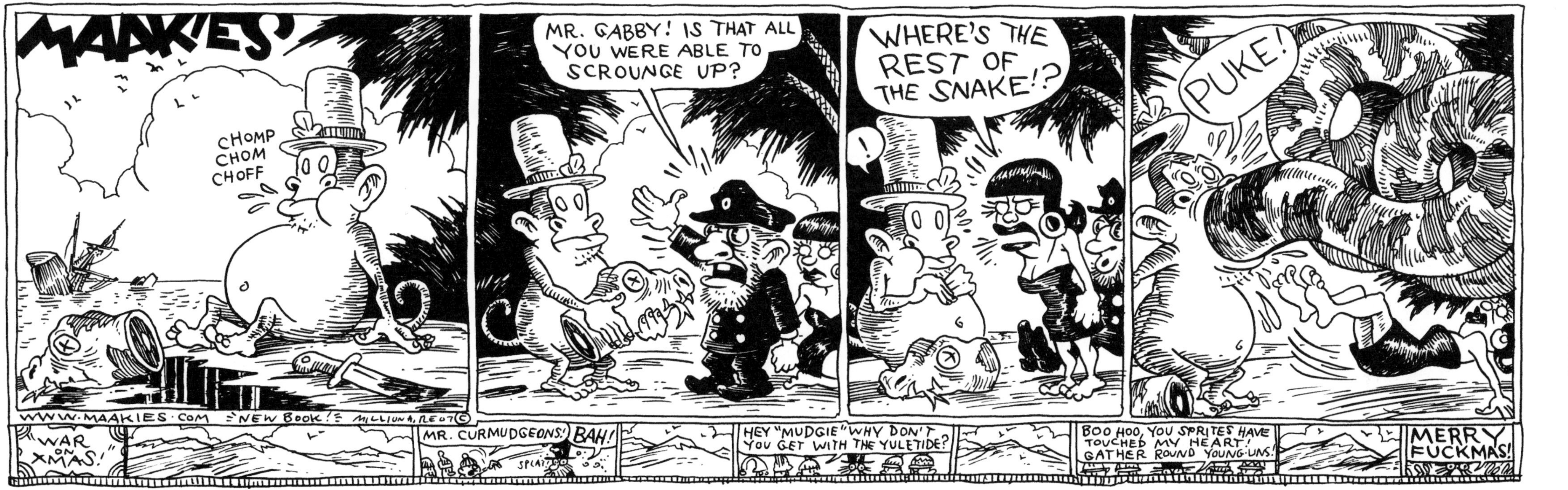
MAAKIES
CHOMP
CHOM
CHOFF
WWW.MAAKIES.COM
NEW BOOK!
MR. GABBY! IS THAT ALL YOU WERE ABLE TO SCROUNGE UP?
!
WHERE'S THE REST OF THE SNAKE!?
PUKE!
"WAR ON XMAS!"
MR. CURMUDGEONS!
BAH!
SPLAT
HEY "MUDGIE" WHY DON'T YOU GET WITH THE YULETIDE?
BOO HOO, YOU SPRITES HAVE TOUCHED MY HEART! GATHER ROUND YOUNG-UNS!
MERRY FUCKMAS!

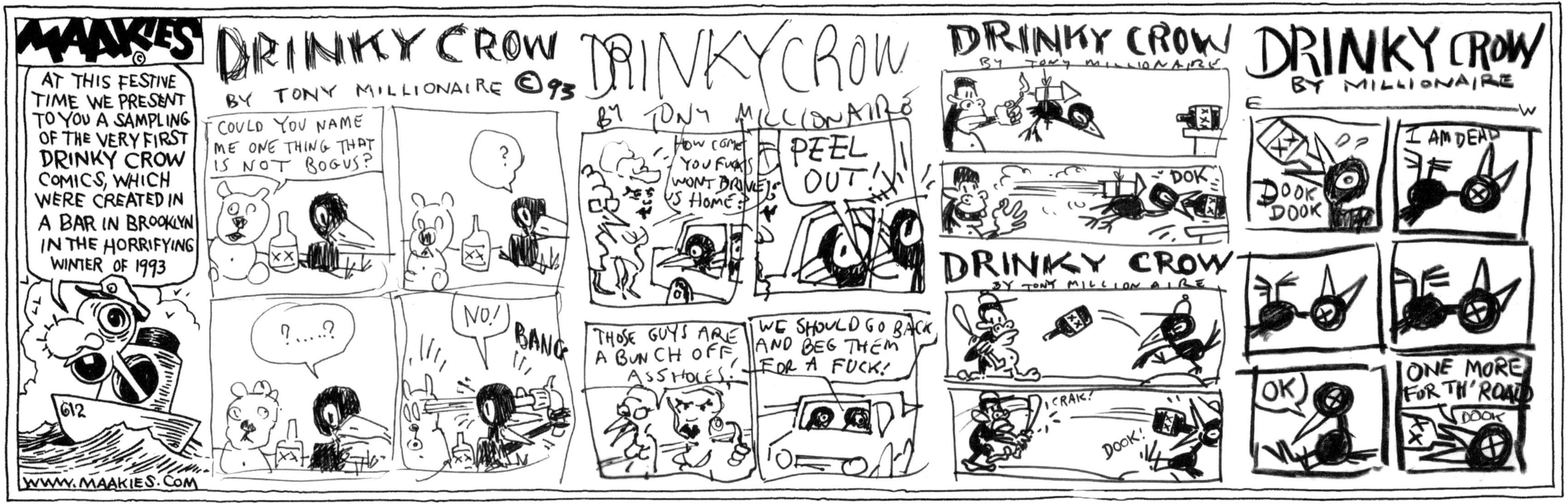
MAAKIES ©
AT THIS FESTIVE TIME WE PRESENT TO YOU A SAMPLING OF THE VERY FIRST DRINKY CROW COMICS, WHICH WERE CREATED IN A BAR IN BROOKLYN IN THE HORRIFYING WINTER OF 1993
612
WWW.MAAKIES.COM
DRINKY CROW
BY TONY MILLIONAIRE ©93
COULD YOU NAME ME ONE THING THAT IS NOT BOGUS?
?
?.....?
NO!
BANG
DRINKY CROW
BY TONY MILLIONAIRE
HOW COME YOU FUCKS WONT DRIVE US HOME?
PEEL OUT!
THOSE GUYS ARE A BUNCH OFF ASSHOLES!
WE SHOULD GO BACK AND BEG THEM FOR A FUCK!
DRINKY CROW
BY TONY MILLIONAIRE
DOK
DRINKY CROW
BY TONY MILLIONAIRE
CRAK!
DOOK!
DRINKY CROW
BY MILLIONAIRE
E
W
DOOK DOOK
I AM DEAD
OK
ONE MORE FOR TH' ROAD
DOOK

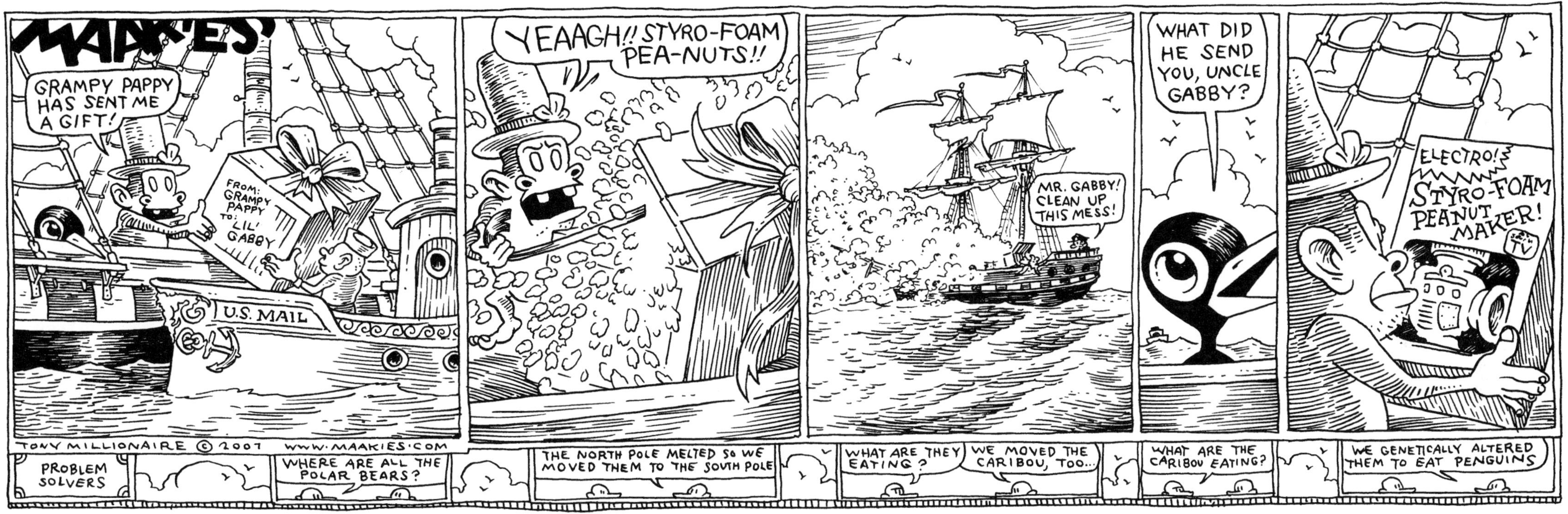

MAAKIES
GRAMPY PAPPY HAS SENT ME A GIFT!
FROM: GRAMPY PAPPY TO: LIL' GABBY
U.S. MAIL
YEAAGH!! STYRO-FOAM PEA-NUTS!!
MR. GABBY! CLEAN UP THIS MESS!
WHAT DID HE SEND YOU, UNCLE GABBY?
ELECTRO! STYRO-FOAM PEANUT MAKER!
TV
TONY MILLIONAIRE © 2007 WWW.MAAKIES.COM
PROBLEM SOLVERS
WHERE ARE ALL THE POLAR BEARS?
THE NORTH POLE MELTED SO WE MOVED THEM TO THE SOUTH POLE
WHAT ARE THEY EATING?
WE MOVED THE CARIBOU, TOO...
WHAT ARE THE CARIBOU EATING?
WE GENETICALLY ALTERED THEM TO EAT PENGUINS

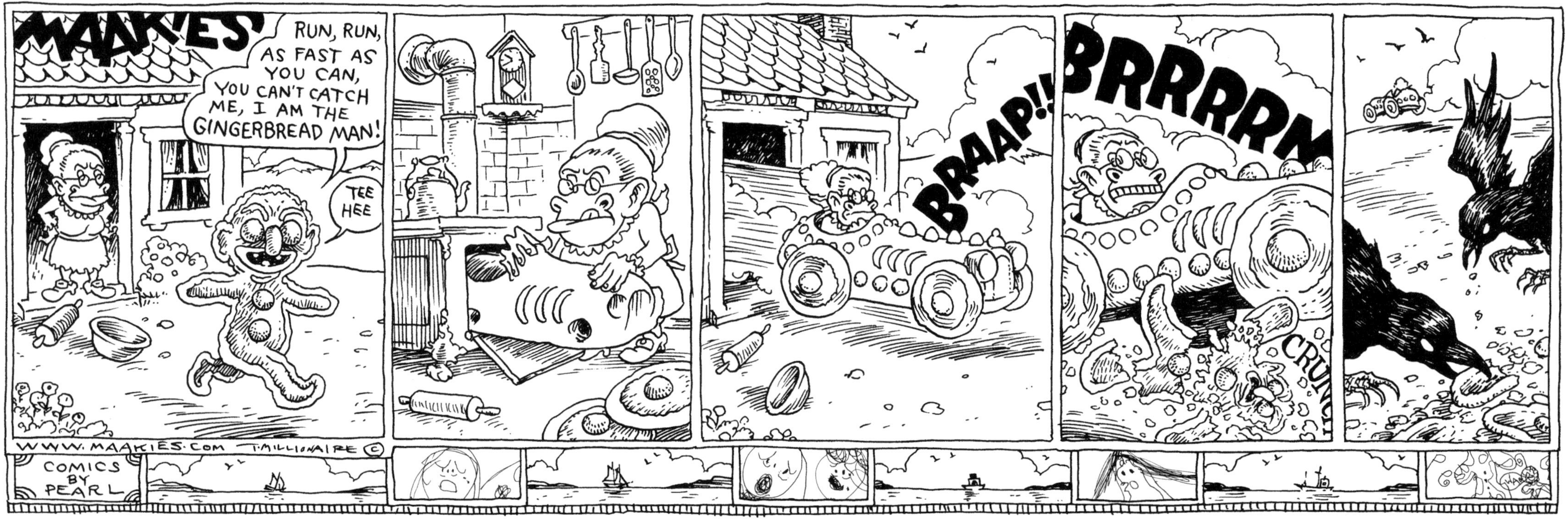
MAAKIES
RUN, RUN, AS FAST AS YOU CAN, YOU CAN'T CATCH ME, I AM THE GINGERBREAD MAN!
TEE HEE
BRAAP!!
BRRRRRM
CRUNCH
WWW.MAAKIES.COM
T.MILLIONAIRE ©
COMICS BY PEARL

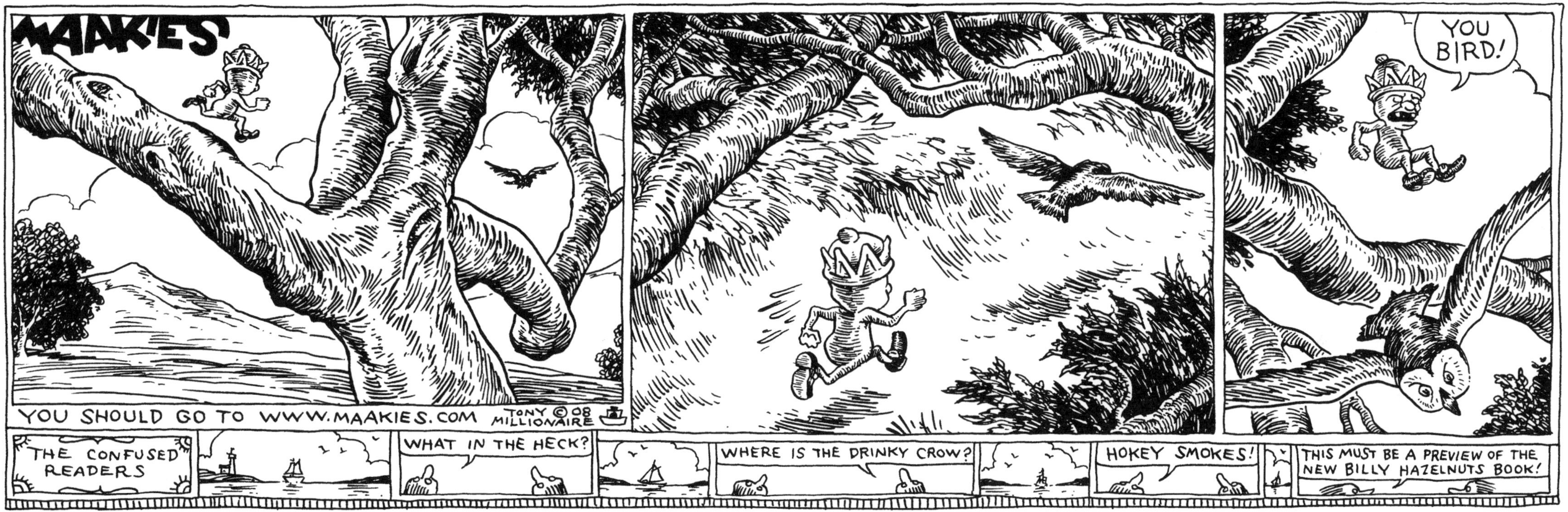
MAAKIES
YOU SHOULD GO TO WWW.MAAKIES.COM
TONY MILLIONAIRE ©08
YOU BIRD!
THE CONFUSED READERS
WHAT IN THE HECK?
WHERE IS THE DRINKY CROW?
HOKEY SMOKES!
THIS MUST BE A PREVIEW OF THE NEW BILLY HAZELNUTS BOOK!

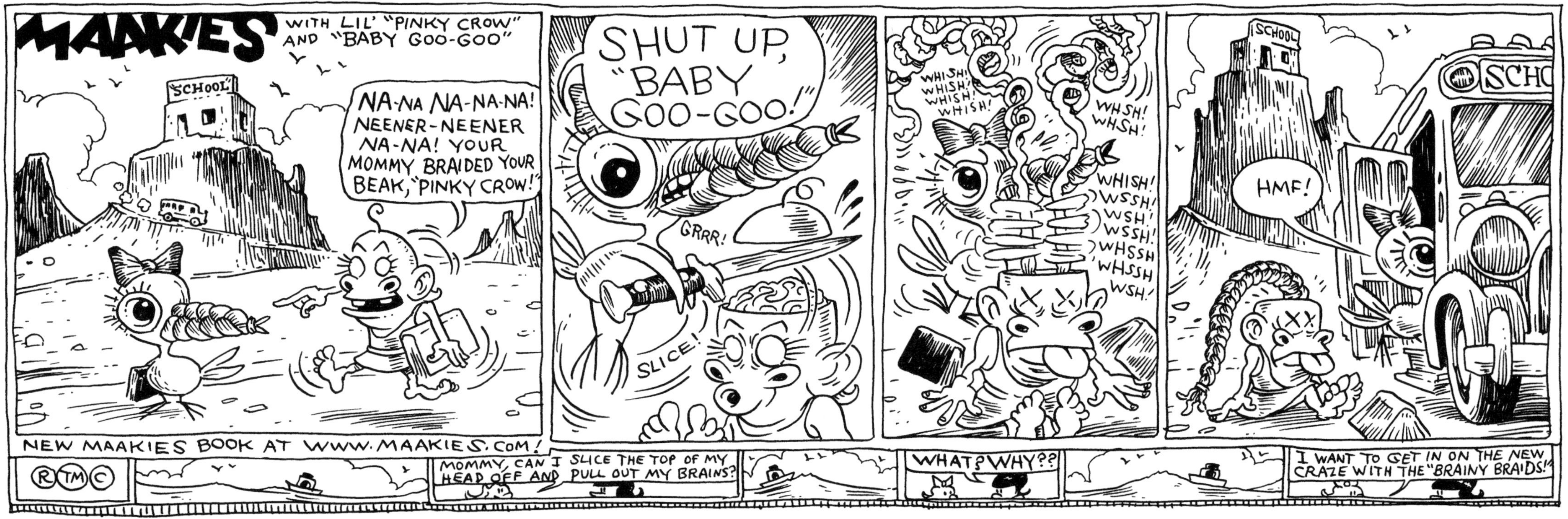
MAAKIES
WITH LIL' "PINKY CROW" AND "BABY GOO-GOO"
SCHOOL
NA-NA NA-NA-NA! NEENER-NEENER NA-NA! YOUR MOMMY BRAIDED YOUR BEAK, "PINKY CROW!"
SHUT UP, "BABY GOO-GOO!"
GRRR!
SLICE!
WHISH! WHISH! WHISH! WHISH!
WHSH! WHSH!
WHISH! WSSH! WSH! WSSH! WHSSH WHSSH WSH!
SCHOOL
SCHO
HMF!
NEW MAAKIES BOOK AT WWW.MAAKIES.COM!
R TM C
MOMMY, CAN I SLICE THE TOP OF MY HEAD OFF AND PULL OUT MY BRAINS?
WHAT? WHY??
I WANT TO GET IN ON THE NEW CRAZE WITH THE "BRAINY BRAIDS!"

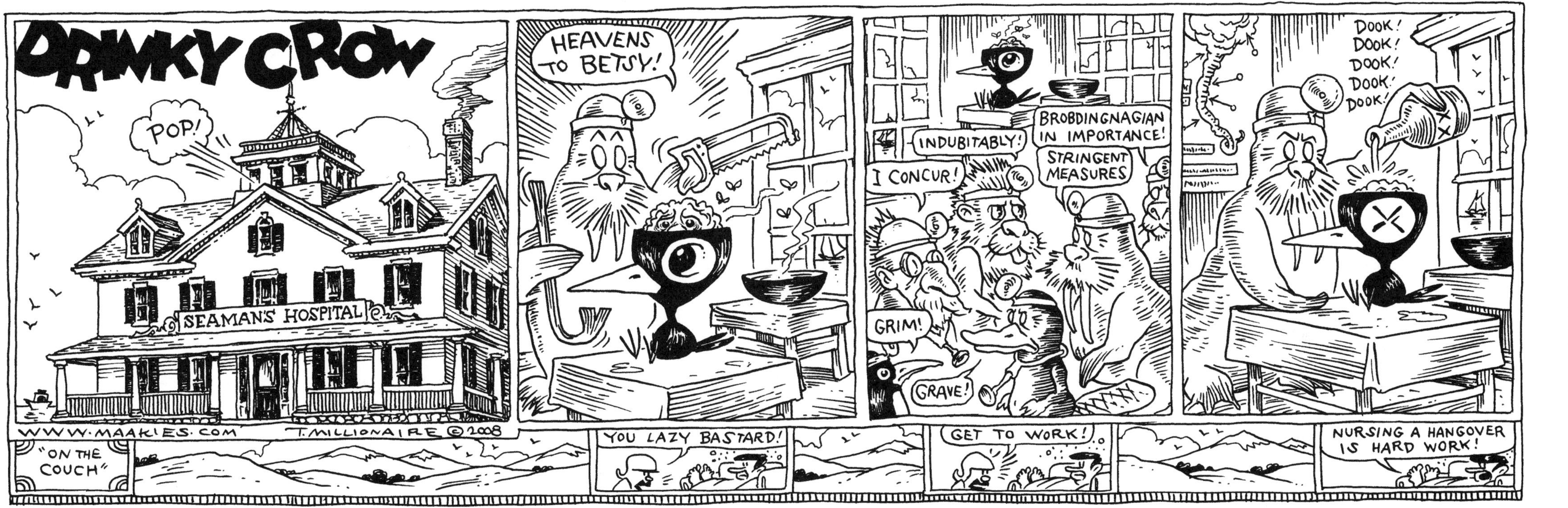
DRINKY CROW
POP!
SEAMAN'S HOSPITAL
HEAVENS TO BETSY!
INDUBITABLY!
BROBDINGNAGIAN IN IMPORTANCE!
I CONCUR!
STRINGENT MEASURES
GRIM!
GRAVE!
DOOK! DOOK! DOOK! DOOK! DOOK!
WWW.MAAKIES.COM
T. MILLIONAIRE ©2008
"ON THE COUCH"
YOU LAZY BASTARD!
GET TO WORK!
NURSING A HANGOVER IS HARD WORK!

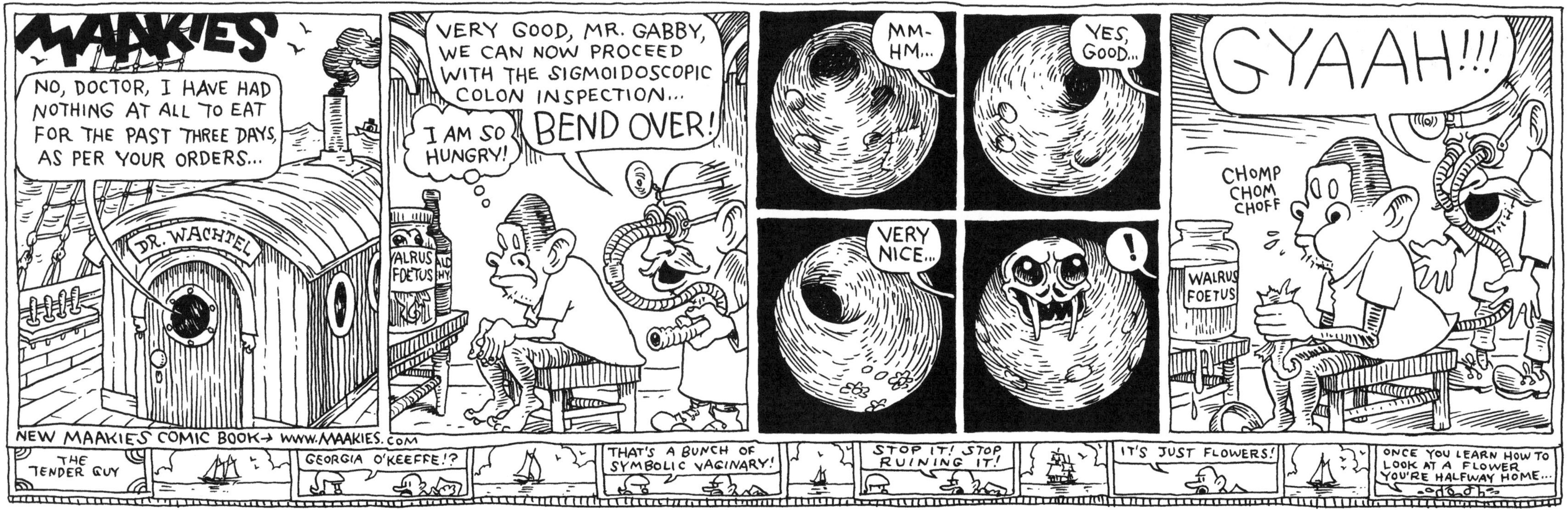
MAAKIES
NO, DOCTOR, I HAVE HAD NOTHING AT ALL TO EAT FOR THE PAST THREE DAYS, AS PER YOUR ORDERS...
DR. WACHTEL
VERY GOOD, MR. GABBY, WE CAN NOW PROCEED WITH THE SIGMOIDOSCOPIC COLON INSPECTION...
I AM SO HUNGRY!
BEND OVER!
WALRUS FOETUS
MM-HM...
YES, GOOD...
VERY NICE...
!
GYAAH!!!
CHOMP CHOM CHOFF
WALRUS FOETUS
NEW MAAKIES COMIC BOOK→ WWW.MAAKIES.COM
THE TENDER GUY
GEORGIA O'KEEFFE!?
THAT'S A BUNCH OF SYMBOLIC VAGINARY!
STOP IT! STOP RUINING IT!
IT'S JUST FLOWERS!
ONCE YOU LEARN HOW TO LOOK AT A FLOWER YOU'RE HALFWAY HOME...

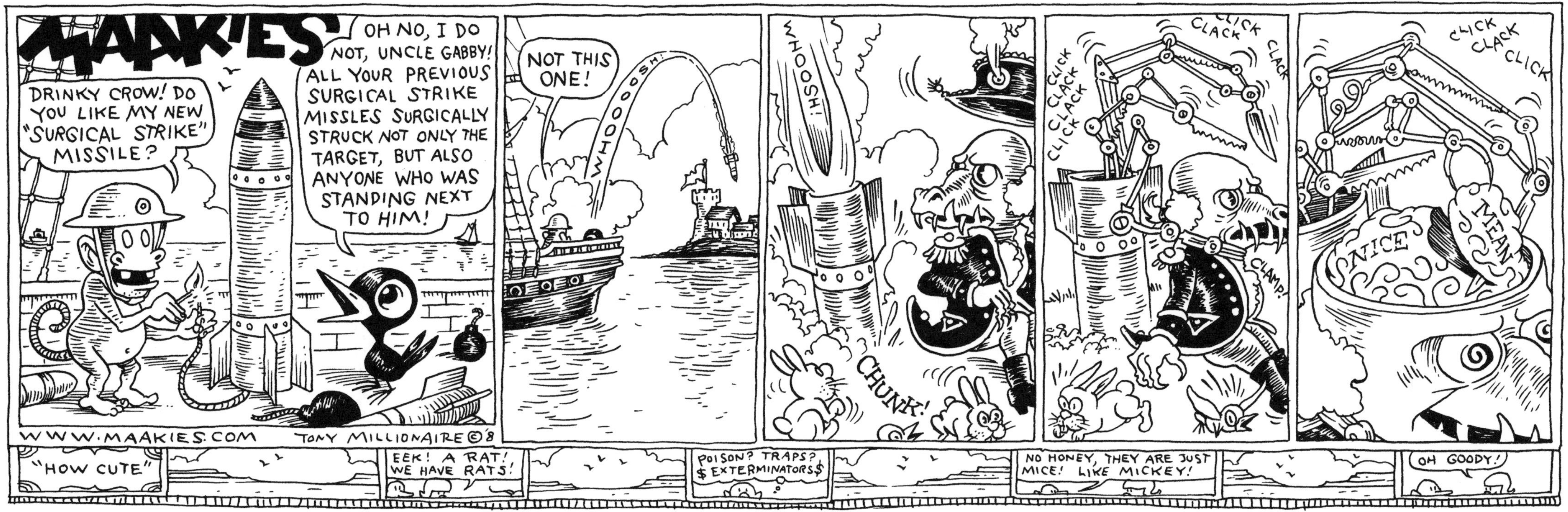
MAAKIES
DRINKY CROW! DO YOU LIKE MY NEW "SURGICAL STRIKE" MISSILE?
OH NO, I DO NOT, UNCLE GABBY! ALL YOUR PREVIOUS SURGICAL STRIKE MISSLES SURGICALLY STRUCK NOT ONLY THE TARGET, BUT ALSO ANYONE WHO WAS STANDING NEXT TO HIM!
WWW.MAAKIES.COM
TONY MILLIONAIRE ©'8
NOT THIS ONE!
WHOOOOOOSH!
WHOOSH!
WHOOSH!
CHUNK!
CLICK CLACK CLICK
CLICK CLACK CLACK
CLICK CLACK CLACK CLICK
CLAMP!
CLICK CLACK CLICK
NICE
MEAN
"HOW CUTE"
EEK! A RAT! WE HAVE RATS!
POISON? TRAPS? $ EXTERMINATORS $
NO HONEY, THEY ARE JUST MICE! LIKE MICKEY!
OH GOODY!

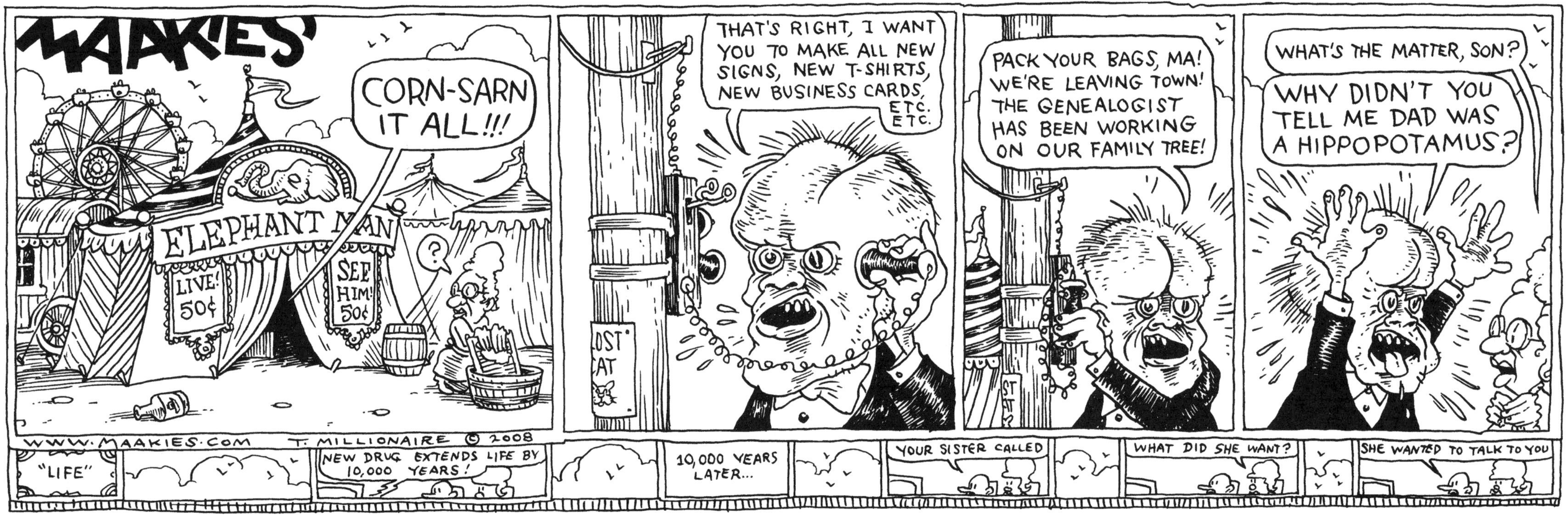
MAAKIES
CORN-SARN IT ALL!!!
ELEPHANT MAN
LIVE! 50¢
SEE HIM! 50¢
?
THAT'S RIGHT, I WANT YOU TO MAKE ALL NEW SIGNS, NEW T-SHIRTS, NEW BUSINESS CARDS, ETC. ETC.
PACK YOUR BAGS, MA! WE'RE LEAVING TOWN! THE GENEALOGIST HAS BEEN WORKING ON OUR FAMILY TREE!
WHAT'S THE MATTER, SON?
WHY DIDN'T YOU TELL ME DAD WAS A HIPPOPOTAMUS?
WWW.MAAKIES.COM T. MILLIONAIRE © 2008
"LIFE"
NEW DRUG EXTENDS LIFE BY 10,000 YEARS!
10,000 YEARS LATER...
YOUR SISTER CALLED
WHAT DID SHE WANT?
SHE WANTED TO TALK TO YOU

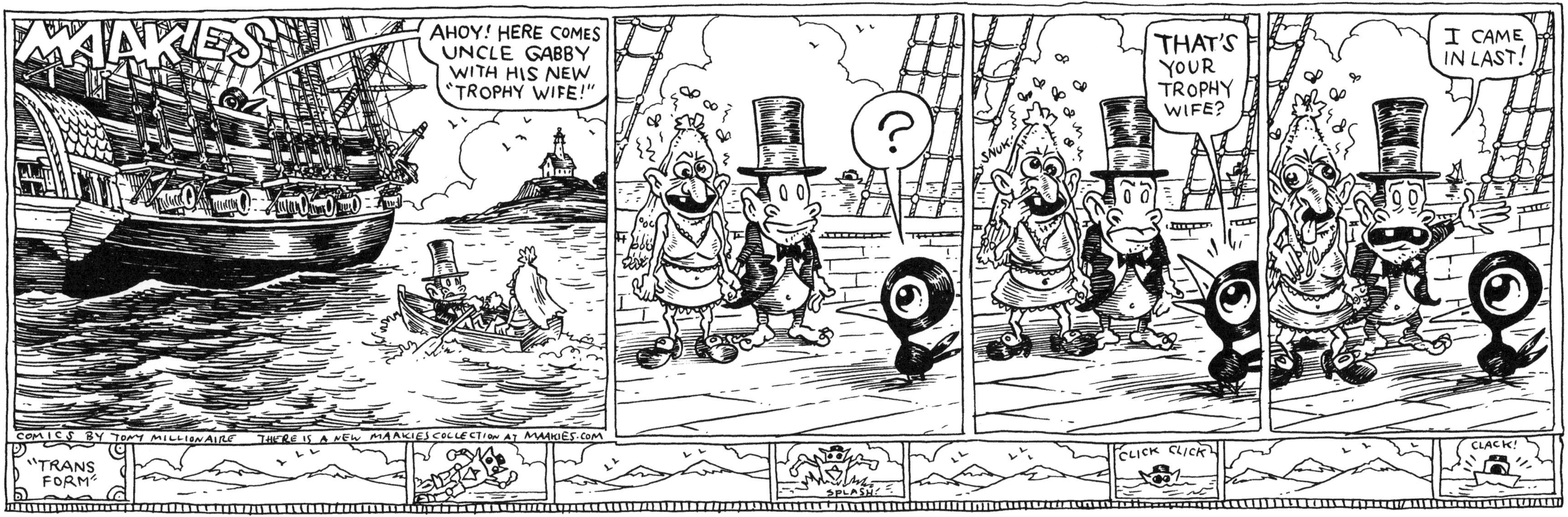
MAAKIES
AHOY! HERE COMES UNCLE GABBY WITH HIS NEW "TROPHY WIFE!"
?
SNUK
THAT'S YOUR TROPHY WIFE?
I CAME IN LAST!
COMICS BY TONY MILLIONAIRE THERE IS A NEW MAAKIES COLLECTION AT MAAKIES.COM
"TRANS FORM"
SPLASH!
CLICK CLICK
CLACK!

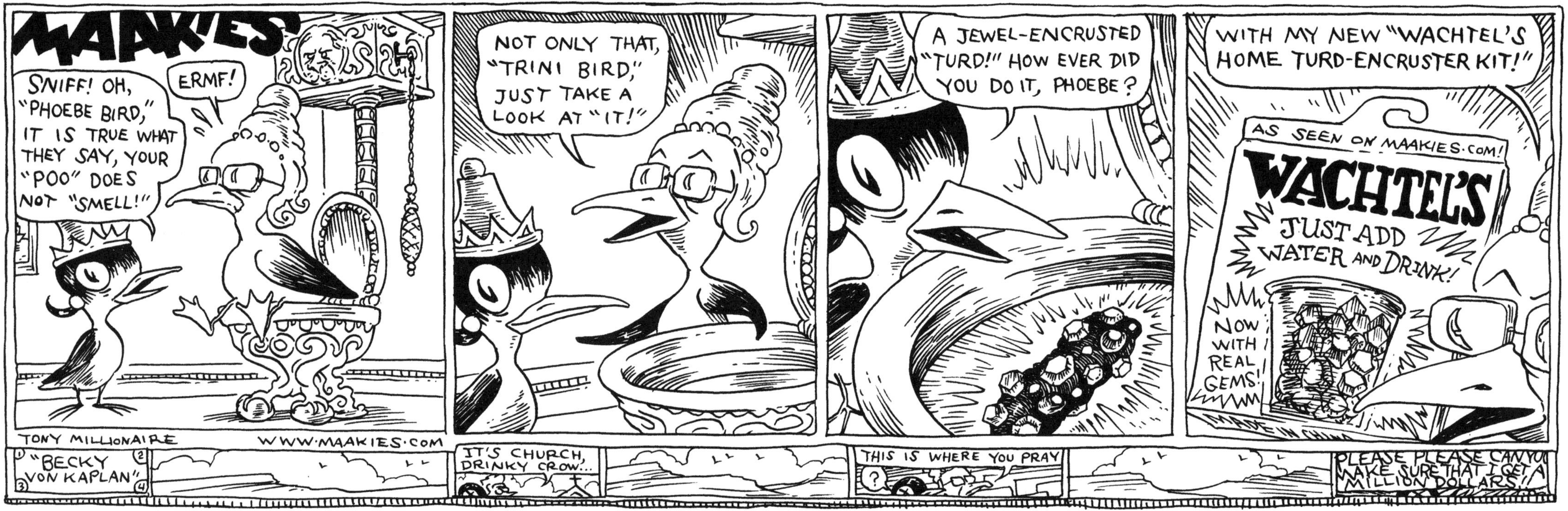
MAAKIES
SNIFF! OH, "PHOEBE BIRD," IT IS TRUE WHAT THEY SAY, YOUR "POO" DOES NOT "SMELL!"
ERMF!
NOT ONLY THAT, "TRINI BIRD," JUST TAKE A LOOK AT "IT!"
A JEWEL-ENCRUSTED "TURD!" HOW EVER DID YOU DO IT, PHOEBE?
WITH MY NEW "WACHTEL'S HOME TURD-ENCRUSTER KIT!"
AS SEEN ON MAAKIES·COM!
WACHTEL'S
JUST ADD WATER AND DRINK!
NOW WITH REAL GEMS!
TONY MILLIONAIRE
WWW·MAAKIES·COM
"BECKY VON KAPLAN"
IT'S CHURCH, DRINKY CROW...
THIS IS WHERE YOU PRAY
?
PLEASE PLEASE CAN YOU MAKE SURE THAT I GET A MILLION DOLLARS!

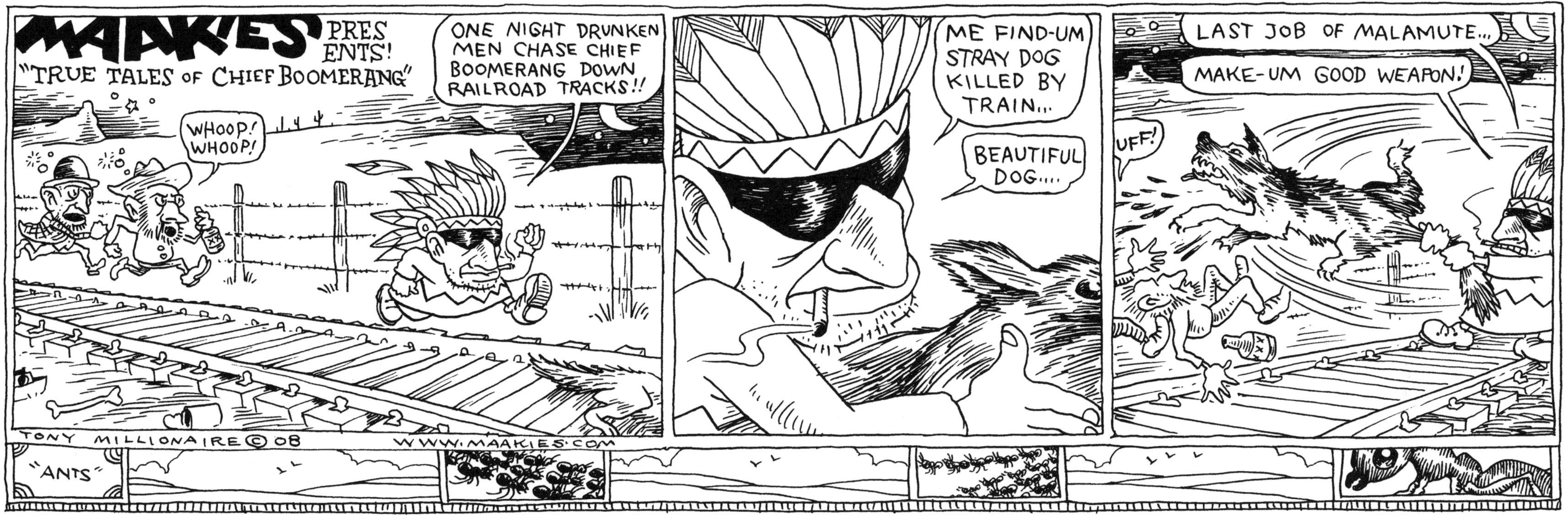

MAAKIES PRESENTS!
"TRUE TALES OF CHIEF BOOMERANG"
ONE NIGHT DRUNKEN MEN CHASE CHIEF BOOMERANG DOWN RAILROAD TRACKS!!
WHOOP! WHOOP!
ME FIND-UM STRAY DOG KILLED BY TRAIN...
BEAUTIFUL DOG....
LAST JOB OF MALAMUTE...
MAKE-UM GOOD WEAPON!
UFF!
TONY MILLIONAIRE © 08
WWW.MAAKIES.COM
"ANTS"

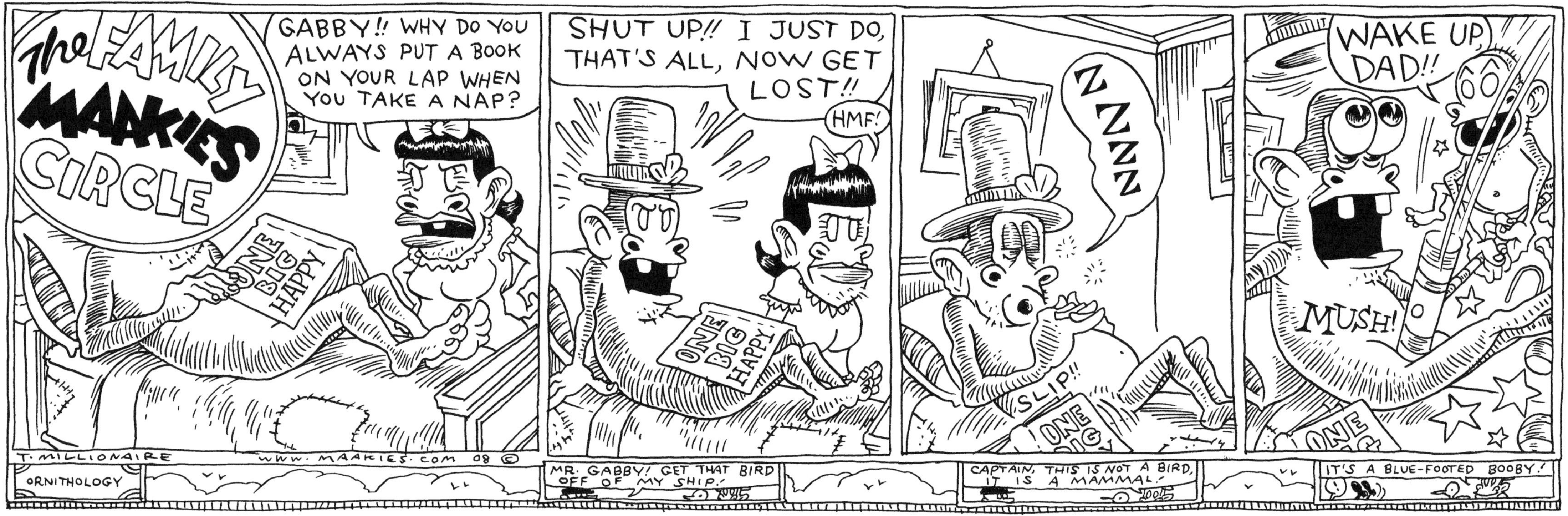

The FAMILY MAAKIES CIRCLE
GABBY!! WHY DO YOU ALWAYS PUT A BOOK ON YOUR LAP WHEN YOU TAKE A NAP?
ONE BIG HAPPY
SHUT UP!! I JUST DO, THAT'S ALL, NOW GET LOST!!
HMF!
ONE BIG HAPPY
ZZZZ
SLIP!!
ONE BIG
WAKE UP, DAD!!
MUSH!
ONE BIG
T. MILLIONAIRE
WWW. MAAKIES. COM 08 ©
ORNITHOLOGY
MR. GABBY! GET THAT BIRD OFF OF MY SHIP!
CAPTAIN, THIS IS NOT A BIRD, IT IS A MAMMAL!
IT'S A BLUE-FOOTED BOOBY!

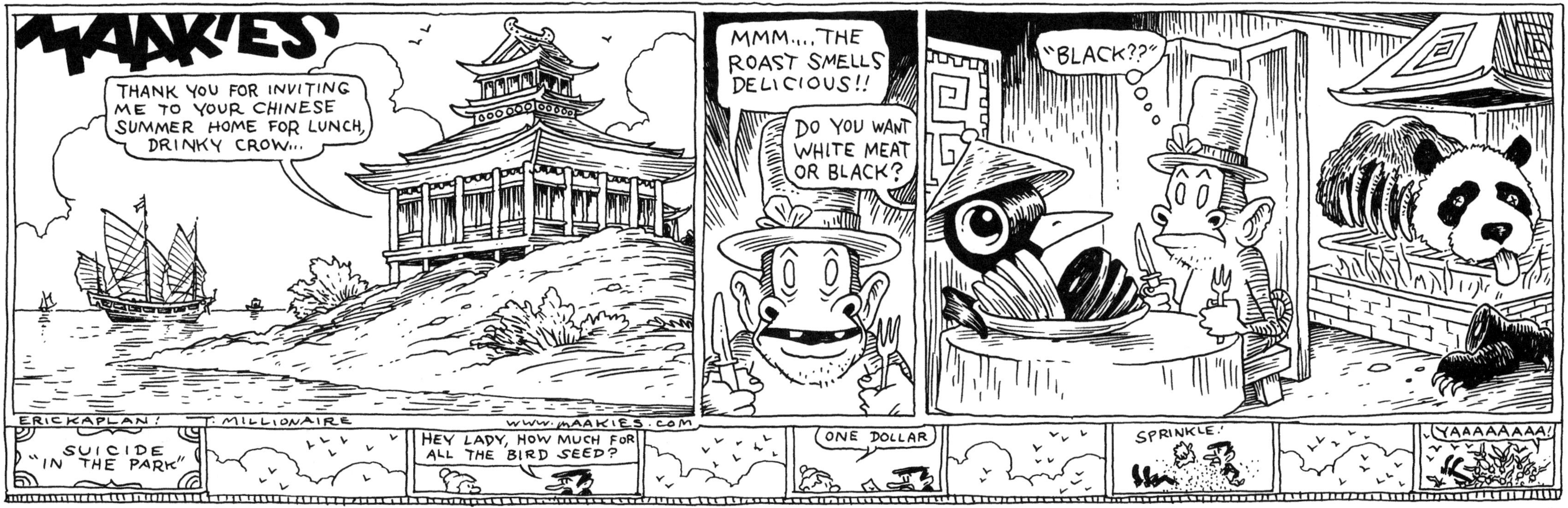

MAAKIES
THANK YOU FOR INVITING ME TO YOUR CHINESE SUMMER HOME FOR LUNCH, DRINKY CROW...
MMM.... THE ROAST SMELLS DELICIOUS!!
DO YOU WANT WHITE MEAT OR BLACK?
"BLACK??"
ERICKAPLAN!
T. MILLIONAIRE
WWW.MAAKIES.COM
SUICIDE "IN THE PARK"
HEY LADY, HOW MUCH FOR ALL THE BIRD SEED?
ONE DOLLAR
SPRINKLE!
YAAAAAAAA!

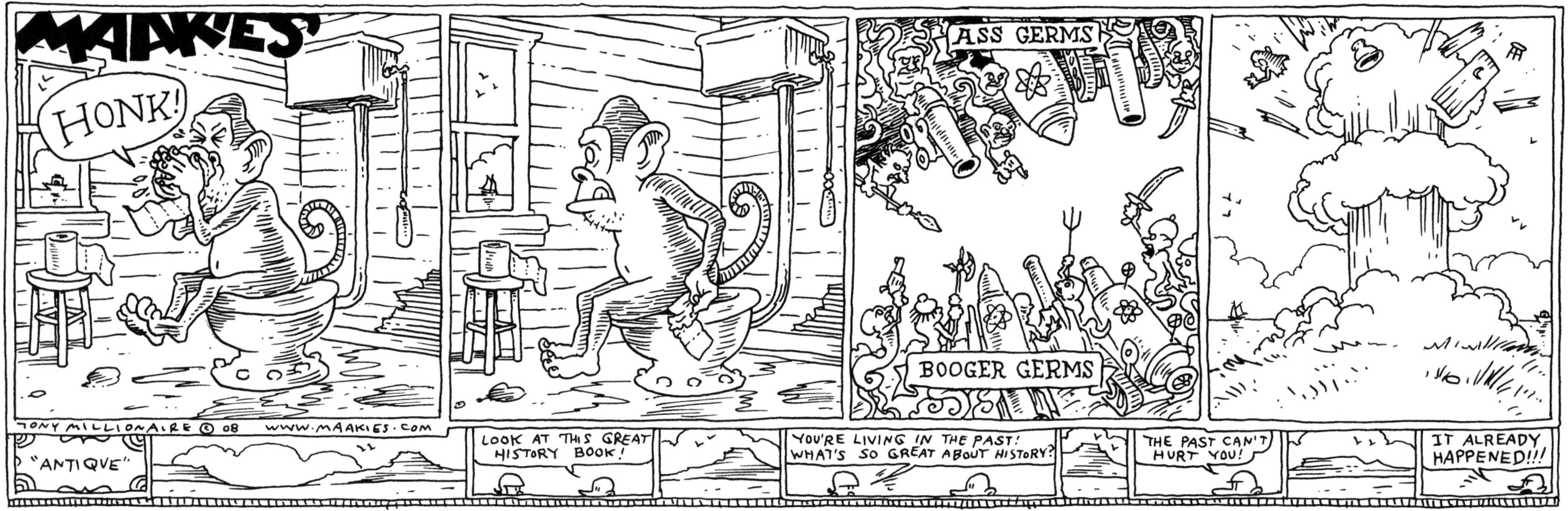
MAAKIES
HONK!
ASS GERMS
BOOGER GERMS
TONY MILLIONAIRE © 08 WWW.MAAKIES.COM
"ANTIQUE"
LOOK AT THIS GREAT HISTORY BOOK!
YOU'RE LIVING IN THE PAST! WHAT'S SO GREAT ABOUT HISTORY?
THE PAST CAN'T HURT YOU!
IT ALREADY HAPPENED!!!

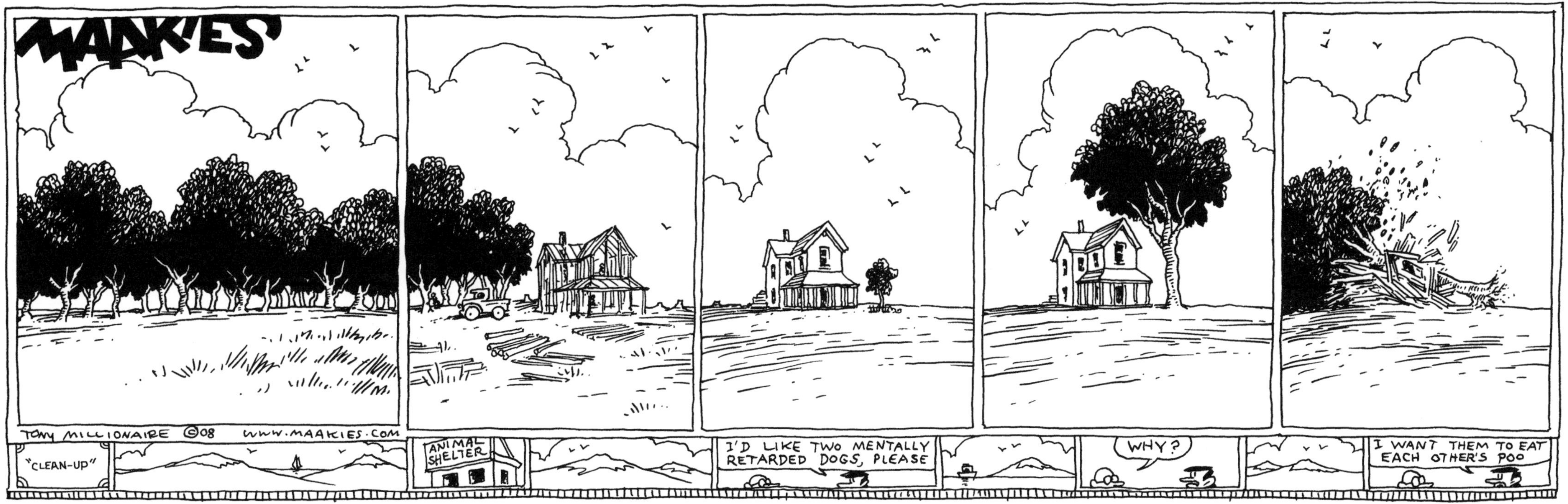
MAAKIES
TONY MILLIONAIRE ©08
WWW.MAAKIES.COM
"CLEAN-UP"
ANIMAL SHELTER
I'D LIKE TWO MENTALLY RETARDED DOGS, PLEASE
WHY?
I WANT THEM TO EAT EACH OTHER'S POO

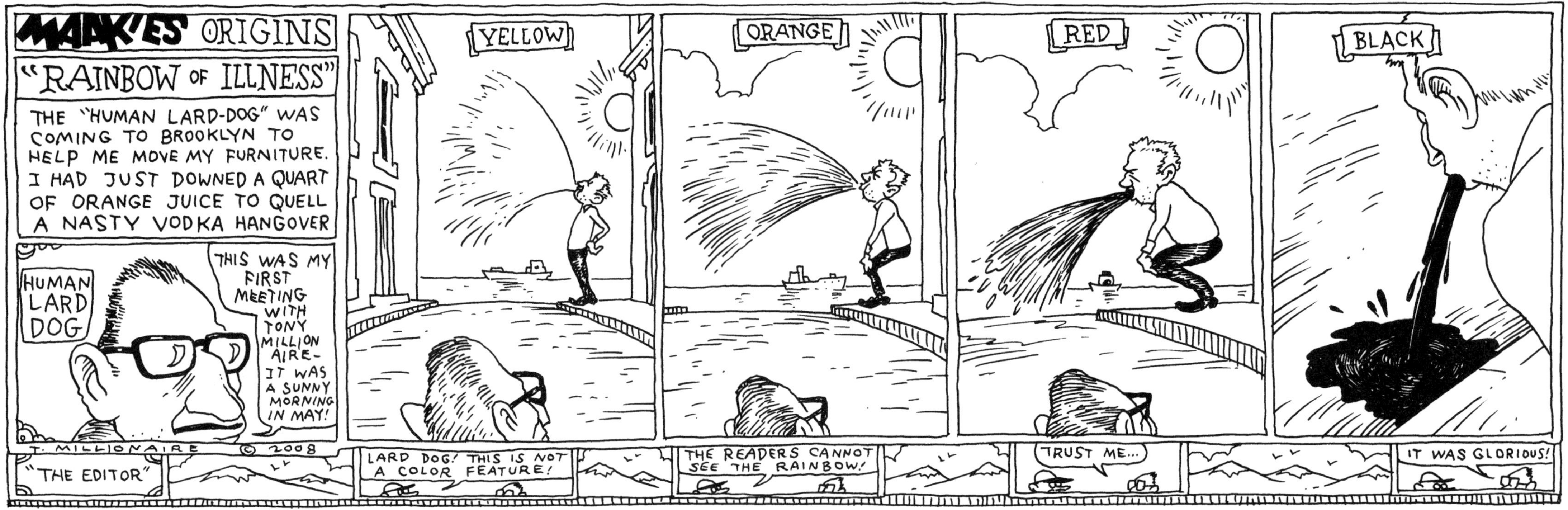
MAAKIES ORIGINS
"RAINBOW OF ILLNESS"
THE "HUMAN LARD-DOG" WAS COMING TO BROOKLYN TO HELP ME MOVE MY FURNITURE. I HAD JUST DOWNED A QUART OF ORANGE JUICE TO QUELL A NASTY VODKA HANGOVER
HUMAN LARD DOG
THIS WAS MY FIRST MEETING WITH TONY MILLIONAIRE- IT WAS A SUNNY MORNING IN MAY!
YELLOW
ORANGE
RED
BLACK
T. MILLIONAIRE © 2008
"THE EDITOR"
LARD DOG! THIS IS NOT A COLOR FEATURE!
THE READERS CANNOT SEE THE RAINBOW!
TRUST ME...
IT WAS GLORIOUS!

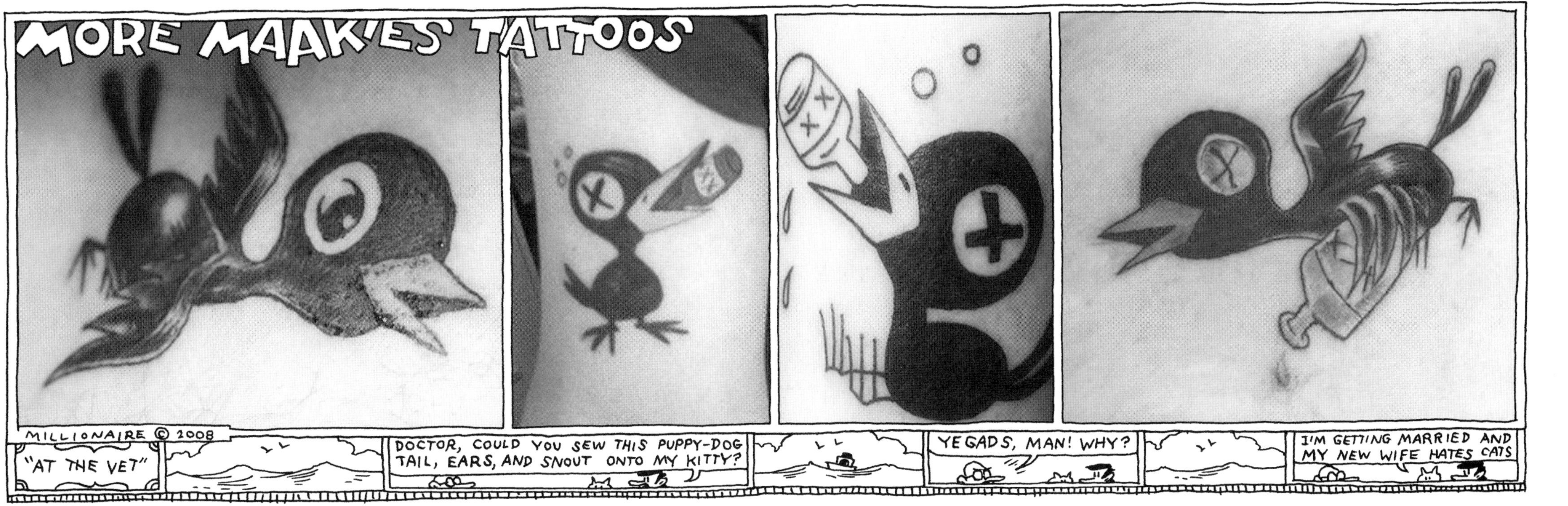
MORE MAAKIES TATTOOS
MILLIONAIRE © 2008
"AT THE VET"
DOCTOR, COULD YOU SEW THIS PUPPY-DOG TAIL, EARS, AND SNOUT ONTO MY KITTY?
YEGADS, MAN! WHY?
I'M GETTING MARRIED AND MY NEW WIFE HATES CATS

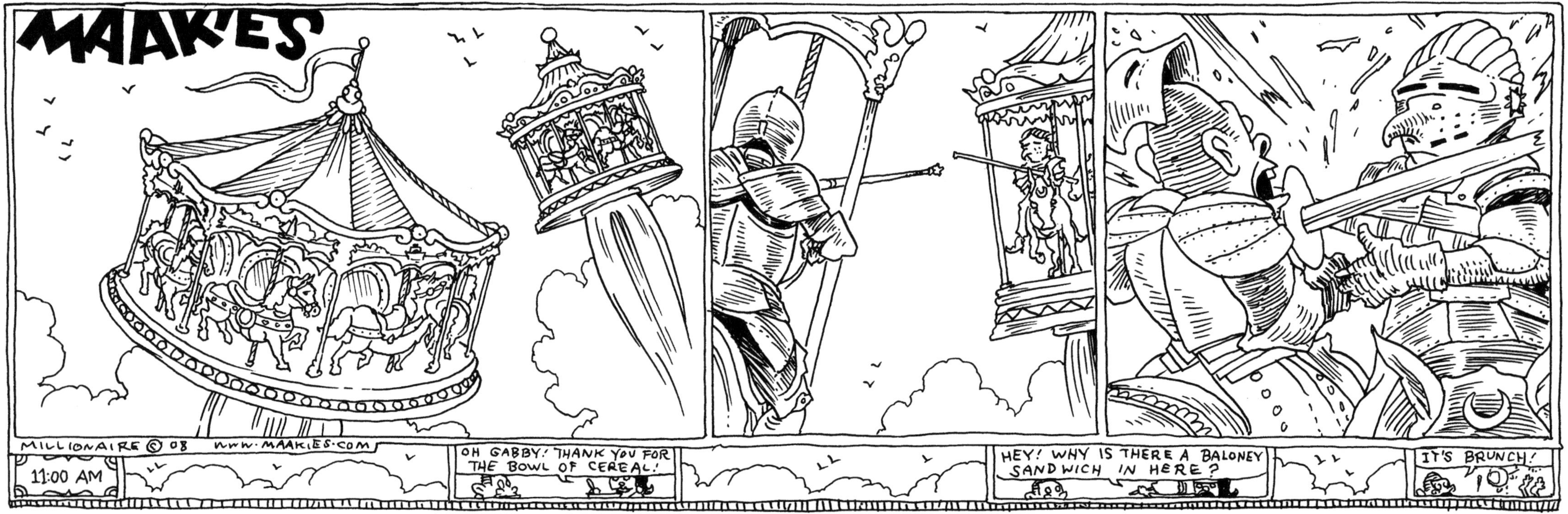

MAAKIES
MILLIONAIRE © 08 WWW.MAAKIES.COM
11:00 AM
OH GABBY! THANK YOU FOR THE BOWL OF CEREAL!
HEY! WHY IS THERE A BALONEY SANDWICH IN HERE?
IT'S BRUNCH!

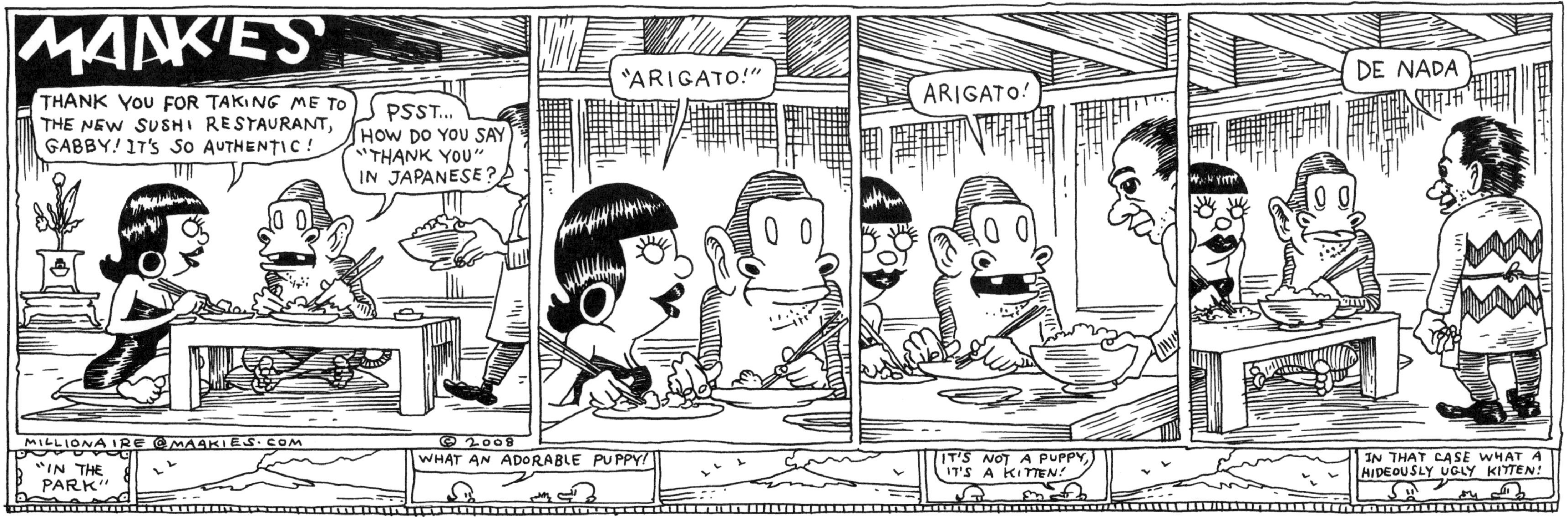
MAAKIES
THANK YOU FOR TAKING ME TO THE NEW SUSHI RESTAURANT, GABBY! IT'S SO AUTHENTIC!
PSST... HOW DO YOU SAY "THANK YOU" IN JAPANESE?
"ARIGATO!"
ARIGATO!
DE NADA
MILLIONAIRE@MAAKIES.COM
© 2008
"IN THE PARK"
WHAT AN ADORABLE PUPPY!
IT'S NOT A PUPPY, IT'S A KITTEN!
IN THAT CASE WHAT A HIDEOUSLY UGLY KITTEN!

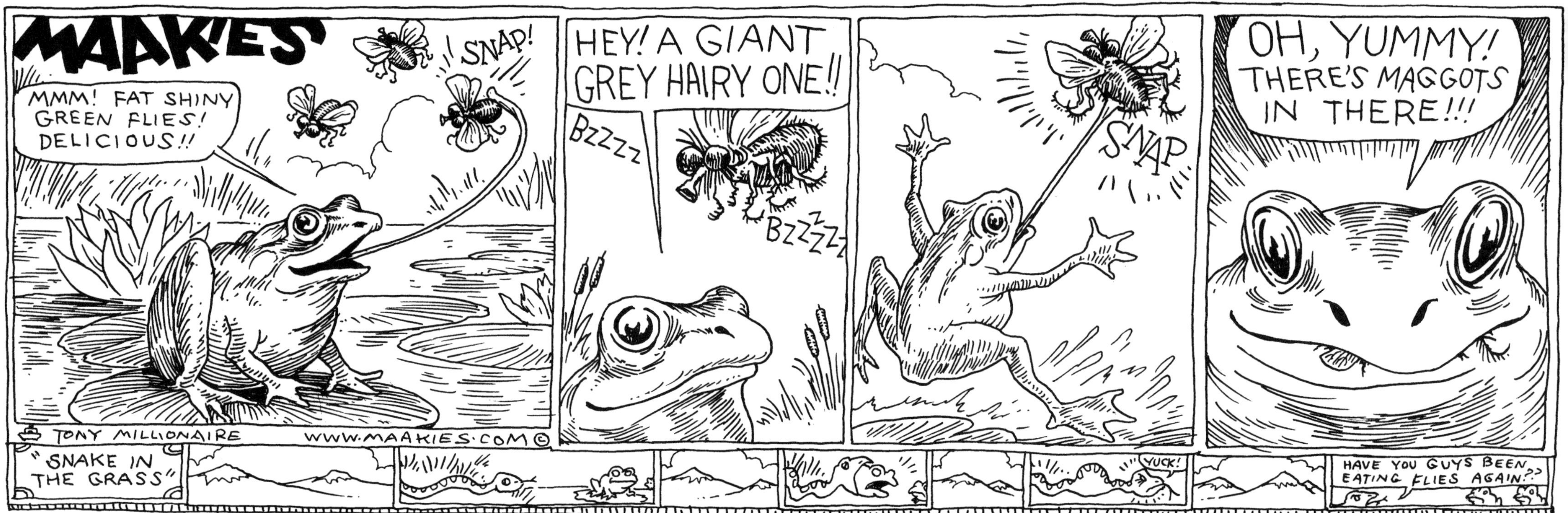
MAAKIES
MMM! FAT SHINY GREEN FLIES! DELICIOUS!!
SNAP!
TONY MILLIONAIRE
WWW.MAAKIES.COM ©
HEY! A GIANT GREY HAIRY ONE!!
BZZZZZ
BZZZZZ
SNAP
OH, YUMMY! THERE'S MAGGOTS IN THERE!!!
"SNAKE IN THE GRASS"
YUCK!
HAVE YOU GUYS BEEN EATING FLIES AGAIN??

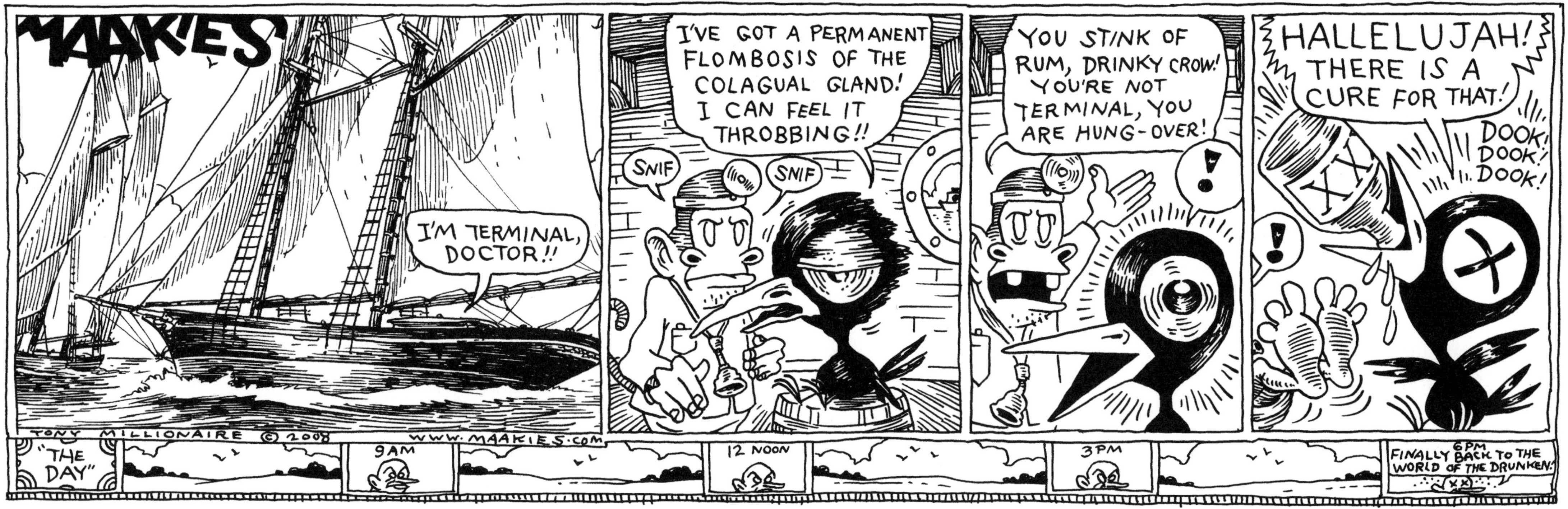

MAAKIES
I'M TERMINAL, DOCTOR!!
TONY MILLIONAIRE © 2008
WWW.MAAKIES.COM
I'VE GOT A PERMANENT FLOMBOSIS OF THE COLAGUAL GLAND! I CAN FEEL IT THROBBING!!
SNIF
SNIF
YOU STINK OF RUM, DRINKY CROW! YOU'RE NOT TERMINAL, YOU ARE HUNG-OVER!
!
HALLELUJAH! THERE IS A CURE FOR THAT!
DOOK! DOOK! DOOK!
!
XX
"THE DAY"
9AM
12 NOON
3PM
6PM
FINALLY BACK TO THE WORLD OF THE DRUNKEN!
XX

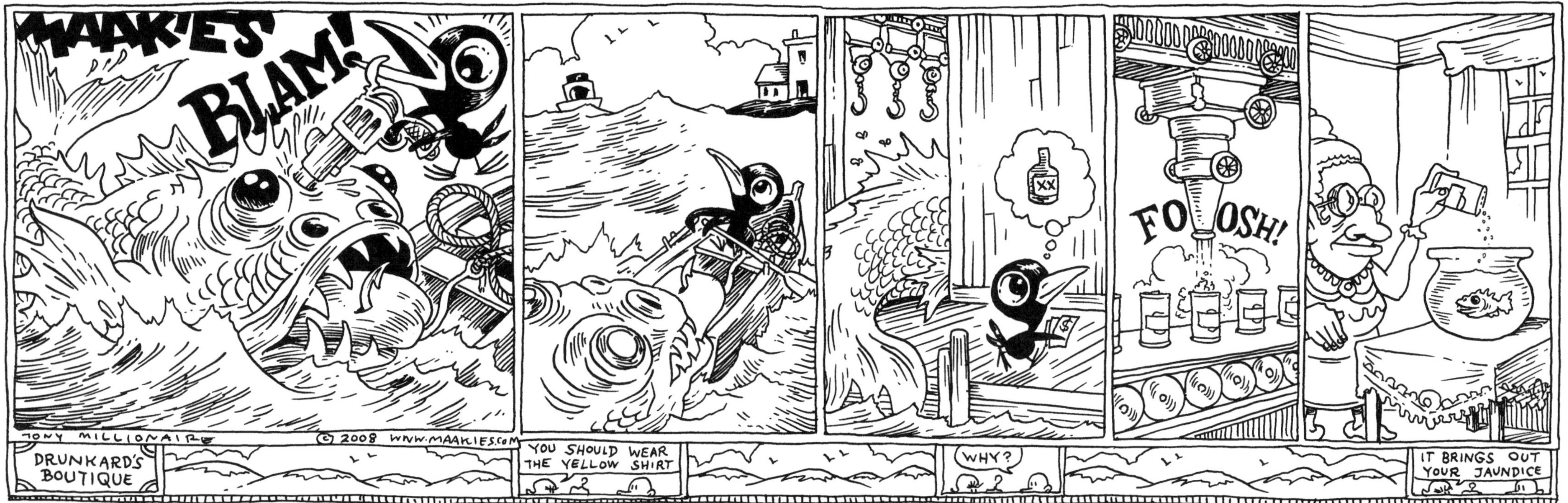
MAAKIES
BLAM!
TONY MILLIONAIRE
© 2008 WWW.MAAKIES.COM
FOOSH!
DRUNKARD'S BOUTIQUE
YOU SHOULD WEAR THE YELLOW SHIRT
WHY?
IT BRINGS OUT YOUR JAUNDICE

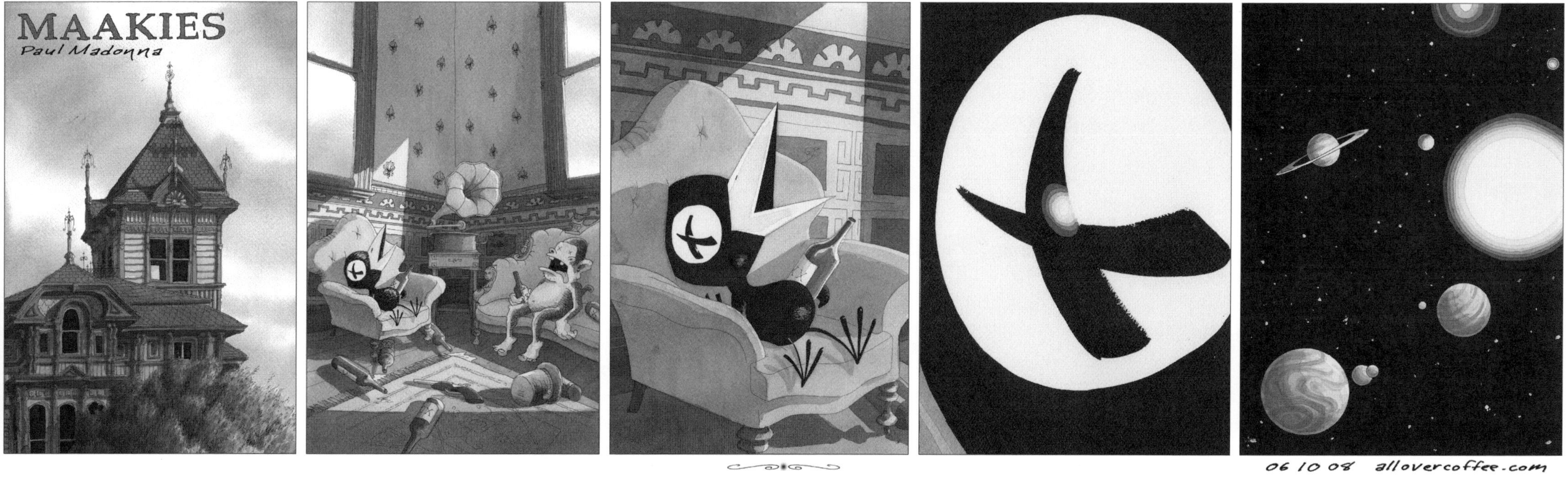
MAAKIES
Paul Madonna
06 10 08 allovercoffee.com

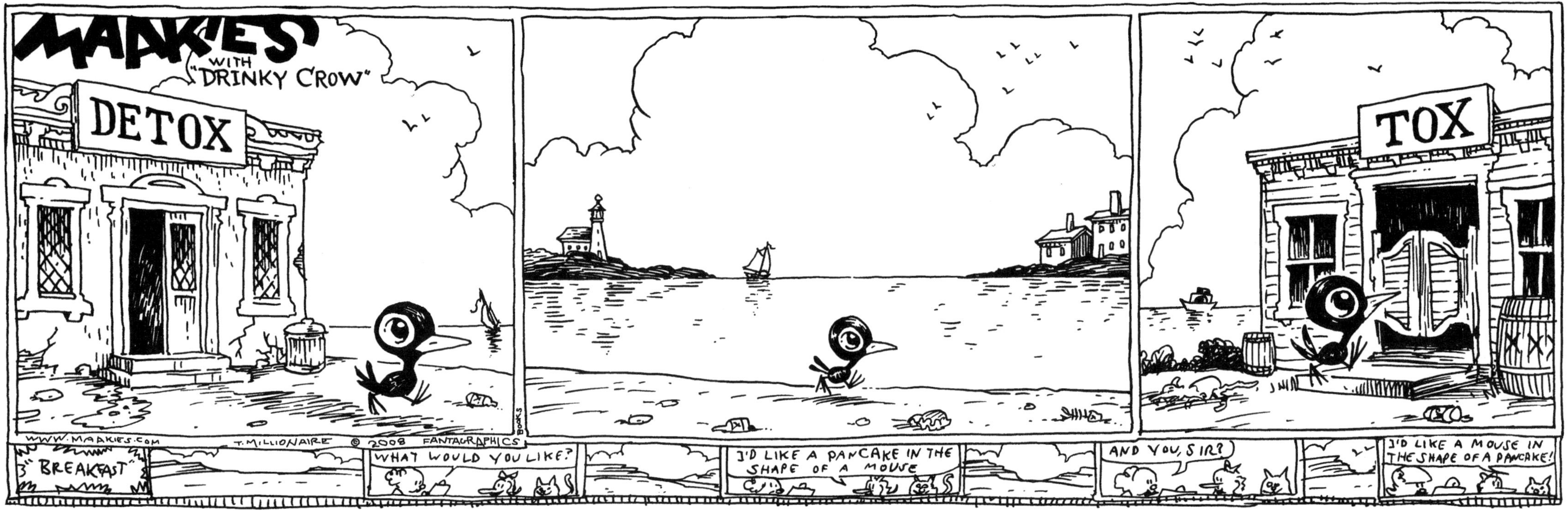
MAAKIES
WITH "DRINKY CROW"
DETOX
TOX
WWW.MAAKIES.COM
T. MILLIONAIRE © 2008 FANTAGRAPHICS BOOKS
"BREAKFAST"
WHAT WOULD YOU LIKE?
I'D LIKE A PANCAKE IN THE SHAPE OF A MOUSE
AND YOU, SIR?
I'D LIKE A MOUSE IN THE SHAPE OF A PANCAKE!

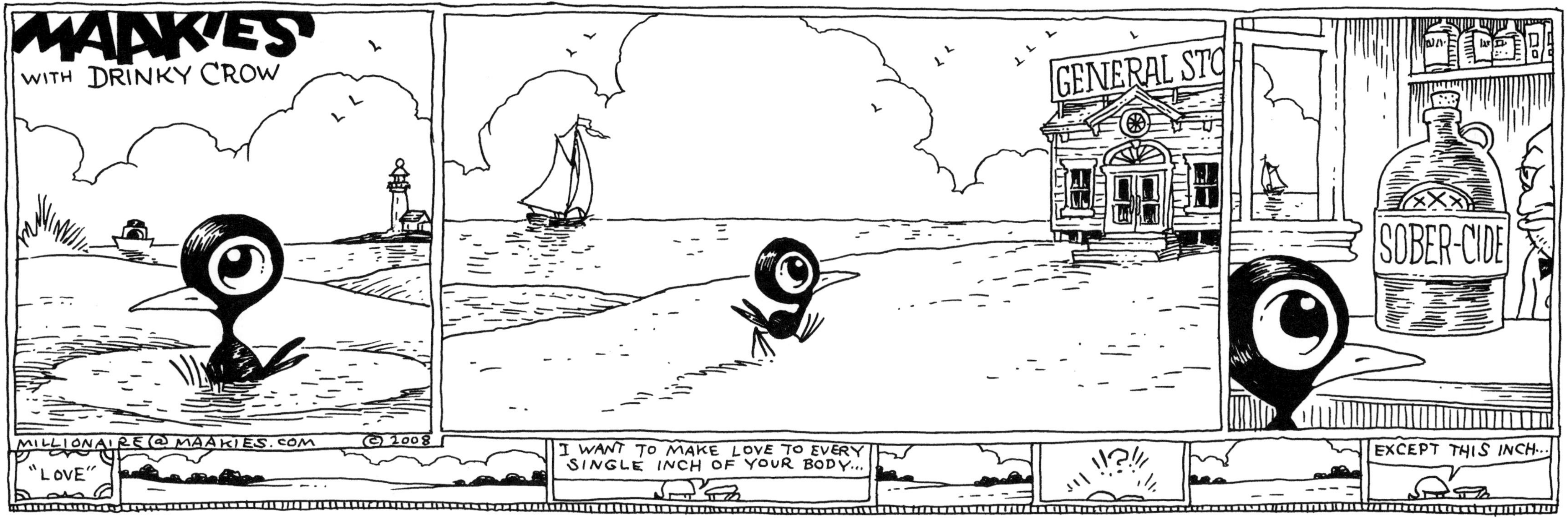
MAAKIES
WITH DRINKY CROW
GENERAL STO
SOBER-CIDE
MILLIONAIRE@MAAKIES.COM
© 2008
"LOVE"
I WANT TO MAKE LOVE TO EVERY SINGLE INCH OF YOUR BODY...
!?
EXCEPT THIS INCH...

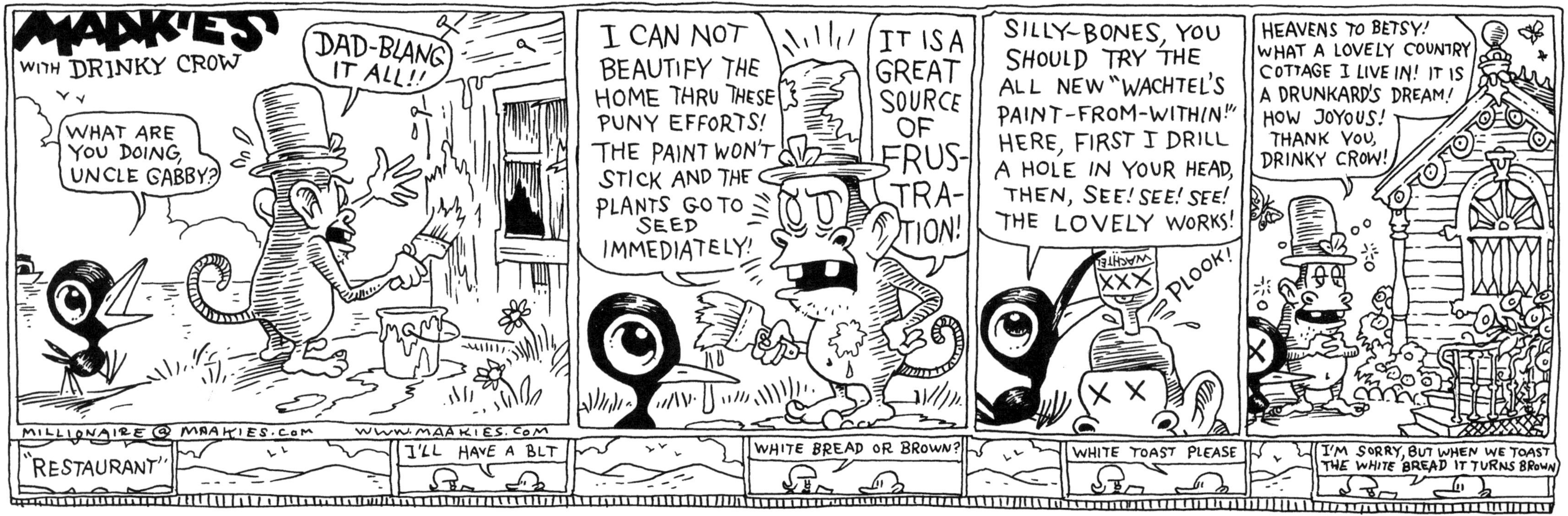
MAAKIES
WITH DRINKY CROW
WHAT ARE YOU DOING, UNCLE GABBY?
DAD-BLANG IT ALL!!
I CAN NOT BEAUTIFY THE HOME THRU THESE PUNY EFFORTS! THE PAINT WON'T STICK AND THE PLANTS GO TO SEED IMMEDIATELY!
IT IS A GREAT SOURCE OF FRUS-TRA-TION!
SILLY-BONES, YOU SHOULD TRY THE ALL NEW "WACHTEL'S PAINT-FROM-WITHIN!" HERE, FIRST I DRILL A HOLE IN YOUR HEAD, THEN, SEE! SEE! SEE! THE LOVELY WORKS!
WACHTEL
XXX
PLOOK!
HEAVENS TO BETSY! WHAT A LOVELY COUNTRY COTTAGE I LIVE IN! IT IS A DRUNKARD'S DREAM! HOW JOYOUS! THANK YOU, DRINKY CROW!
MILLIONAIRE@MAAKIES.COM
WWW.MAAKIES.COM
"RESTAURANT"
I'LL HAVE A BLT
WHITE BREAD OR BROWN?
WHITE TOAST PLEASE
I'M SORRY, BUT WHEN WE TOAST THE WHITE BREAD IT TURNS BROWN

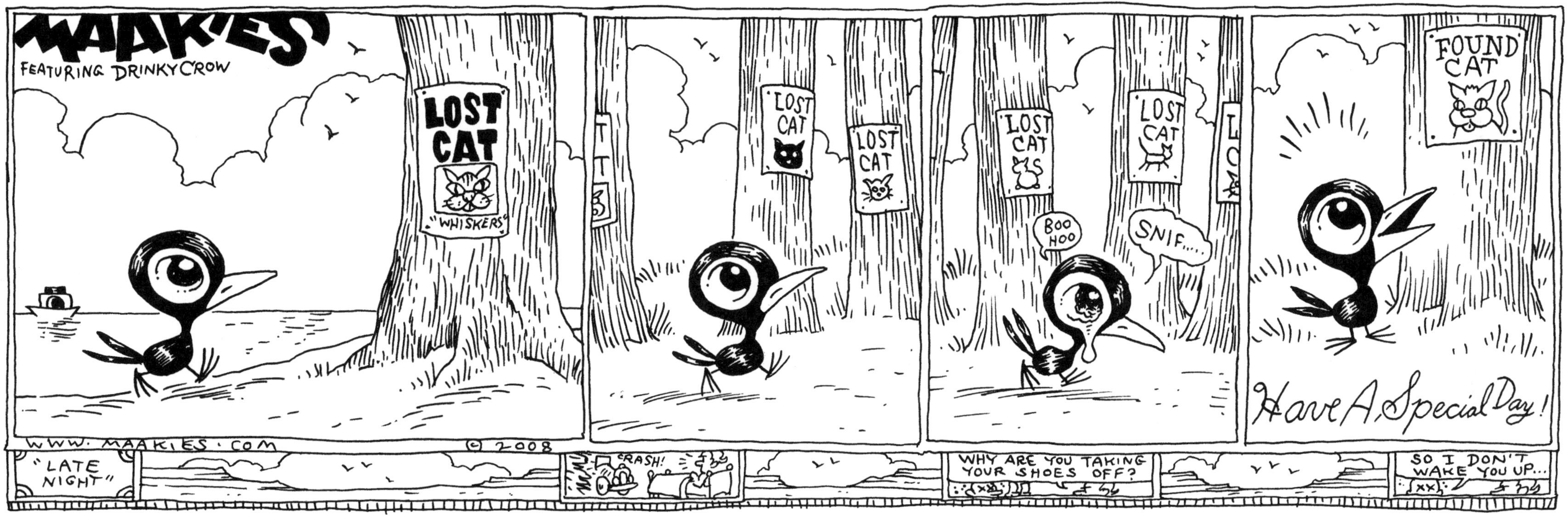
MAAKIES
FEATURING DRINKY CROW
LOST CAT
"WHISKERS"
WWW. MAAKIES. COM
© 2008
LOST CAT
LOST CAT
LOST CAT
LOST CAT
BOO HOO
SNIF....
FOUND CAT
Have A Special Day!
"LATE NIGHT"
CRASH!
WHY ARE YOU TAKING YOUR SHOES OFF?
SO I DON'T WAKE YOU UP...

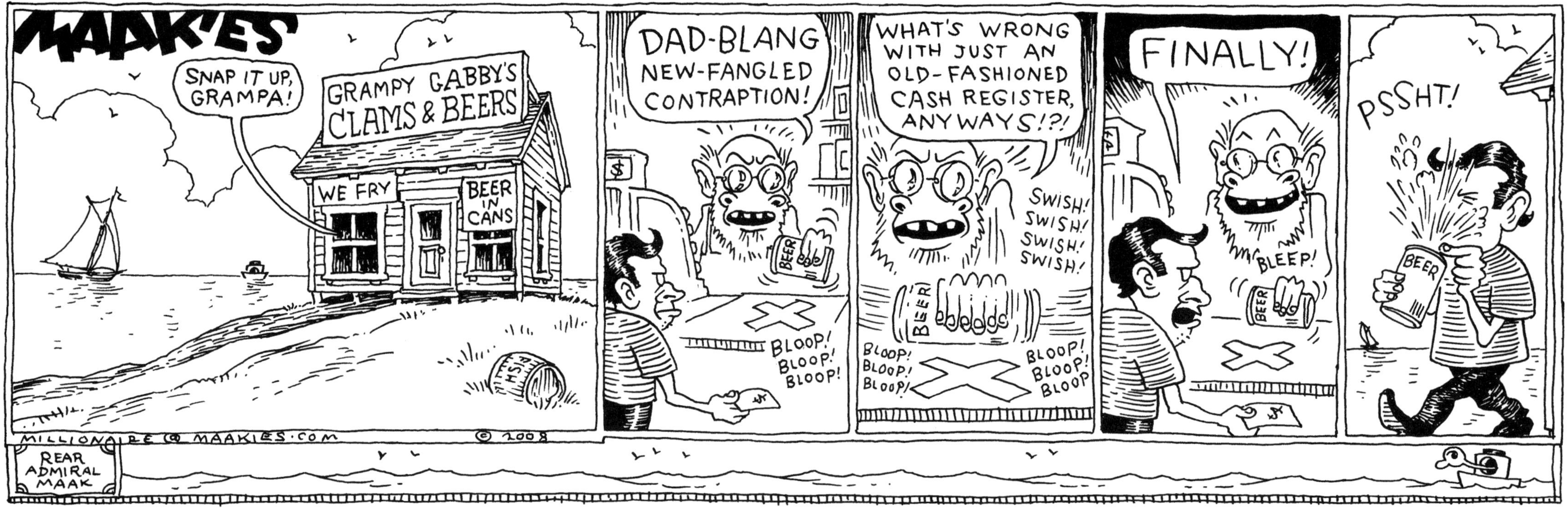
MAAK'ES
SNAP IT UP, GRAMPA!
GRAMPY GABBY'S CLAMS & BEERS
WE FRY
BEER IN CANS
DAD-BLANG NEW-FANGLED CONTRAPTION!
BEER
BLOOP! BLOOP! BLOOP!
WHAT'S WRONG WITH JUST AN OLD-FASHIONED CASH REGISTER, ANYWAYS!?!
SWISH! SWISH! SWISH! SWISH!
BEER
BLOOP! BLOOP! BLOOP!
BLOOP! BLOOP! BLOOP
FINALLY!
BLEEP!
BEER
PSSHT!
BEER
MILLIONAIRE @ MAAKIES.COM
© 2008
REAR ADMIRAL MAAK

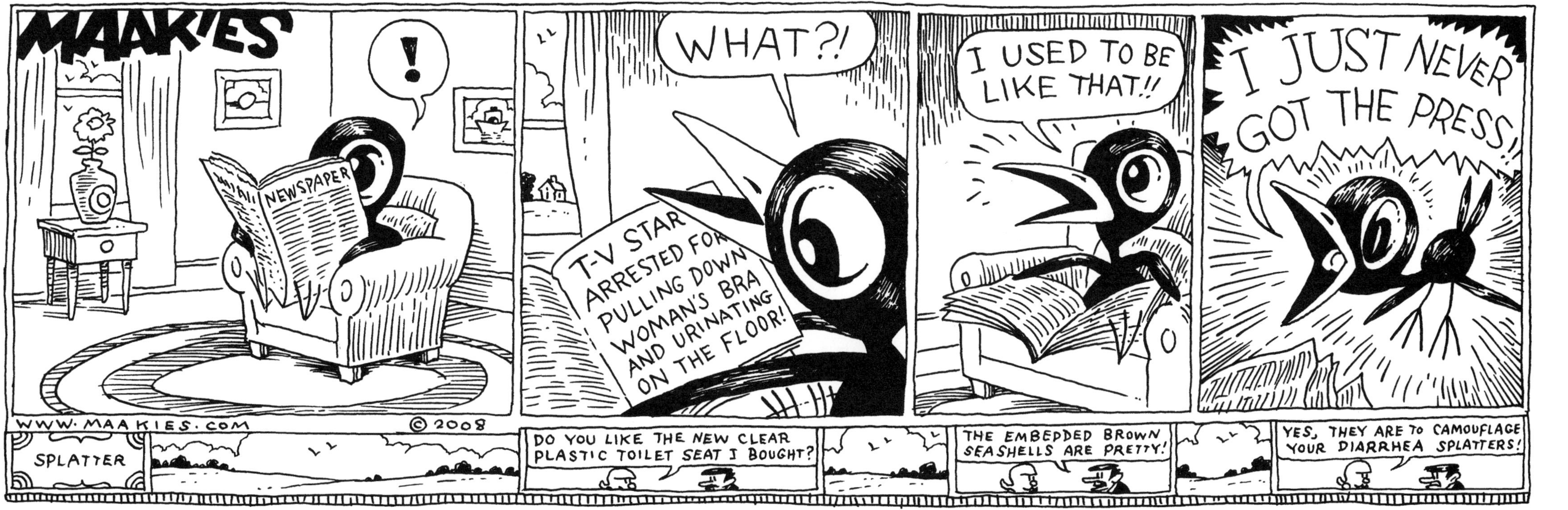
MAAKIES
!
NEWSPAPER
WHAT?!
T-V STAR ARRESTED FOR PULLING DOWN WOMAN'S BRA AND URINATING ON THE FLOOR!
I USED TO BE LIKE THAT!!
I JUST NEVER GOT THE PRESS!
WWW. MAAKIES.COM
© 2008
SPLATTER
DO YOU LIKE THE NEW CLEAR PLASTIC TOILET SEAT I BOUGHT?
THE EMBEDDED BROWN SEASHELLS ARE PRETTY!
YES, THEY ARE TO CAMOUFLAGE YOUR DIARRHEA SPLATTERS!

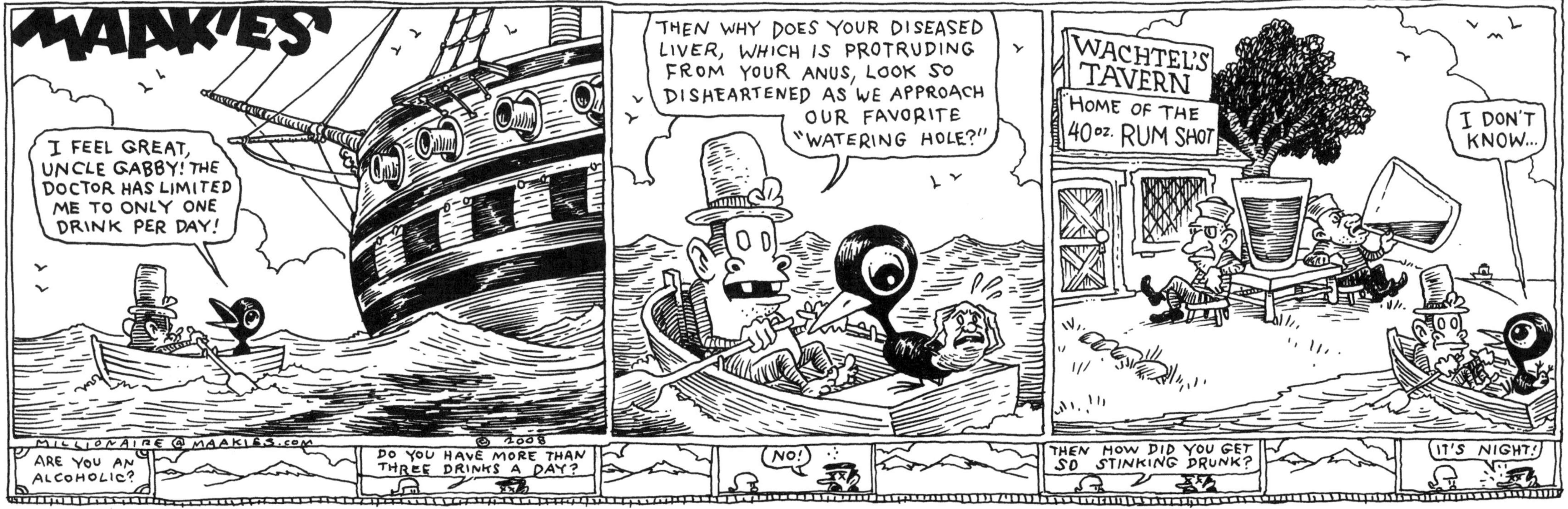
MAAKIES
I FEEL GREAT, UNCLE GABBY! THE DOCTOR HAS LIMITED ME TO ONLY ONE DRINK PER DAY!
THEN WHY DOES YOUR DISEASED LIVER, WHICH IS PROTRUDING FROM YOUR ANUS, LOOK SO DISHEARTENED AS WE APPROACH OUR FAVORITE "WATERING HOLE?"
WACHTEL'S TAVERN
"HOME OF THE 40 OZ. RUM SHOT
I DON'T KNOW...
MILLIONAIRE@MAAKIES.COM
© 2008
ARE YOU AN ALCOHOLIC?
DO YOU HAVE MORE THAN THREE DRINKS A DAY?
NO!
THEN HOW DID YOU GET SO STINKING DRUNK?
IT'S NIGHT!

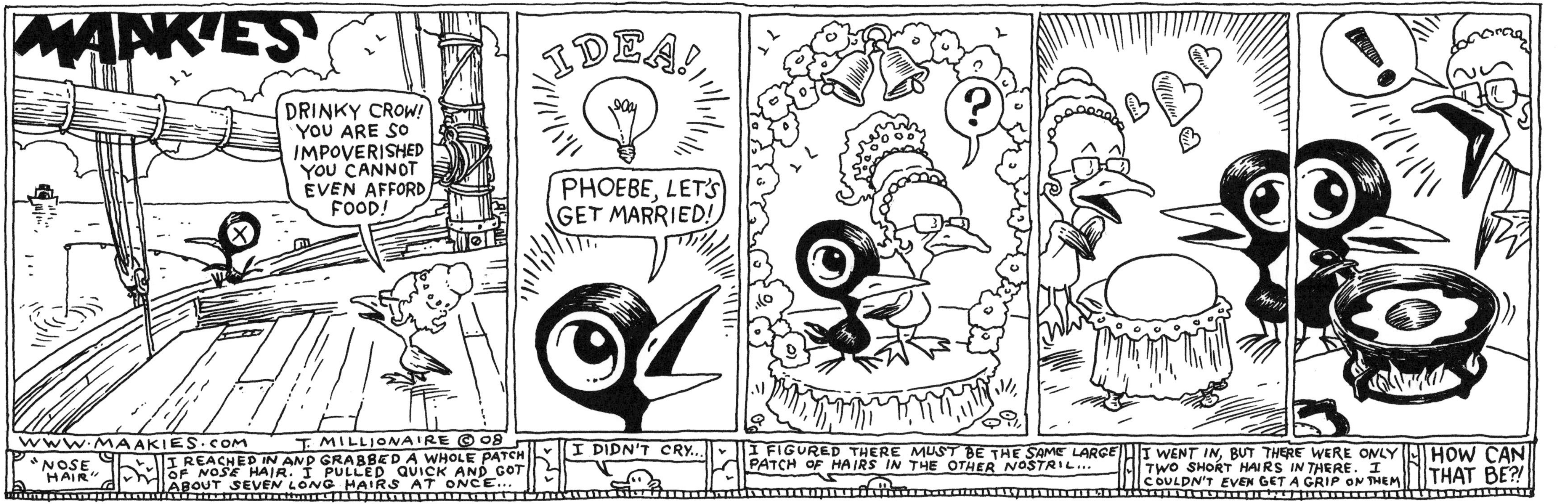
MAAKIES
DRINKY CROW! YOU ARE SO IMPOVERISHED YOU CANNOT EVEN AFFORD FOOD!
WWW.MAAKIES.COM
T. MILLIONAIRE © 08
IDEA!
PHOEBE, LET'S GET MARRIED!
?
!
"NOSE HAIR"
I REACHED IN AND GRABBED A WHOLE PATCH OF NOSE HAIR. I PULLED QUICK AND GOT ABOUT SEVEN LONG HAIRS AT ONCE...
I DIDN'T CRY...
I FIGURED THERE MUST BE THE SAME LARGE PATCH OF HAIRS IN THE OTHER NOSTRIL...
I WENT IN, BUT THERE WERE ONLY TWO SHORT HAIRS IN THERE. I COULDN'T EVEN GET A GRIP ON THEM
HOW CAN THAT BE?!

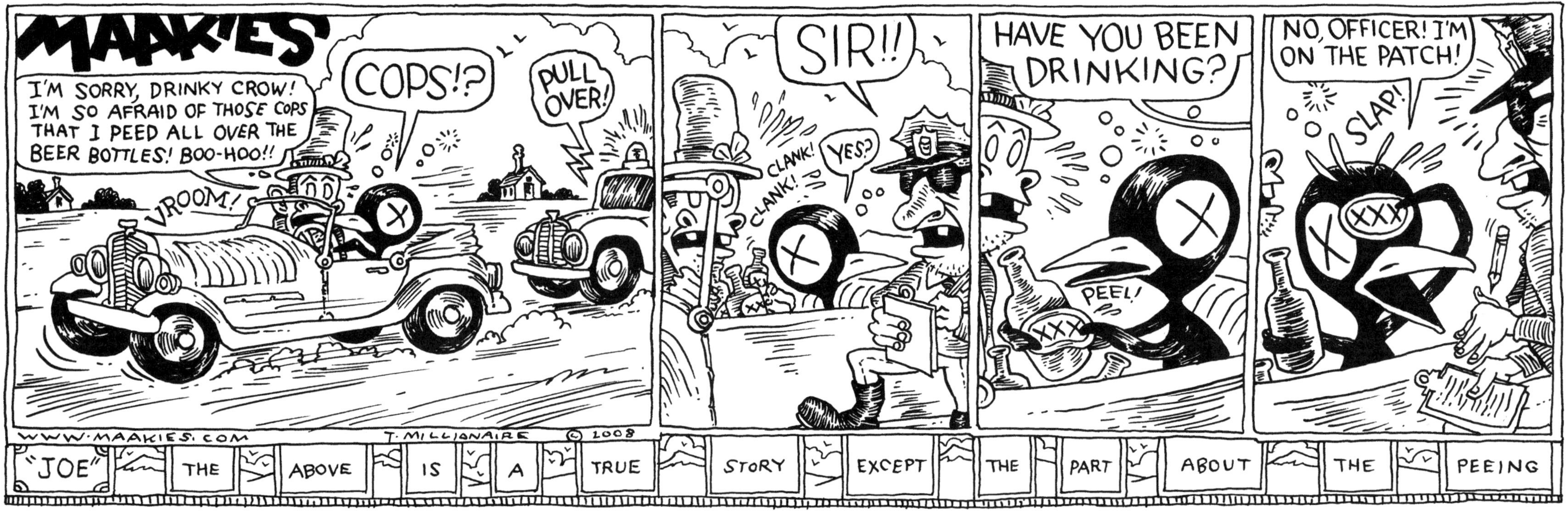
MAAKIES
I'M SORRY, DRINKY CROW! I'M SO AFRAID OF THOSE COPS THAT I PEED ALL OVER THE BEER BOTTLES! BOO-HOO!!
COPS!?
PULL OVER!
VROOM!
SIR!!
CLANK! CLANK!
YES?
HAVE YOU BEEN DRINKING?
PEEL!
XXX
NO, OFFICER! I'M ON THE PATCH!
SLAP!
WWW.MAAKIES.COM
T. MILLIONAIRE
© 2008
"JOE" THE ABOVE IS A TRUE STORY EXCEPT THE PART ABOUT THE PEEING

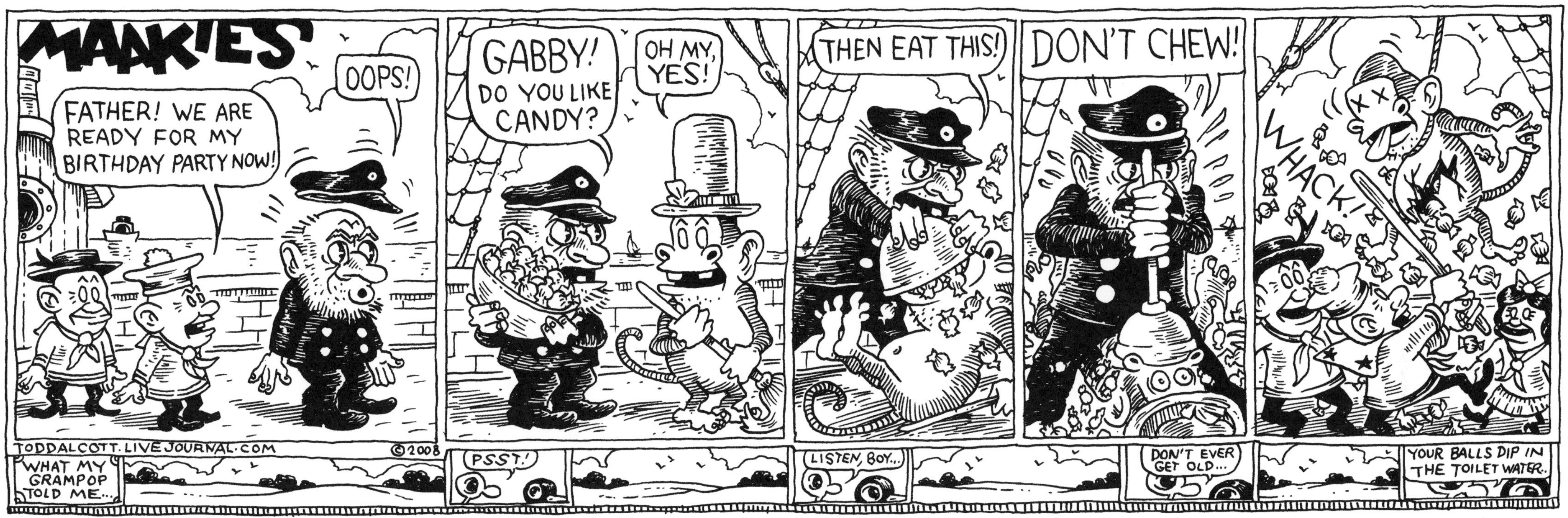
MAAKIES
FATHER! WE ARE READY FOR MY BIRTHDAY PARTY NOW!
OOPS!
GABBY! DO YOU LIKE CANDY?
OH MY, YES!
THEN EAT THIS!
DON'T CHEW!
WHACK!
TODDALCOTT.LIVEJOURNAL.COM
©2008
WHAT MY GRAMPOP TOLD ME...
PSST!
LISTEN, BOY...
DON'T EVER GET OLD...
YOUR BALLS DIP IN THE TOILET WATER..

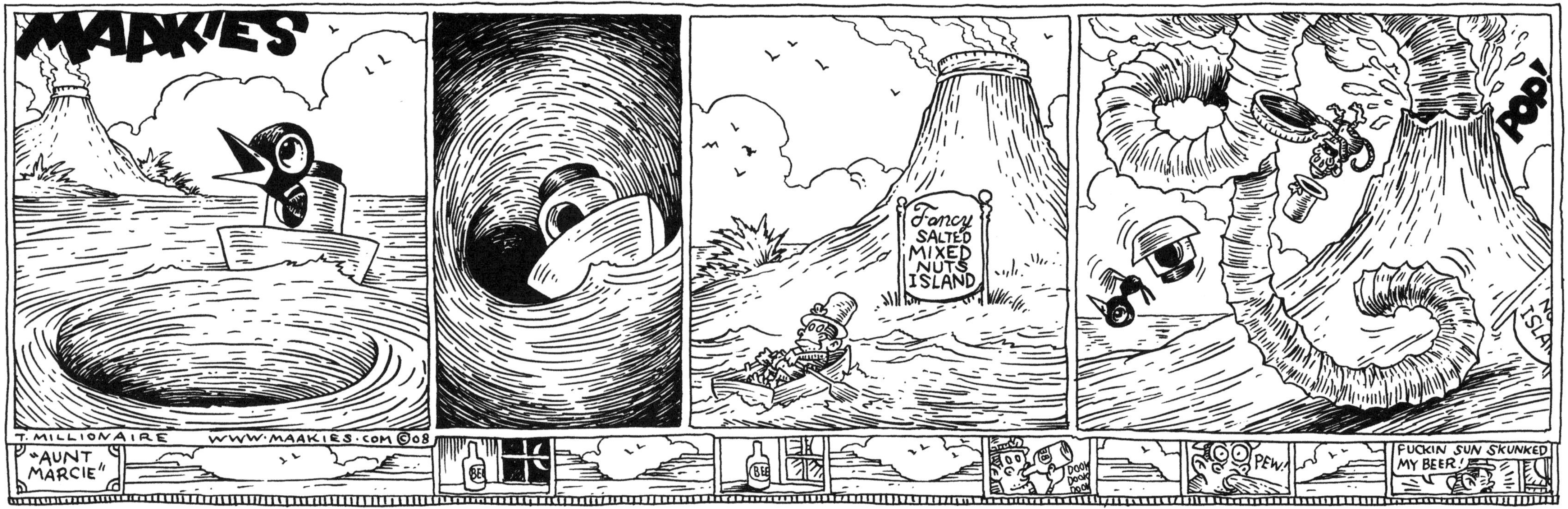
MAAKIES
T. MILLIONAIRE
WWW.MAAKIES.COM ©08
Fancy SALTED MIXED NUTS ISLAND
POP!
"AUNT MARCIE"
PEW!
FUCKIN SUN SKUNKED MY BEER!

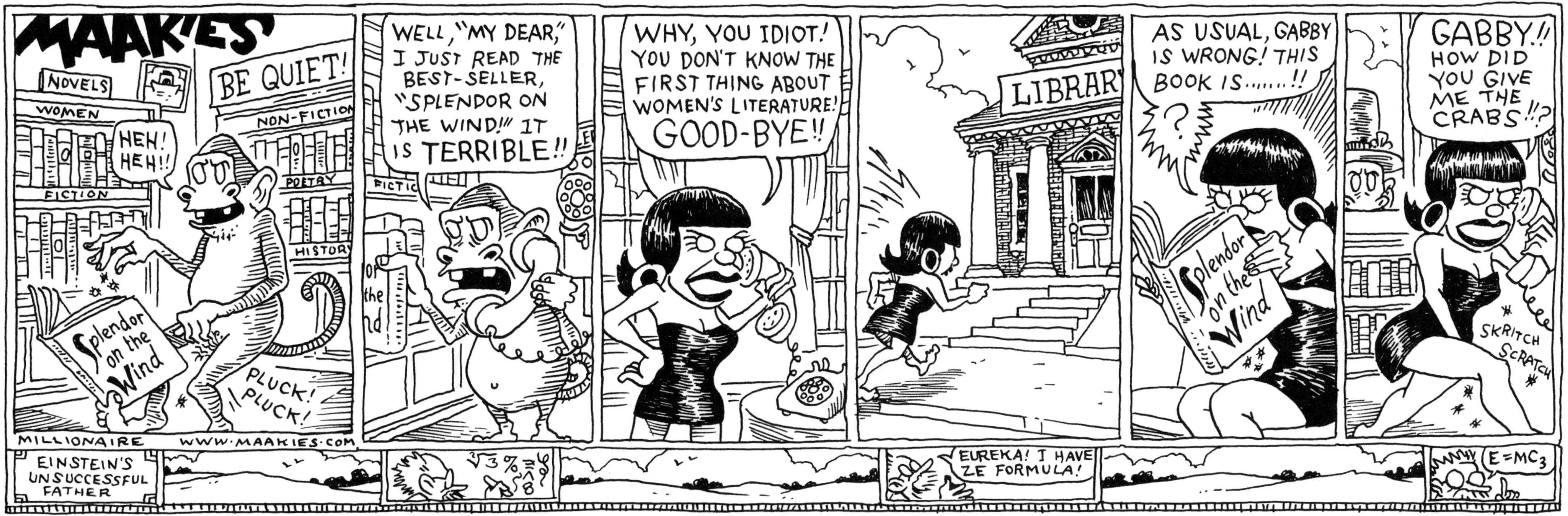
MAAKIES
NOVELS
WOMEN
FICTION
BE QUIET!
NON-FICTION
POETRY
HISTORY
HEH! HEH!!
Splendor on the Wind
PLUCK! PLUCK!
MILLIONAIRE
WWW.MAAKIES.COM
WELL, "MY DEAR," I JUST READ THE BEST-SELLER, "SPLENDOR ON THE WIND!" IT IS TERRIBLE!!
WHY, YOU IDIOT! YOU DON'T KNOW THE FIRST THING ABOUT WOMEN'S LITERATURE! GOOD-BYE!!
LIBRARY
AS USUAL, GABBY IS WRONG! THIS BOOK IS.......!!
?
Splendor on the Wind
GABBY!! HOW DID YOU GIVE ME THE CRABS!!?
SKRITCH SCRATCH
EINSTEIN'S UNSUCCESSFUL FATHER
EUREKA! I HAVE ZE FORMULA!
E=MC3

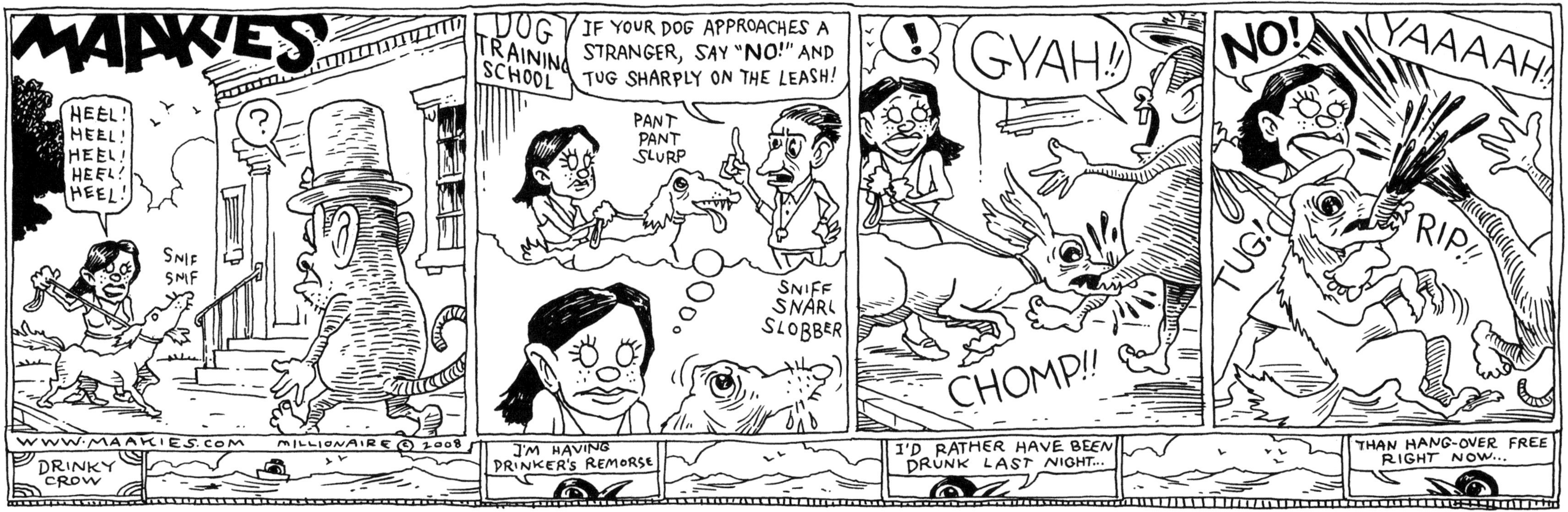
MAAKIES
HEEL! HEEL! HEEL! HEEL! HEEL!
?
SNIF SNIF
DOG TRAINING SCHOOL
IF YOUR DOG APPROACHES A STRANGER, SAY "NO!" AND TUG SHARPLY ON THE LEASH!
PANT PANT SLURP
SNIFF SNARL SLOBBER
!
GYAH!!
CHOMP!!
NO!
YAAAAH!!
TUG!
RIP!!
WWW.MAAKIES.COM
MILLIONAIRE © 2008
DRINKY CROW
I'M HAVING DRINKER'S REMORSE
I'D RATHER HAVE BEEN DRUNK LAST NIGHT...
THAN HANG-OVER FREE RIGHT NOW...

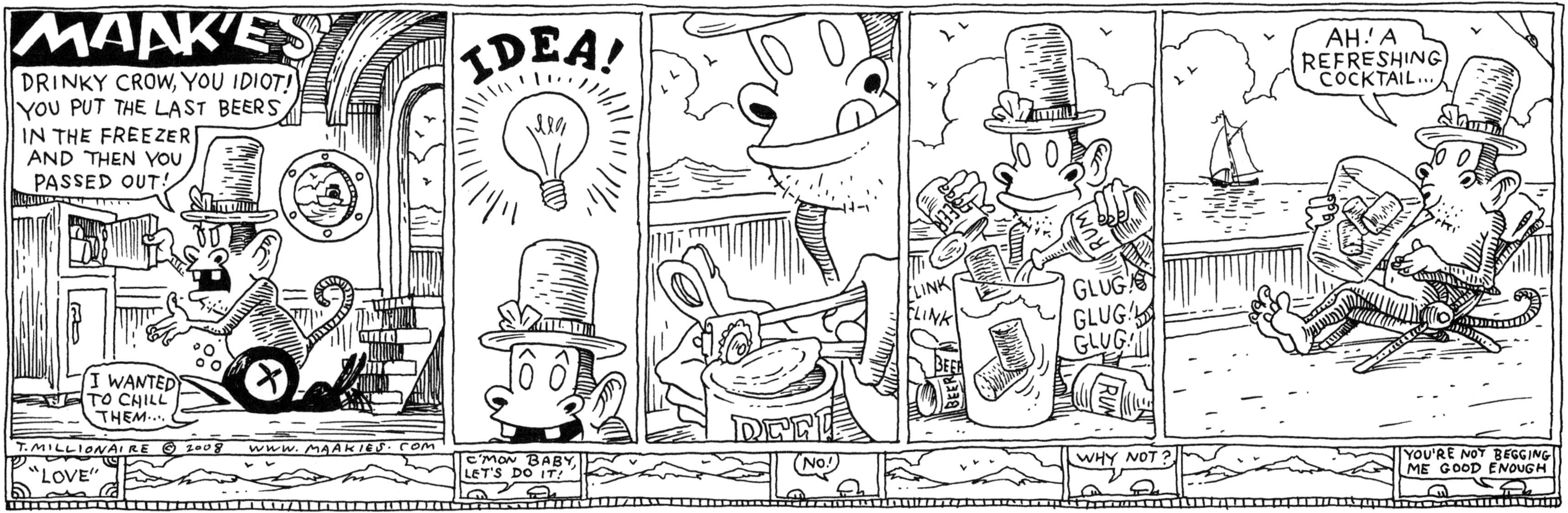
MAAKIES
DRINKY CROW, YOU IDIOT! YOU PUT THE LAST BEERS IN THE FREEZER AND THEN YOU PASSED OUT!
I WANTED TO CHILL THEM....
IDEA!
CLINK CLINK
GLUG! GLUG! GLUG!
BEER
RUM
AH! A REFRESHING COCKTAIL...
T. MILLIONAIRE © 2008 WWW.MAAKIES.COM
"LOVE"
C'MON BABY, LET'S DO IT!
NO!
WHY NOT?
YOU'RE NOT BEGGING ME GOOD ENOUGH

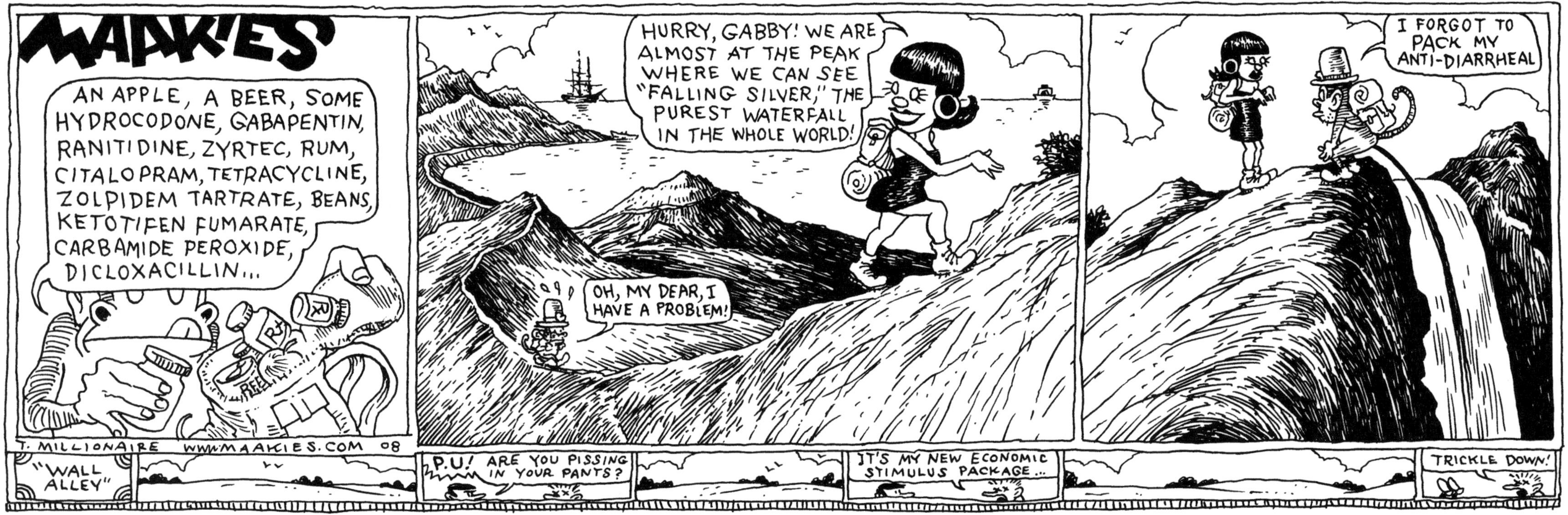
MAAKIES
AN APPLE, A BEER, SOME HYDROCODONE, GABAPENTIN, RANITIDINE, ZYRTEC, RUM, CITALOPRAM, TETRACYCLINE, ZOLPIDEM TARTRATE, BEANS, KETOTIFEN FUMARATE, CARBAMIDE PEROXIDE, DICLOXACILLIN...
HURRY, GABBY! WE ARE ALMOST AT THE PEAK WHERE WE CAN SEE "FALLING SILVER," THE PUREST WATERFALL IN THE WHOLE WORLD!
OH, MY DEAR, I HAVE A PROBLEM!
I FORGOT TO PACK MY ANTI-DIARRHEAL
T. MILLIONAIRE WWW.MAAKIES.COM 08
"WALL ALLEY"
P.U! ARE YOU PISSING IN YOUR PANTS?
IT'S MY NEW ECONOMIC STIMULUS PACKAGE...
TRICKLE DOWN!

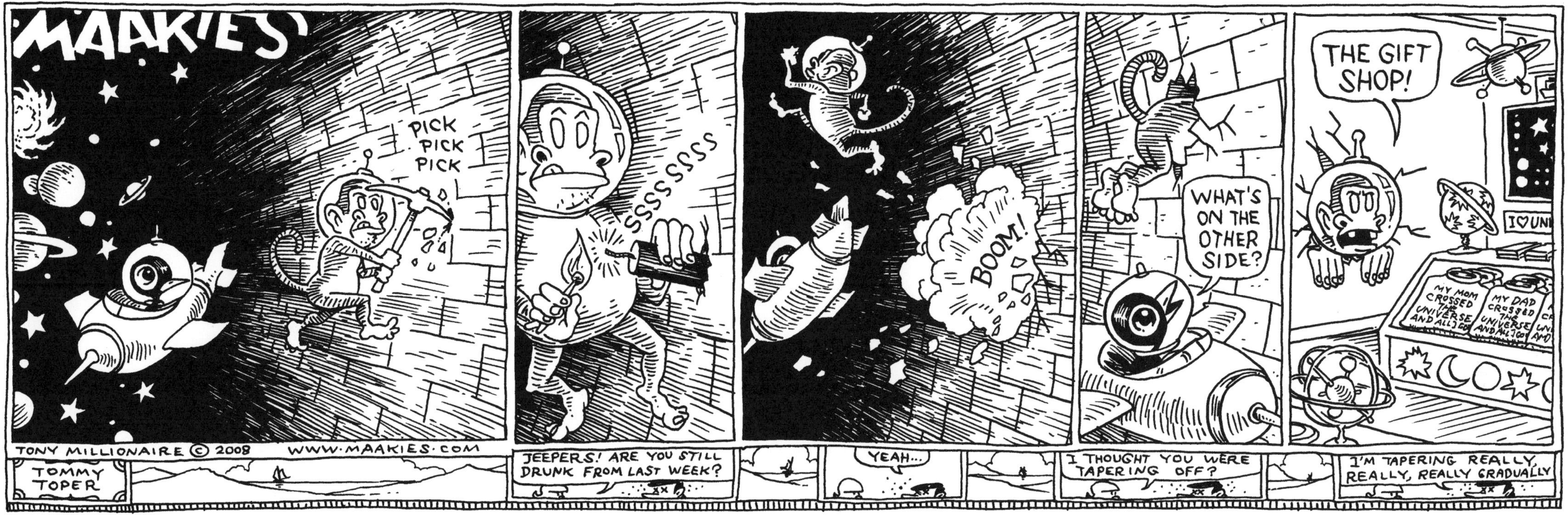
MAAKIES
PICK PICK PICK
SSSSSSSSS
BOOM!
WHAT'S ON THE OTHER SIDE?
THE GIFT SHOP!
I♡UNI
MY MOM CROSSED THE UNIVERSE AND ALL I GOT
MY DAD CROSSED THE UNIVERSE AND ALL I GOT
TONY MILLIONAIRE © 2008 WWW.MAAKIES.COM
TOMMY TOPER
JEEPERS! ARE YOU STILL DRUNK FROM LAST WEEK?
YEAH...
I THOUGHT YOU WERE TAPERING OFF?
I'M TAPERING REALLY, REALLY, REALLY GRADUALLY

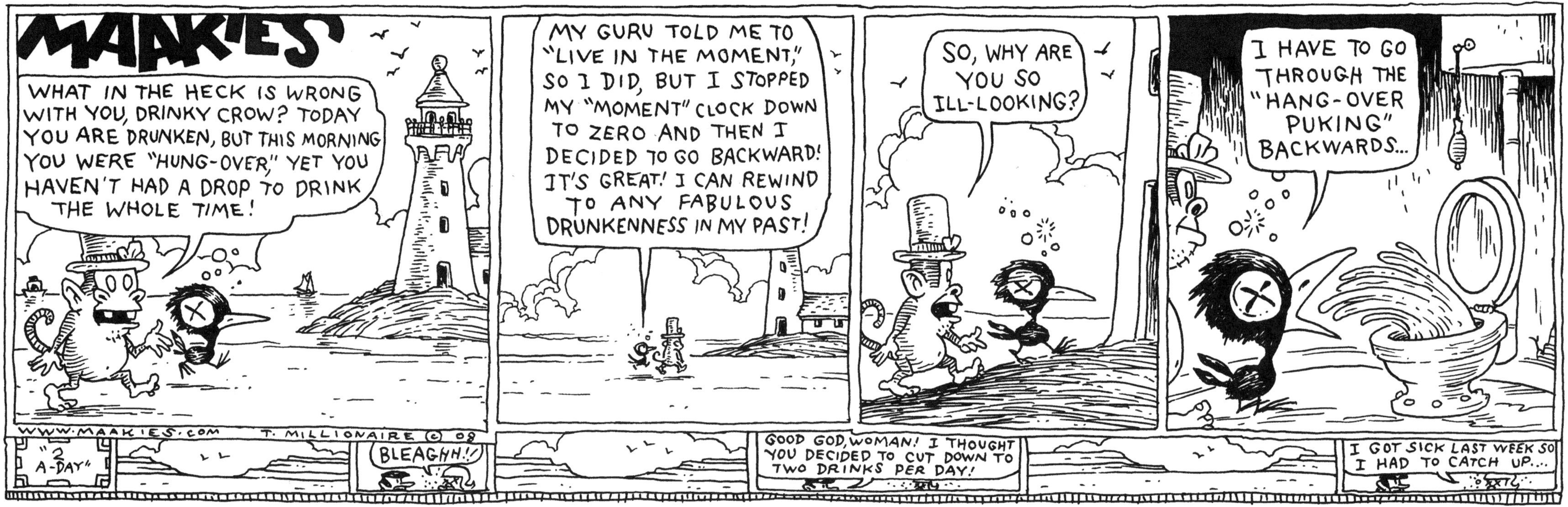
MAAKIES
WHAT IN THE HECK IS WRONG WITH YOU, DRINKY CROW? TODAY YOU ARE DRUNKEN, BUT THIS MORNING YOU WERE "HUNG-OVER," YET YOU HAVEN'T HAD A DROP TO DRINK THE WHOLE TIME!
MY GURU TOLD ME TO "LIVE IN THE MOMENT," SO I DID, BUT I STOPPED MY "MOMENT" CLOCK DOWN TO ZERO AND THEN I DECIDED TO GO BACKWARD! IT'S GREAT! I CAN REWIND TO ANY FABULOUS DRUNKENNESS IN MY PAST!
SO, WHY ARE YOU SO ILL-LOOKING?
I HAVE TO GO THROUGH THE "HANG-OVER PUKING" BACKWARDS...
WWW.MAAKIES.COM
T. MILLIONAIRE © 08
"2 A-DAY"
BLEAGHH!!
GOOD GOD, WOMAN! I THOUGHT YOU DECIDED TO CUT DOWN TO TWO DRINKS PER DAY!
I GOT SICK LAST WEEK SO I HAD TO CATCH UP...

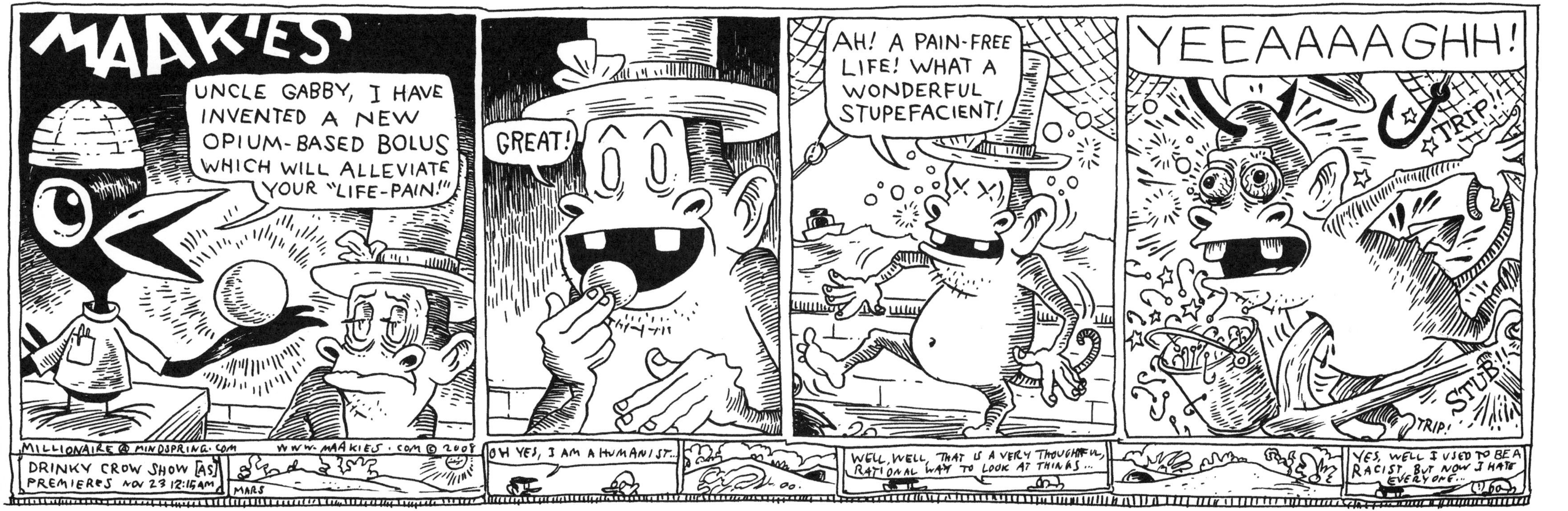
MAAKIES
UNCLE GABBY, I HAVE INVENTED A NEW OPIUM-BASED BOLUS WHICH WILL ALLEVIATE YOUR "LIFE-PAIN!"
GREAT!
AH! A PAIN-FREE LIFE! WHAT A WONDERFUL STUPEFACIENT!
YEEAAAAGHH!
TRIP!
TRIP!
STUB!
MILLIONAIRE@MINDSPRING.COM
WWW.MAAKIES.COM © 2008
DRINKY CROW SHOW [AS] PREMIERES NOV 23 12:15AM
MARS
OH YES, I AM A HUMANIST...
WELL, WELL, THAT IS A VERY THOUGHTFUL, RATIONAL WAY TO LOOK AT THINGS...
YES, WELL I USED TO BE A RACIST, BUT NOW I HATE EVERYONE...

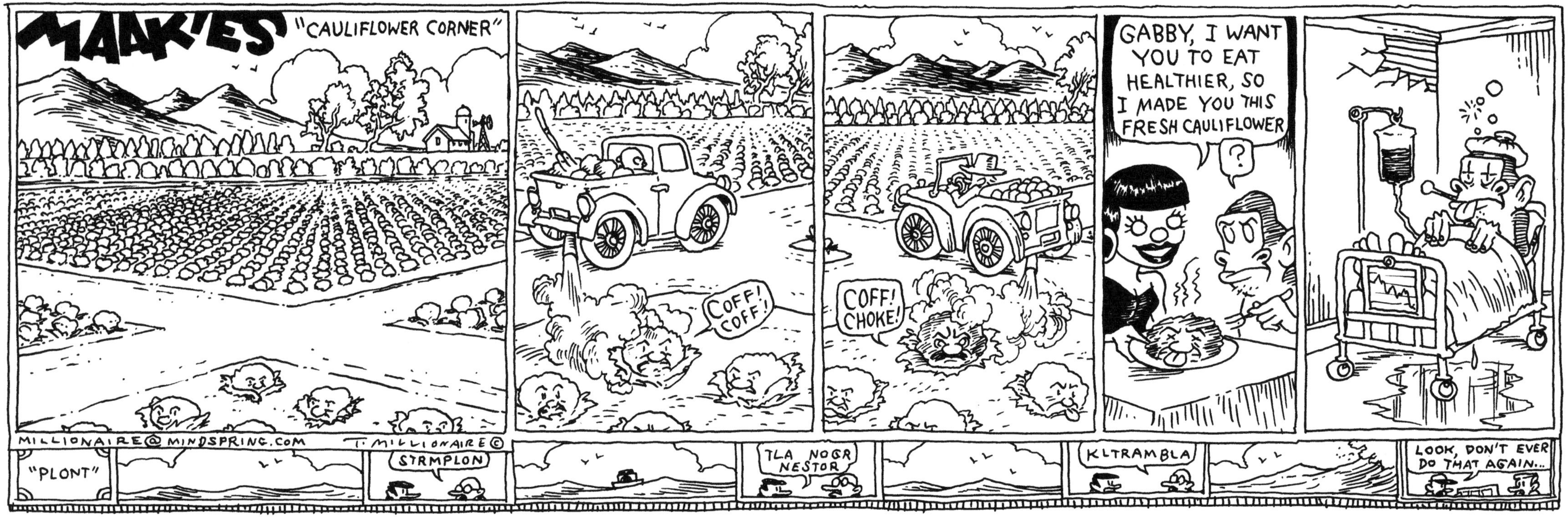

MAAKIES
"CAULIFLOWER CORNER"
COFF! COFF!
COFF! CHOKE!
GABBY, I WANT YOU TO EAT HEALTHIER, SO I MADE YOU THIS FRESH CAULIFLOWER
?
MILLIONAIRE@MINDSPRING.COM
T. MILLIONAIRE©
"PLONT"
STRMPLON
TLA NOGR NESTOR
KLTRAMBLA
LOOK, DON'T EVER DO THAT AGAIN...

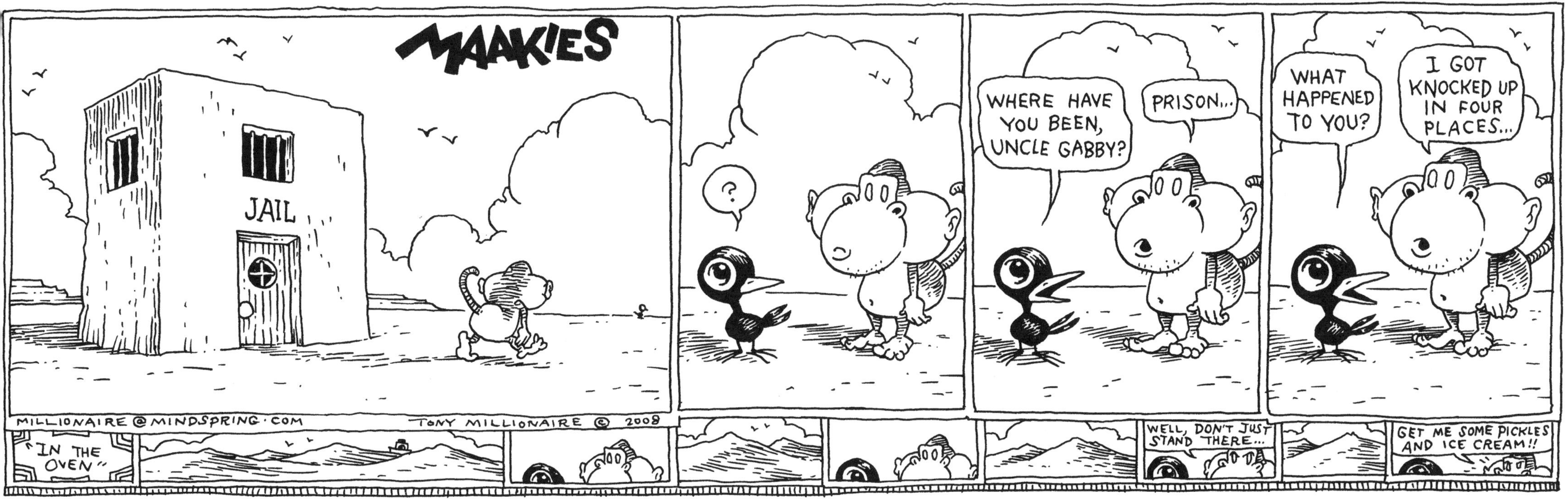
MAAKIES
JAIL
MILLIONAIRE@MINDSPRING·COM
TONY MILLIONAIRE © 2008
?
WHERE HAVE YOU BEEN, UNCLE GABBY?
PRISON...
WHAT HAPPENED TO YOU?
I GOT KNOCKED UP IN FOUR PLACES...
"IN THE OVEN"
WELL, DON'T JUST STAND THERE...
GET ME SOME PICKLES AND ICE CREAM!!

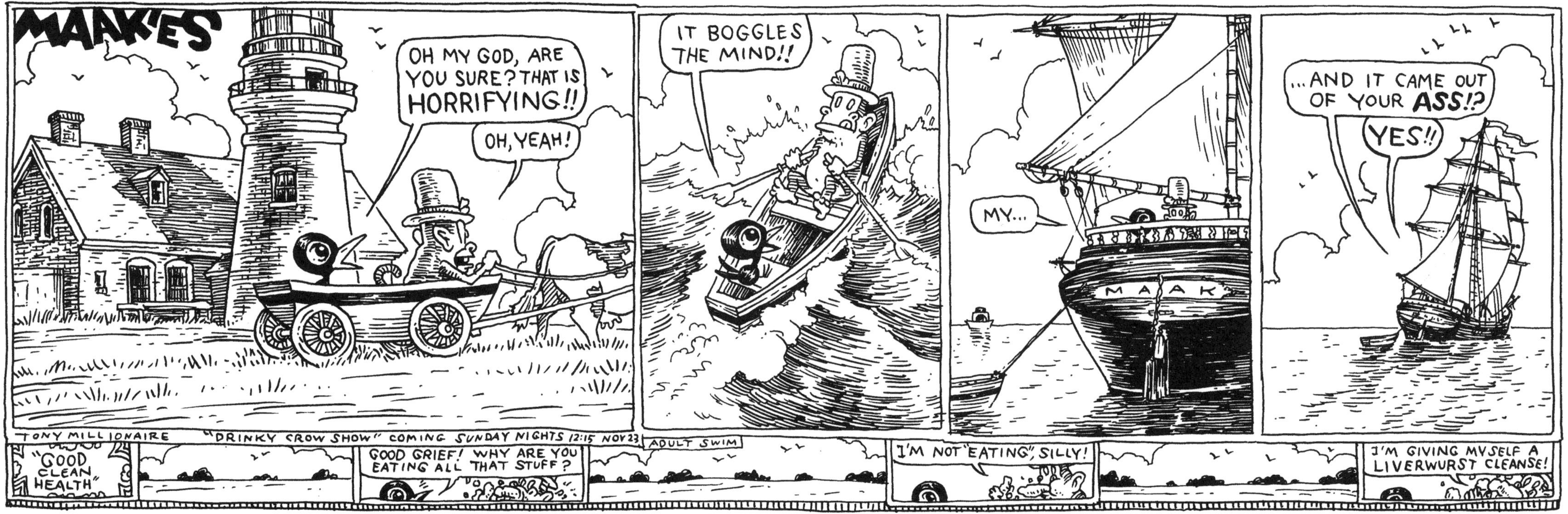
MAAK'ES
OH MY GOD, ARE YOU SURE? THAT IS HORRIFYING!!
OH, YEAH!
IT BOGGLES THE MIND!!
MY...
MAAK
...AND IT CAME OUT OF YOUR ASS!?
YES!!
TONY MILLIONAIRE "DRINKY CROW SHOW" COMING SUNDAY NIGHTS 12:15 NOV 23 ADULT SWIM
"GOOD CLEAN HEALTH"
GOOD GRIEF! WHY ARE YOU EATING ALL THAT STUFF?
I'M NOT "EATING", SILLY!
I'M GIVING MYSELF A LIVERWURST CLEANSE!

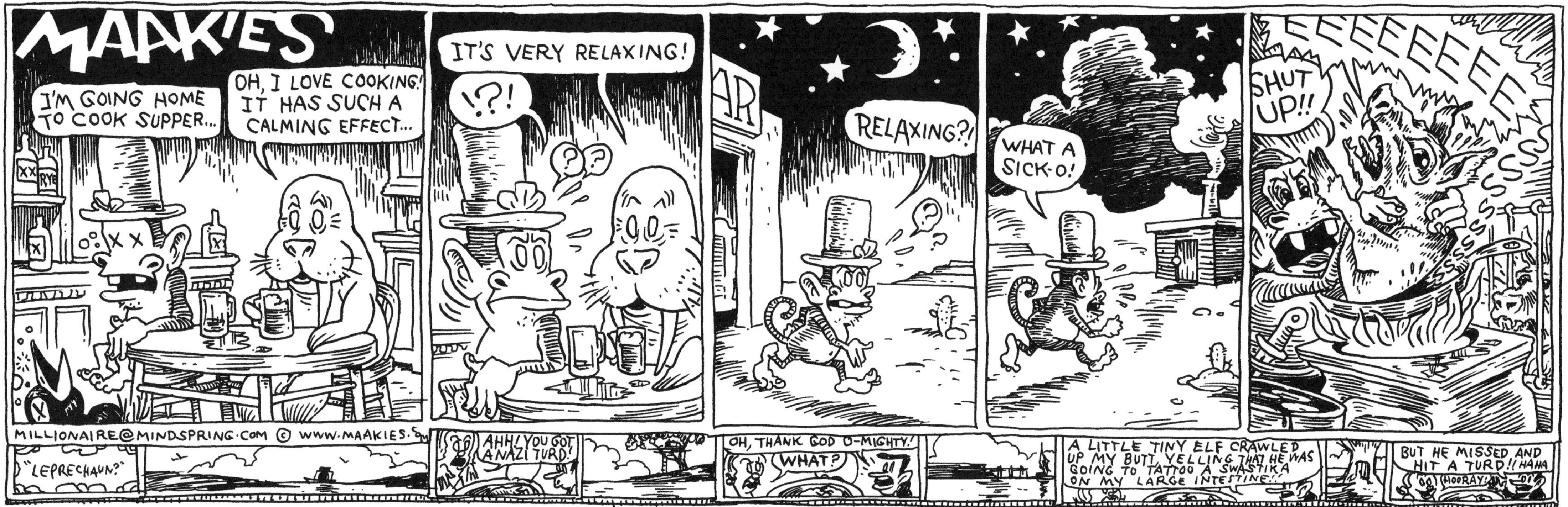
MAAKIES
I'M GOING HOME TO COOK SUPPER...
OH, I LOVE COOKING! IT HAS SUCH A CALMING EFFECT...
XX
RYE
IT'S VERY RELAXING!
!?!
AR
RELAXING?!
WHAT A SICK-O!
SHUT UP!!
EEEEEEEEE
SSSSSSSSSS
MILLIONAIRE@MINDSPRING.COM © WWW.MAAKIES.COM
"LEPRECHAUN?"
AHH! YOU GOT A NAZI TURD!
OH, THANK GOD O-MIGHTY!
WHAT?
A LITTLE TINY ELF CRAWLED UP MY BUTT YELLING THAT HE WAS GOING TO TATTOO A SWASTIKA ON MY LARGE INTESTINE!
BUT HE MISSED AND HIT A TURD!! HAHA
HOORAY!

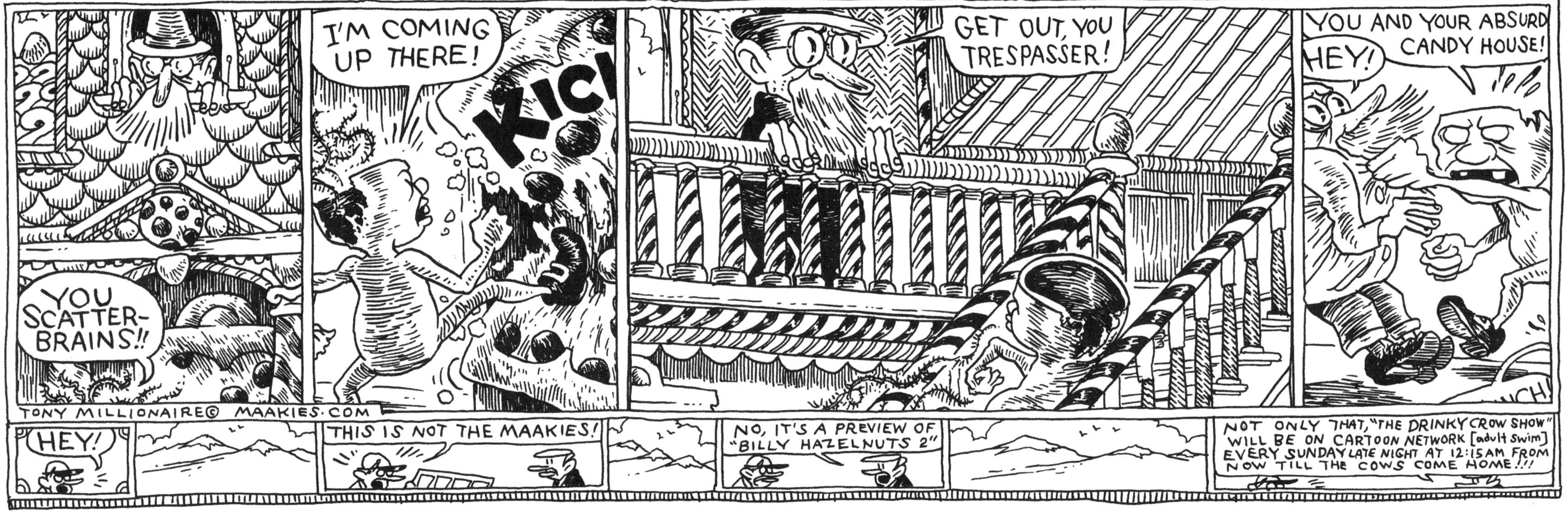
YOU SCATTER-BRAINS!!
I'M COMING UP THERE!
KIC
GET OUT, YOU TRESPASSER!
HEY!
YOU AND YOUR ABSURD CANDY HOUSE!
TONY MILLIONAIRE© MAAKIES.COM
HEY!
THIS IS NOT THE MAAKIES!
NO, IT'S A PREVIEW OF "BILLY HAZELNUTS 2"
NOT ONLY THAT, "THE DRINKY CROW SHOW" WILL BE ON CARTOON NETWORK [adult swim] EVERY SUNDAY LATE NIGHT AT 12:15AM FROM NOW TILL THE COWS COME HOME!!!

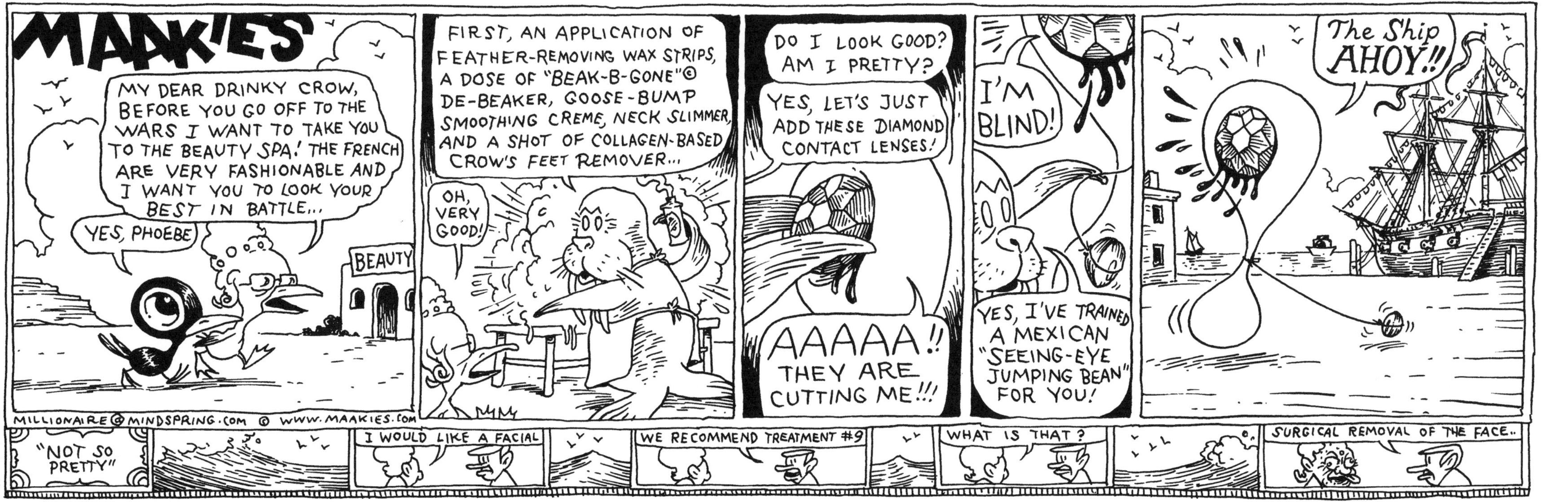

MAAKIES
MY DEAR DRINKY CROW, BEFORE YOU GO OFF TO THE WARS I WANT TO TAKE YOU TO THE BEAUTY SPA! THE FRENCH ARE VERY FASHIONABLE AND I WANT YOU TO LOOK YOUR BEST IN BATTLE...
YES, PHOEBE
BEAUTY
FIRST, AN APPLICATION OF FEATHER-REMOVING WAX STRIPS, A DOSE OF "BEAK-B-GONE"© DE-BEAKER, GOOSE-BUMP SMOOTHING CREME, NECK SLIMMER, AND A SHOT OF COLLAGEN-BASED CROW'S FEET REMOVER...
OH, VERY GOOD!
DO I LOOK GOOD? AM I PRETTY?
YES, LET'S JUST ADD THESE DIAMOND CONTACT LENSES!
AAAAA!! THEY ARE CUTTING ME!!!
I'M BLIND!
YES, I'VE TRAINED A MEXICAN "SEEING-EYE JUMPING BEAN" FOR YOU!
The Ship AHOY!!
MILLIONAIRE@MINDSPRING.COM © WWW.MAAKIES.COM
"NOT SO PRETTY"
I WOULD LIKE A FACIAL
WE RECOMMEND TREATMENT #9
WHAT IS THAT?
SURGICAL REMOVAL OF THE FACE..

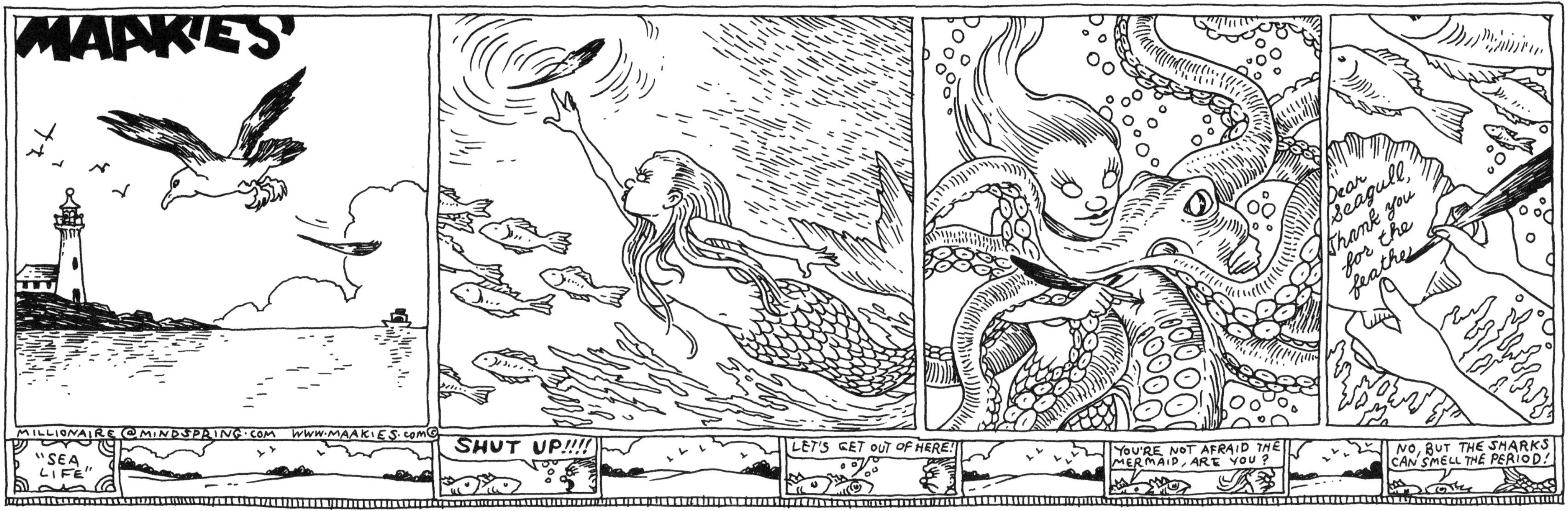
MAAKIES
Dear Seagull, thank you for the feather
MILLIONAIRE@MINDSPRING·COM
WWW·MAAKIES·COM©
"SEA LIFE"
SHUT UP!!!!
LET'S GET OUT OF HERE!
YOU'RE NOT AFRAID THE MERMAID, ARE YOU?
NO, BUT THE SHARKS CAN SMELL THE PERIOD!

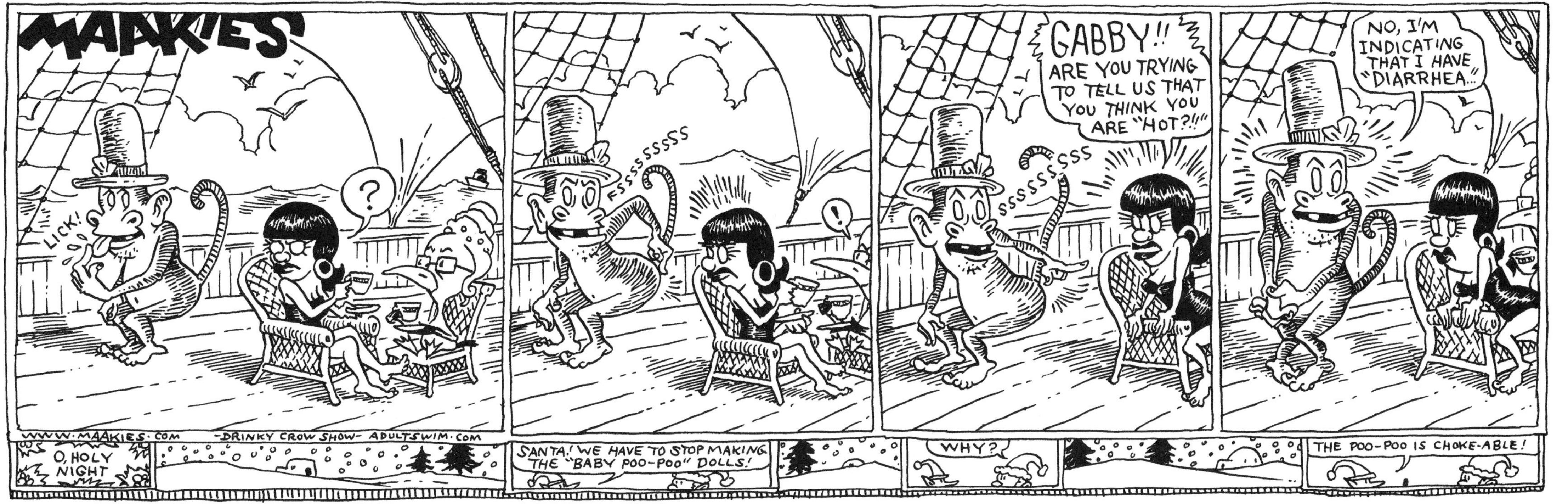
MAAKIES
LICK!
?
FSSSSSSSSS
!
SSSSSSSSSS
GABBY!! ARE YOU TRYING TO TELL US THAT YOU THINK YOU ARE "HOT?!"
NO, I'M INDICATING THAT I HAVE "DIARRHEA"...
WWW.MAAKIES.COM -DRINKY CROW SHOW- ADULTSWIM.COM
O, HOLY NIGHT
SANTA! WE HAVE TO STOP MAKING THE "BABY POO-POO" DOLLS!
WHY?
THE POO-POO IS CHOKE-ABLE!

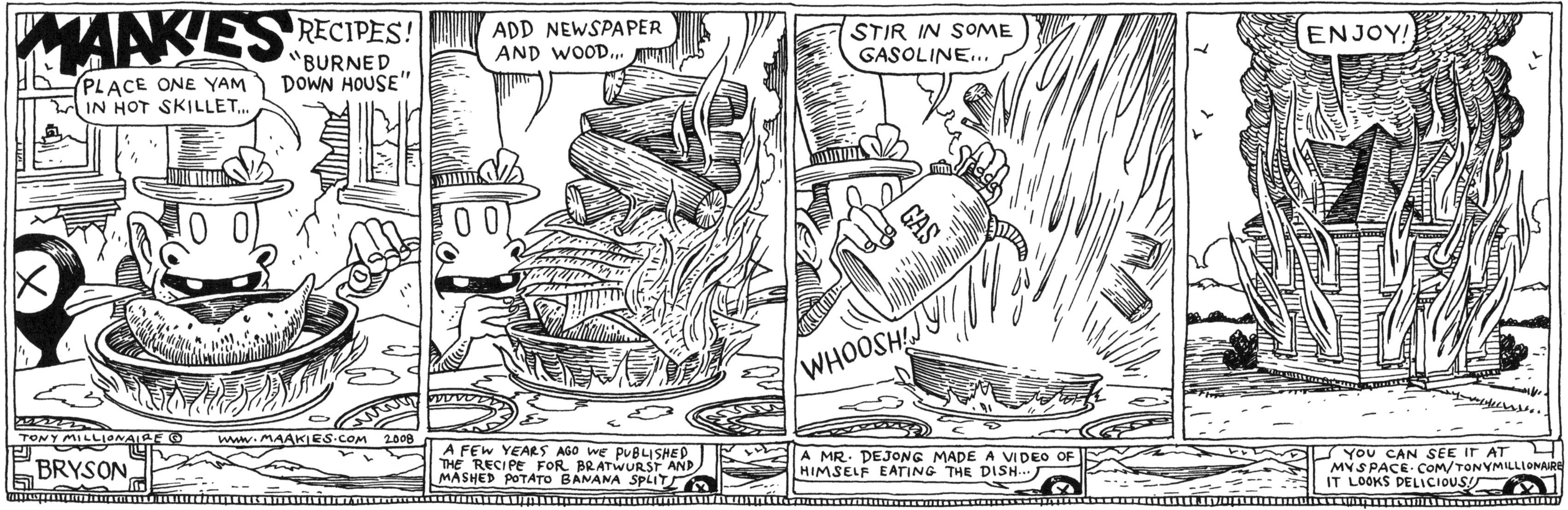
MAAKIES
RECIPES! "BURNED DOWN HOUSE"
PLACE ONE YAM IN HOT SKILLET...
ADD NEWSPAPER AND WOOD...
STIR IN SOME GASOLINE...
GAS
WHOOSH!
ENJOY!
TONY MILLIONAIRE © WWW.MAAKIES.COM 2008
BRYSON
A FEW YEARS AGO WE PUBLISHED THE RECIPE FOR BRATWURST AND MASHED POTATO BANANA SPLIT
A MR. DEJONG MADE A VIDEO OF HIMSELF EATING THE DISH...
YOU CAN SEE IT AT MYSPACE.COM/TONYMILLIONAIRE IT LOOKS DELICIOUS!

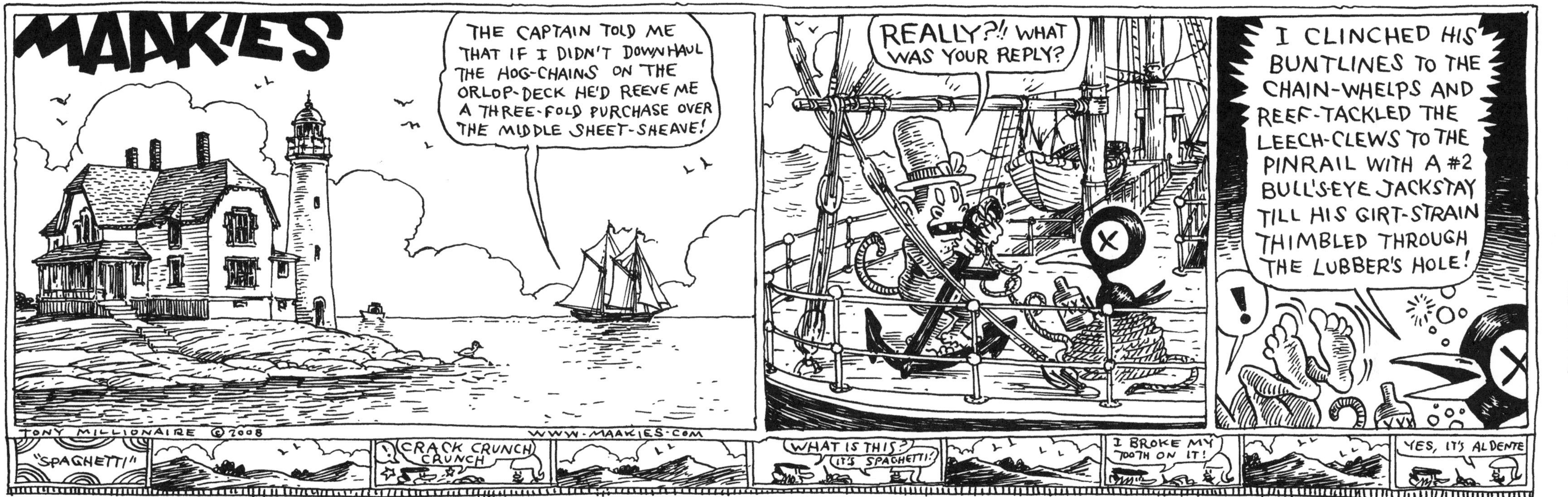
MAAKIES
THE CAPTAIN TOLD ME THAT IF I DIDN'T DOWNHAUL THE HOG-CHAINS ON THE ORLOP-DECK HE'D REEVE ME A THREE-FOLD PURCHASE OVER THE MIDDLE SHEET-SHEAVE!
REALLY?!! WHAT WAS YOUR REPLY?
I CLINCHED HIS BUNTLINES TO THE CHAIN-WHELPS AND REEF-TACKLED THE LEECH-CLEWS TO THE PINRAIL WITH A #2 BULL'S-EYE JACKSTAY TILL HIS GIRT-STRAIN THIMBLED THROUGH THE LUBBER'S HOLE!
!
TONY MILLIONAIRE © 2008
WWW.MAAKIES.COM
"SPAGHETTI"
!
CRACK CRUNCH CRUNCH
WHAT IS THIS?
IT'S SPAGHETTI!
I BROKE MY TOOTH ON IT!
YES, IT'S ALDENTE

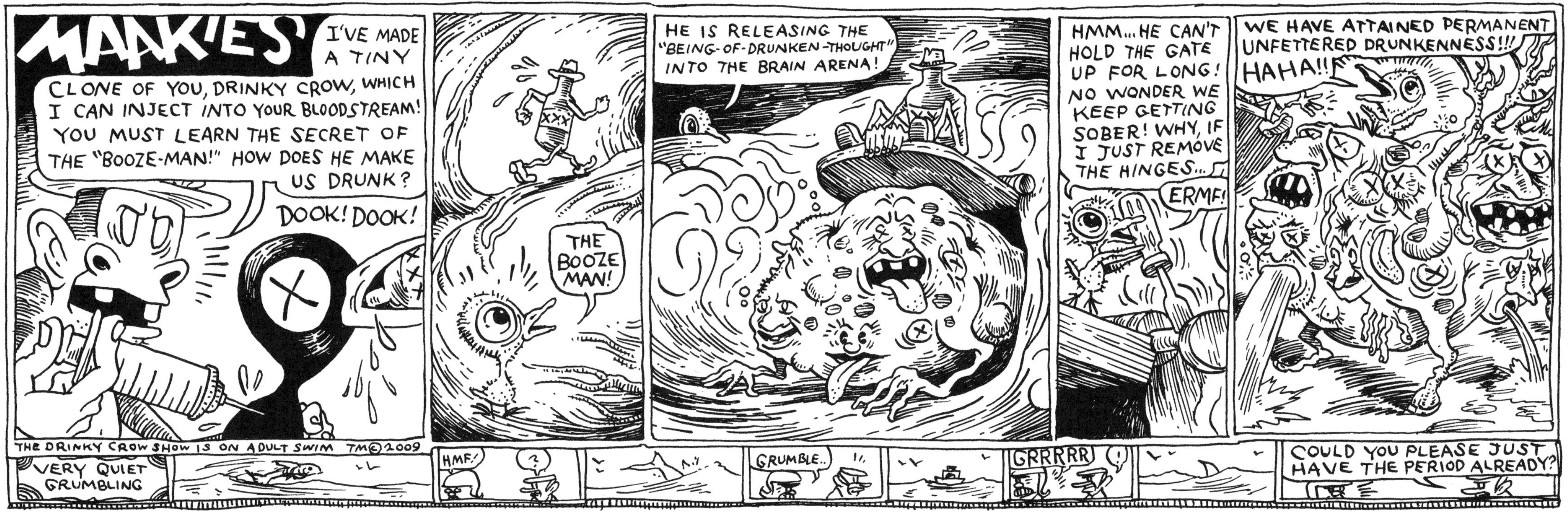
MAAKIES
I'VE MADE A TINY CLONE OF YOU, DRINKY CROW, WHICH I CAN INJECT INTO YOUR BLOODSTREAM! YOU MUST LEARN THE SECRET OF THE "BOOZE-MAN!" HOW DOES HE MAKE US DRUNK?
DOOK! DOOK!
THE BOOZE MAN!
HE IS RELEASING THE "BEING-OF-DRUNKEN-THOUGHT" INTO THE BRAIN ARENA!
HMM... HE CAN'T HOLD THE GATE UP FOR LONG! NO WONDER WE KEEP GETTING SOBER! WHY, IF I JUST REMOVE THE HINGES...
ERMF!
WE HAVE ATTAINED PERMANENT UNFETTERED DRUNKENNESS!!! HAHA!!
THE DRINKY CROW SHOW IS ON ADULT SWIM TM© 2009
VERY QUIET GRUMBLING
HMF!
?
GRUMBLE..
GRRRRRR
!
COULD YOU PLEASE JUST HAVE THE PERIOD ALREADY?

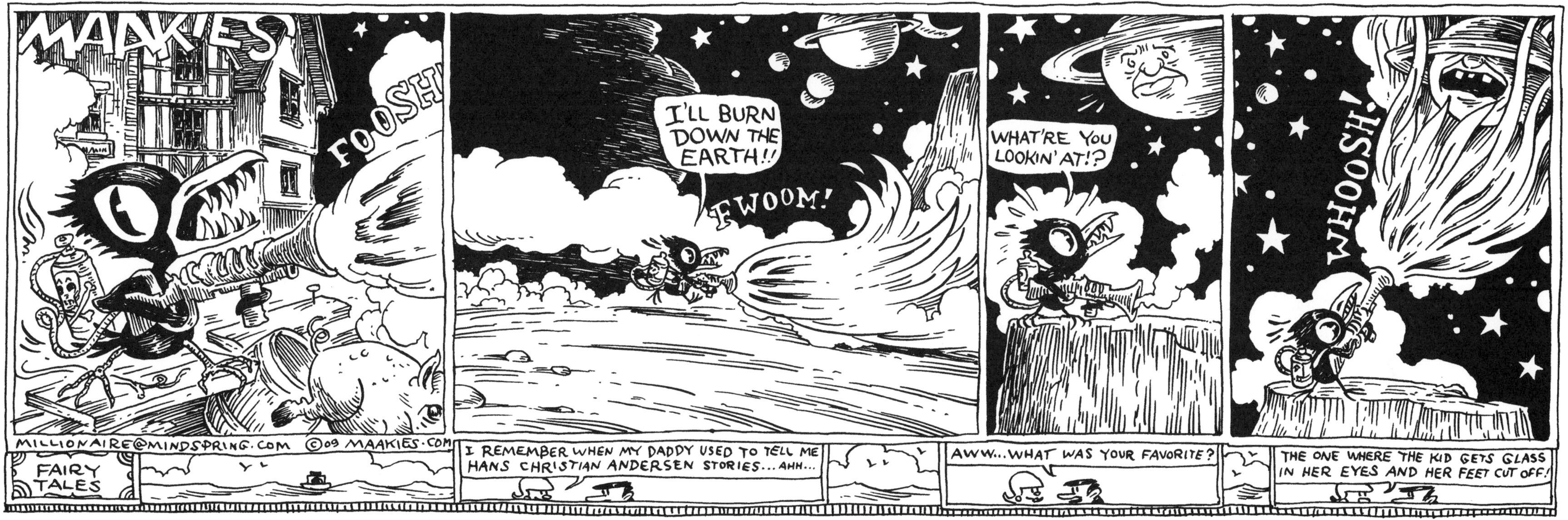
MAAKIES
FOOSH!
I'LL BURN DOWN THE EARTH!!
FWOOM!
WHAT'RE YOU LOOKIN' AT!?
WHOOSH!
MILLIONAIRE@MINDSPRING.COM ©09 MAAKIES.COM
FAIRY TALES
I REMEMBER WHEN MY DADDY USED TO TELL ME HANS CHRISTIAN ANDERSEN STORIES... AHH...
AWW... WHAT WAS YOUR FAVORITE?
THE ONE WHERE THE KID GETS GLASS IN HER EYES AND HER FEET CUT OFF!

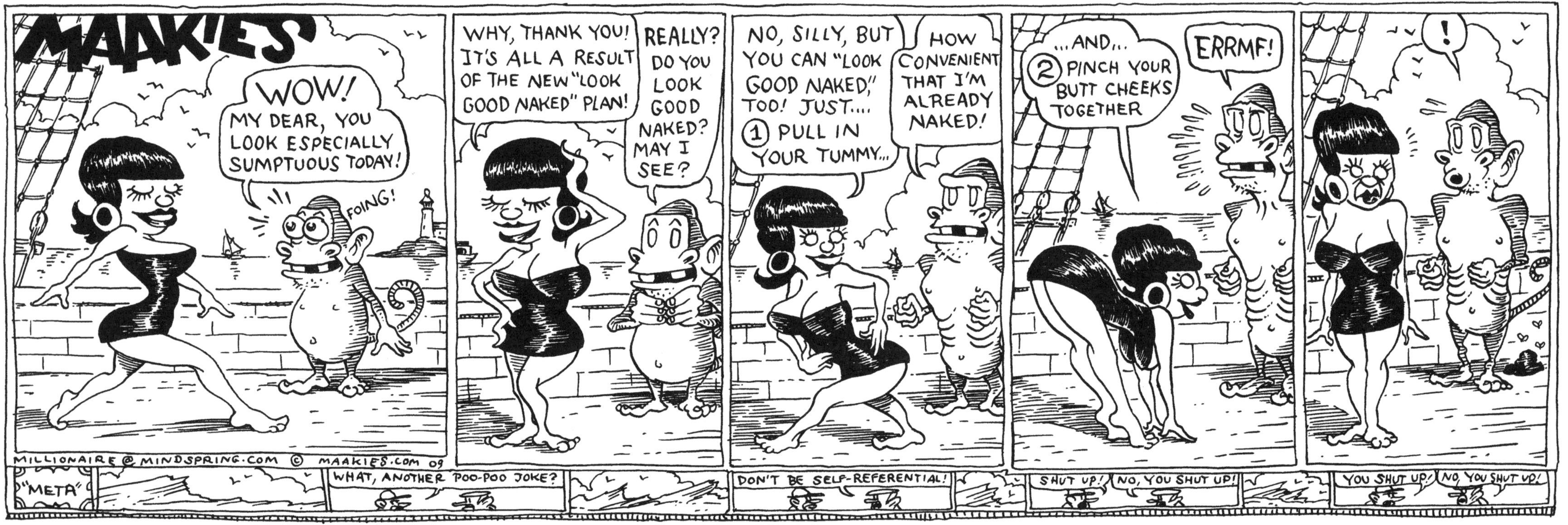
MAAKIES
WOW! MY DEAR, YOU LOOK ESPECIALLY SUMPTUOUS TODAY!
FOING!
WHY, THANK YOU! IT'S ALL A RESULT OF THE NEW "LOOK GOOD NAKED" PLAN!
REALLY? DO YOU LOOK GOOD NAKED? MAY I SEE?
NO, SILLY, BUT YOU CAN "LOOK GOOD NAKED," TOO! JUST.... (1) PULL IN YOUR TUMMY...
HOW CONVENIENT THAT I'M ALREADY NAKED!
...AND... (2) PINCH YOUR BUTT CHEEKS TOGETHER
ERRMF!
!
MILLIONAIRE@MINDSPRING.COM © MAAKIES.COM 09
"META"
WHAT, ANOTHER POO-POO JOKE?
DON'T BE SELF-REFERENTIAL!
SHUT UP!
NO, YOU SHUT UP!
YOU SHUT UP!
NO, YOU SHUT UP!

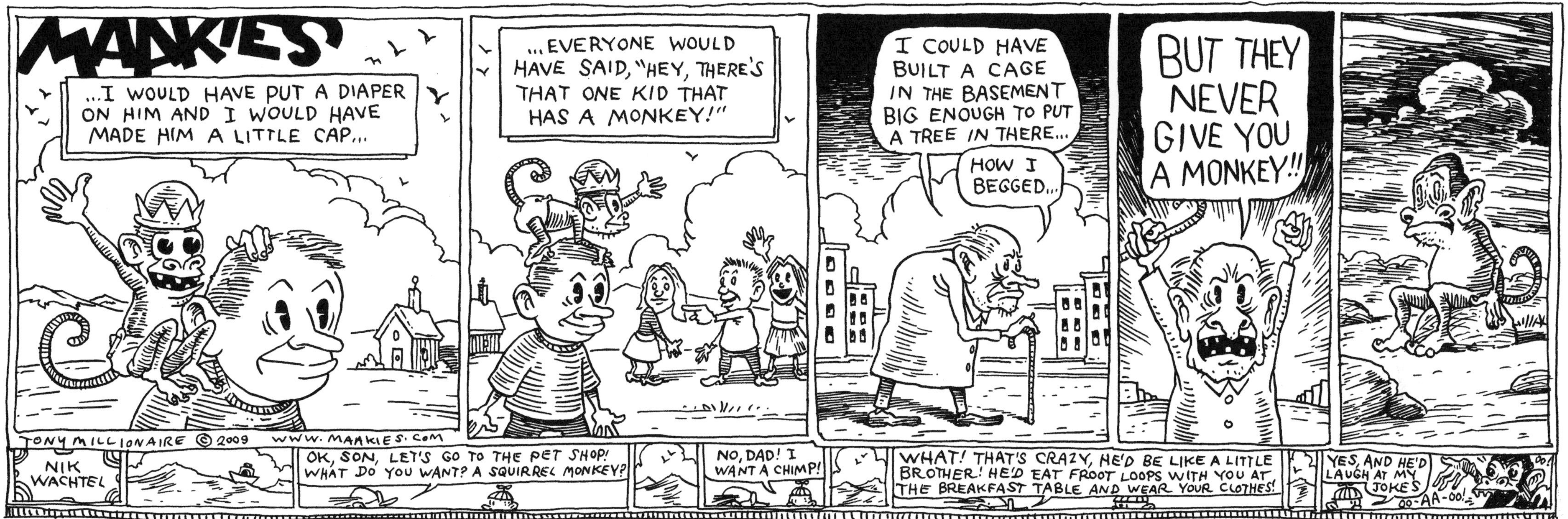
MAAKIES
...I WOULD HAVE PUT A DIAPER ON HIM AND I WOULD HAVE MADE HIM A LITTLE CAP...
...EVERYONE WOULD HAVE SAID, "HEY, THERE'S THAT ONE KID THAT HAS A MONKEY!"
I COULD HAVE BUILT A CAGE IN THE BASEMENT BIG ENOUGH TO PUT A TREE IN THERE...
HOW I BEGGED...
BUT THEY NEVER GIVE YOU A MONKEY!!
TONY MILLIONAIRE © 2009 WWW.MAAKIES.COM
NIK WACHTEL
OK, SON, LET'S GO TO THE PET SHOP! WHAT DO YOU WANT? A SQUIRREL MONKEY?
NO, DAD! I WANT A CHIMP!
WHAT! THAT'S CRAZY, HE'D BE LIKE A LITTLE BROTHER! HE'D EAT FROOT LOOPS WITH YOU AT THE BREAKFAST TABLE AND WEAR YOUR CLOTHES!
YES, AND HE'D LAUGH AT MY JOKES
OO-AA-OO!

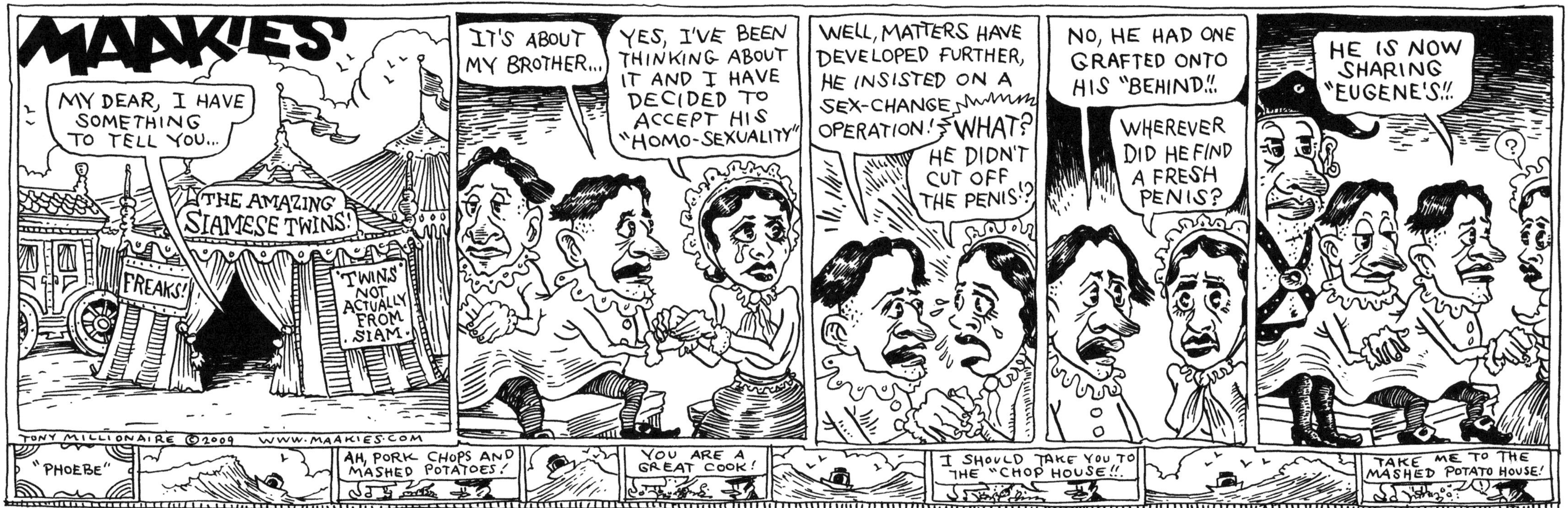
MAAKIES
MY DEAR, I HAVE SOMETHING TO TELL YOU...
THE AMAZING SIAMESE TWINS!
FREAKS!
TWINS NOT ACTUALLY FROM SIAM.
IT'S ABOUT MY BROTHER...
YES, I'VE BEEN THINKING ABOUT IT AND I HAVE DECIDED TO ACCEPT HIS "HOMO-SEXUALITY"
WELL, MATTERS HAVE DEVELOPED FURTHER, HE INSISTED ON A SEX-CHANGE OPERATION!
WHAT? HE DIDN'T CUT OFF THE PENIS!?
NO, HE HAD ONE GRAFTED ONTO HIS "BEHIND"!!
WHEREVER DID HE FIND A FRESH PENIS?
HE IS NOW SHARING "EUGENE'S"!!
?
TONY MILLIONAIRE ©2009 WWW.MAAKIES.COM
"PHOEBE"
AH, PORK CHOPS AND MASHED POTATOES!
YOU ARE A GREAT COOK!
I SHOULD TAKE YOU TO THE "CHOP HOUSE"!!
TAKE ME TO THE MASHED POTATO HOUSE!

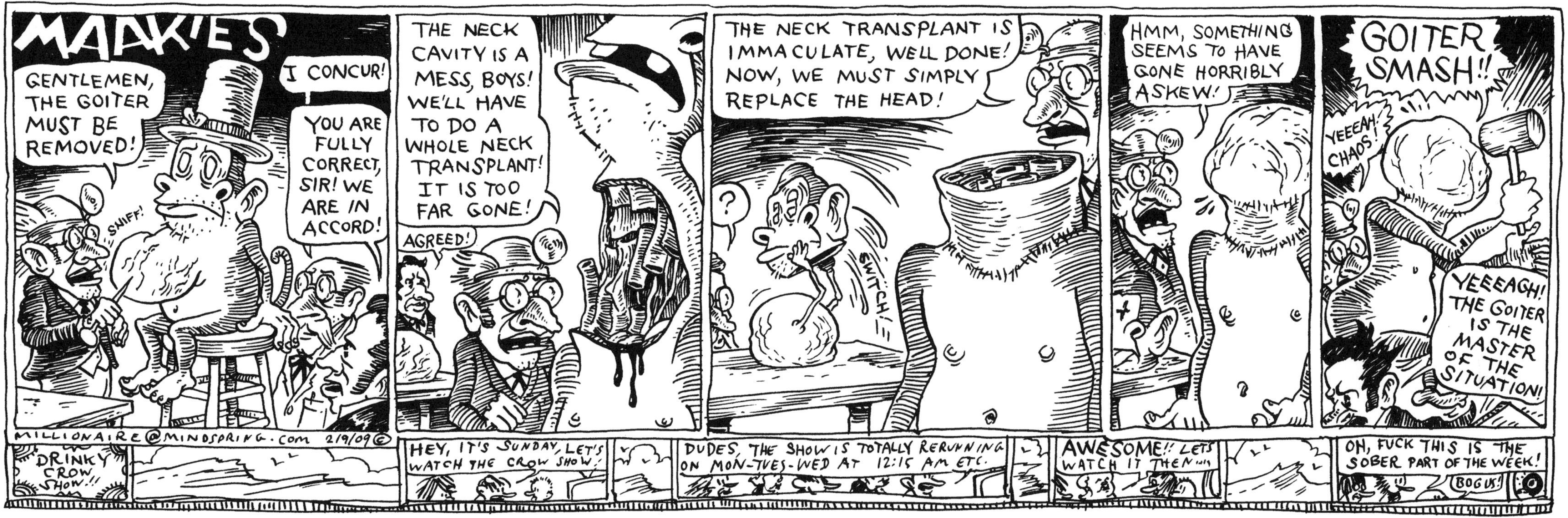
MAAKIES
GENTLEMEN, THE GOITER MUST BE REMOVED!
SNIFF!
I CONCUR!
YOU ARE FULLY CORRECT, SIR! WE ARE IN ACCORD!
THE NECK CAVITY IS A MESS, BOYS! WE'LL HAVE TO DO A WHOLE NECK TRANSPLANT! IT IS TOO FAR GONE!
AGREED!
THE NECK TRANSPLANT IS IMMACULATE, WELL DONE! NOW, WE MUST SIMPLY REPLACE THE HEAD!
?
SWITCH!
HMM, SOMETHING SEEMS TO HAVE GONE HORRIBLY ASKEW!
GOITER SMASH!!
YEEEAH! CHAOS!
YEEEAGH! THE GOITER IS THE MASTER OF THE SITUATION!
MILLIONAIRE@MINDSPRING.COM 2/19/09©
DRINKY CROW SHOW!!
HEY, IT'S SUNDAY, LET'S WATCH THE CROW SHOW.
DUDES, THE SHOW IS TOTALLY RERUNNING ON MON-TUES-WED AT 12:15 AM ETC.
AWESOME!! LETS WATCH IT THEN
OH, FUCK THIS IS THE SOBER PART OF THE WEEK!
BOGUS!

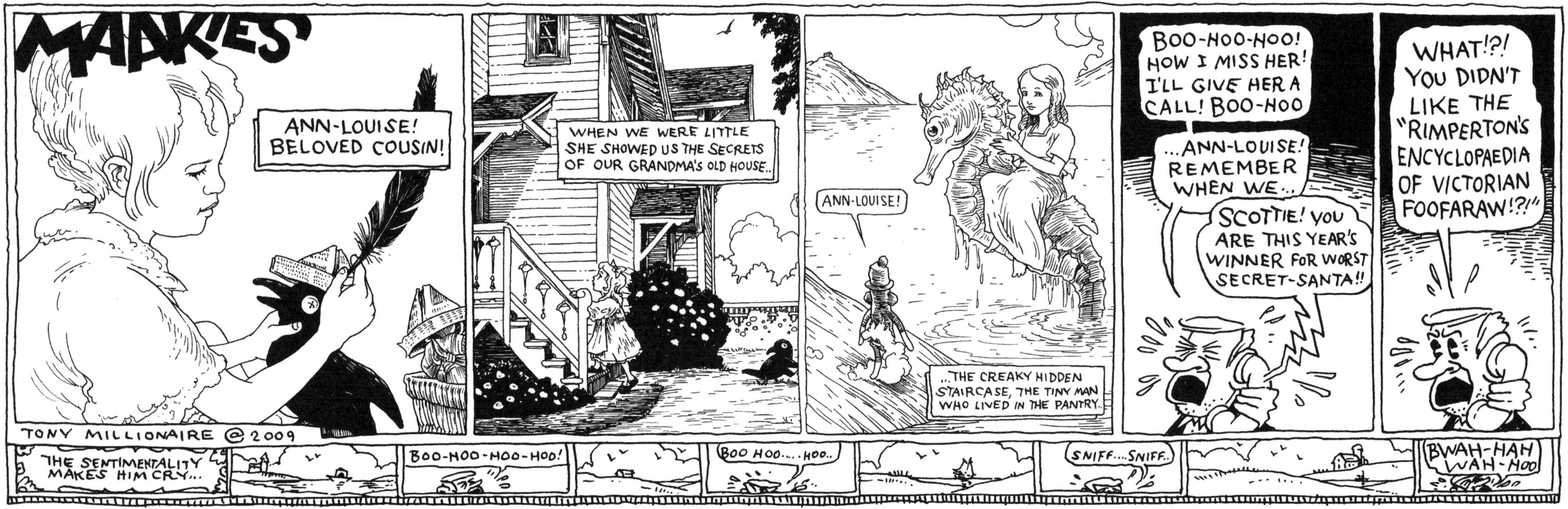
MAAKIES
ANN-LOUISE! BELOVED COUSIN!
TONY MILLIONAIRE @ 2009
WHEN WE WERE LITTLE SHE SHOWED US THE SECRETS OF OUR GRANDMA'S OLD HOUSE..
ANN-LOUISE!
...THE CREAKY HIDDEN STAIRCASE, THE TINY MAN WHO LIVED IN THE PANTRY..
BOO-HOO-HOO! HOW I MISS HER! I'LL GIVE HER A CALL! BOO-HOO
...ANN-LOUISE! REMEMBER WHEN WE...
SCOTTIE! YOU ARE THIS YEAR'S WINNER FOR WORST SECRET-SANTA!!
WHAT!?! YOU DIDN'T LIKE THE "RIMPERTON'S ENCYCLOPAEDIA OF VICTORIAN FOOFARAW!?!"
THE SENTIMENTALITY MAKES HIM CRY...
BOO-HOO-HOO-HOO!
BOO HOO.... HOO..
SNIFF.... SNIFF..
BWAH-HAH WAH-HOO

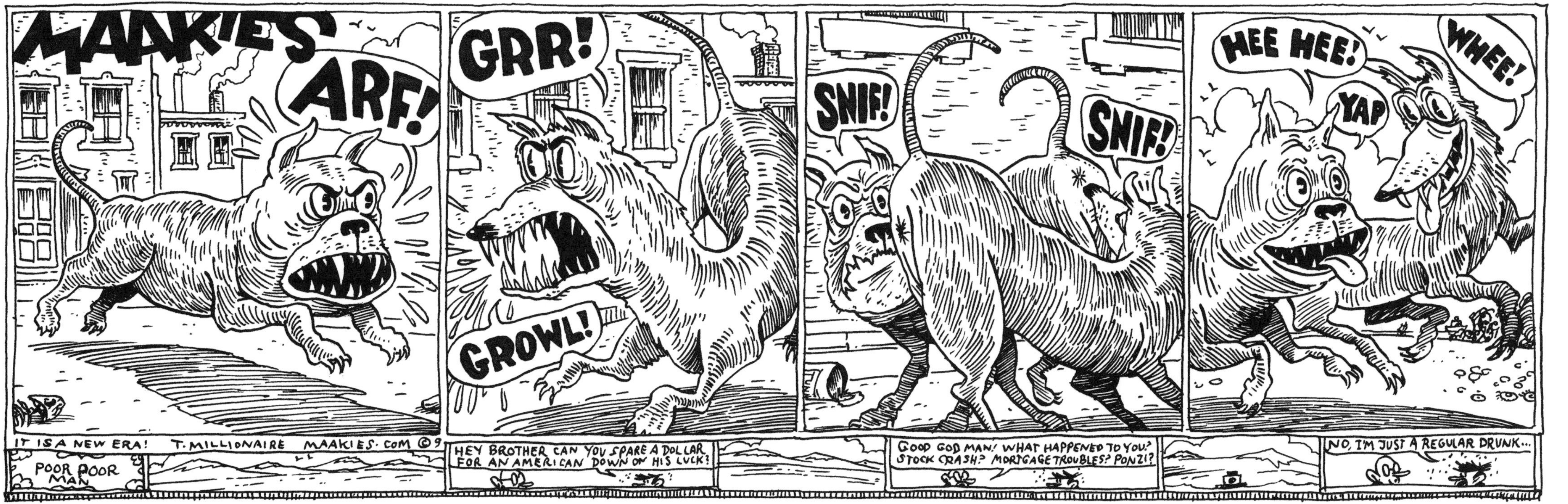
MAAKIES
ARF!
GRR!
GROWL!
SNIF!
SNIF!
HEE HEE!
YAP
WHEE!
IT IS A NEW ERA!
T. MILLIONAIRE
MAAKIES.COM ©9
POOR POOR MAN
HEY BROTHER CAN YOU SPARE A DOLLAR FOR AN AMERICAN DOWN ON HIS LUCK!
GOOD GOD MAN! WHAT HAPPENED TO YOU? STOCK CRASH? MORTGAGE TROUBLES? PONZI?
NO, I'M JUST A REGULAR DRUNK...

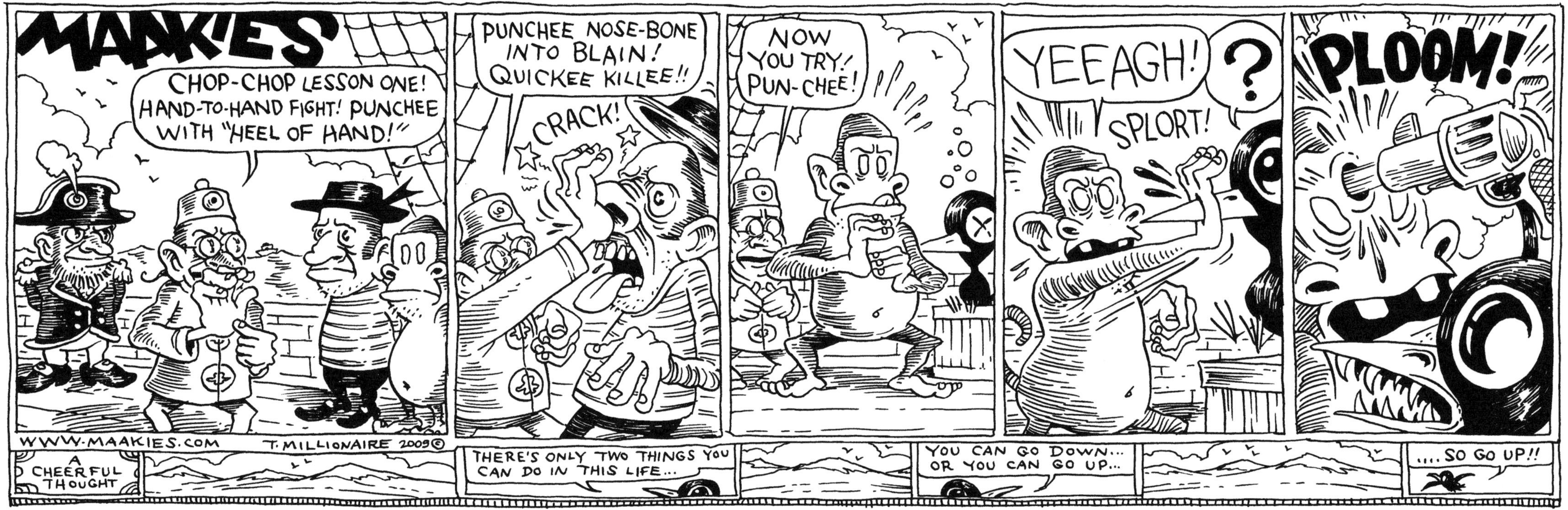
MAAKIES
CHOP-CHOP LESSON ONE! HAND-TO-HAND FIGHT! PUNCHEE WITH "HEEL OF HAND!"
PUNCHEE NOSE-BONE INTO BLAIN! QUICKEE KILLEE!!
CRACK!
NOW YOU TRY! PUN-CHEE!
YEEAGH!
?
SPLORT!
PLOOM!
WWW.MAAKIES.COM
T. MILLIONAIRE 2009©
A CHEERFUL THOUGHT
THERE'S ONLY TWO THINGS YOU CAN DO IN THIS LIFE...
YOU CAN GO DOWN... OR YOU CAN GO UP...
....SO GO UP!!

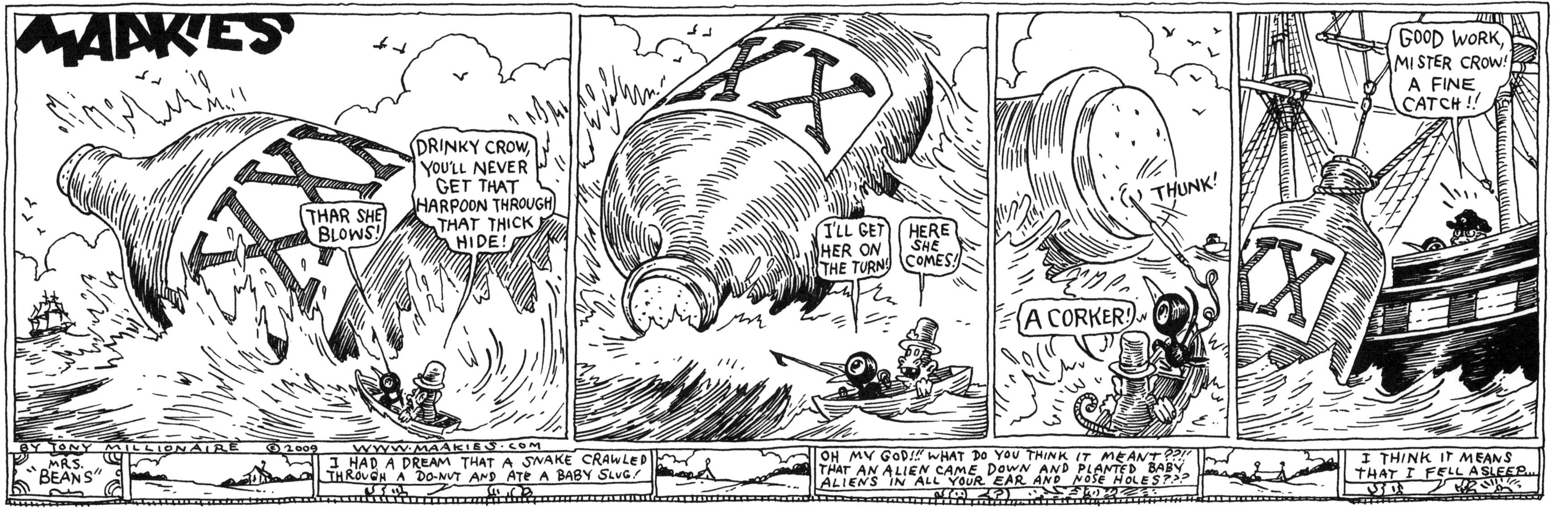
MAAKIES
THAR SHE BLOWS!
DRINKY CROW, YOU'LL NEVER GET THAT HARPOON THROUGH THAT THICK HIDE!
I'LL GET HER ON THE TURN!
HERE SHE COMES!
THUNK!
A CORKER!
GOOD WORK, MISTER CROW! A FINE CATCH!!
BY TONY MILLIONAIRE ©2009 WWW.MAAKIES.COM
"MRS. BEANS"
I HAD A DREAM THAT A SNAKE CRAWLED THROUGH A DO-NUT AND ATE A BABY SLUG!
OH MY GOD!!! WHAT DO YOU THINK IT MEANT??!! THAT AN ALIEN CAME DOWN AND PLANTED BABY ALIENS IN ALL YOUR EAR AND NOSE HOLES???
I THINK IT MEANS THAT I FELL ASLEEP...

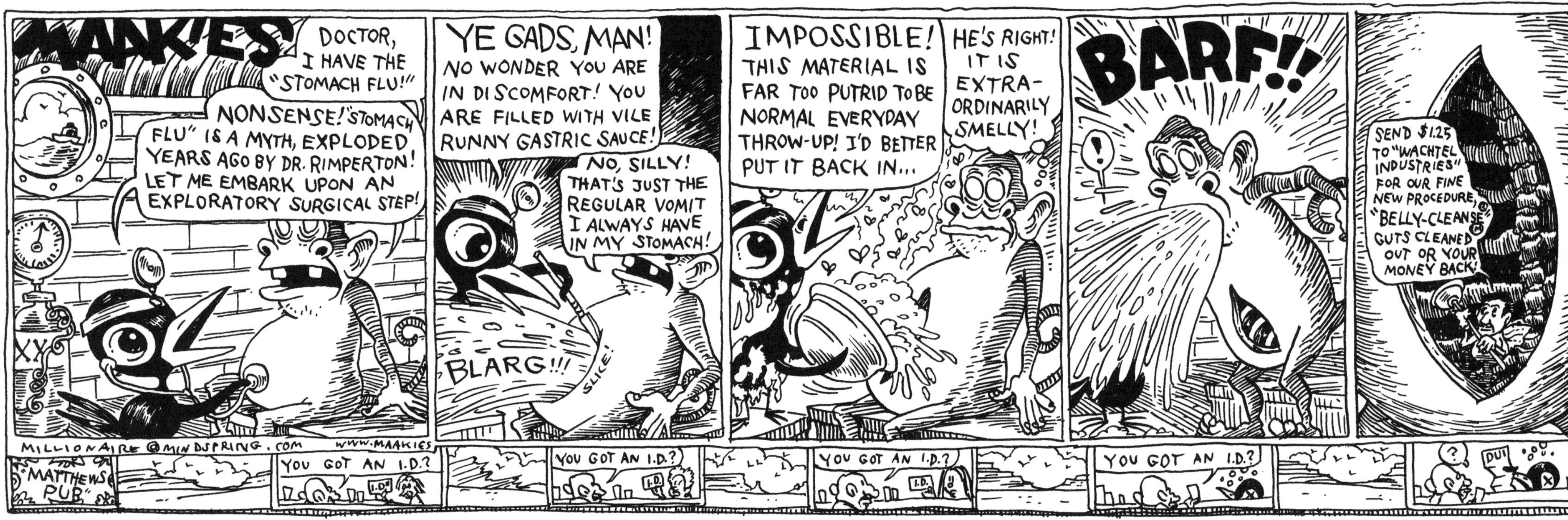
MAAKIES
DOCTOR, I HAVE THE "STOMACH FLU!"
NONSENSE! "STOMACH FLU" IS A MYTH, EXPLODED YEARS AGO BY DR. RIMPERTON! LET ME EMBARK UPON AN EXPLORATORY SURGICAL STEP!
YE GADS, MAN! NO WONDER YOU ARE IN DISCOMFORT! YOU ARE FILLED WITH VILE RUNNY GASTRIC SAUCE!
NO, SILLY! THAT'S JUST THE REGULAR VOMIT I ALWAYS HAVE IN MY STOMACH!
BLARG!!!
SLICE!
IMPOSSIBLE! THIS MATERIAL IS FAR TOO PUTRID TO BE NORMAL EVERYDAY THROW-UP! I'D BETTER PUT IT BACK IN...
HE'S RIGHT! IT IS EXTRA-ORDINARILY SMELLY!
BARF!!
!
SEND $1.25 TO "WACHTEL INDUSTRIES" FOR OUR FINE NEW PROCEDURE, "BELLY-CLEANSE"® GUTS CLEANED OUT OR YOUR MONEY BACK!
MILLIONAIRE@MINDSPRING.COM
WWW.MAAKIES
"MATTHEWS PUB"
YOU GOT AN I.D.?
I.D.
YOU GOT AN I.D.?
I.D.
YOU GOT AN I.D.?
I.D.
YOU GOT AN I.D.?
?
DUI

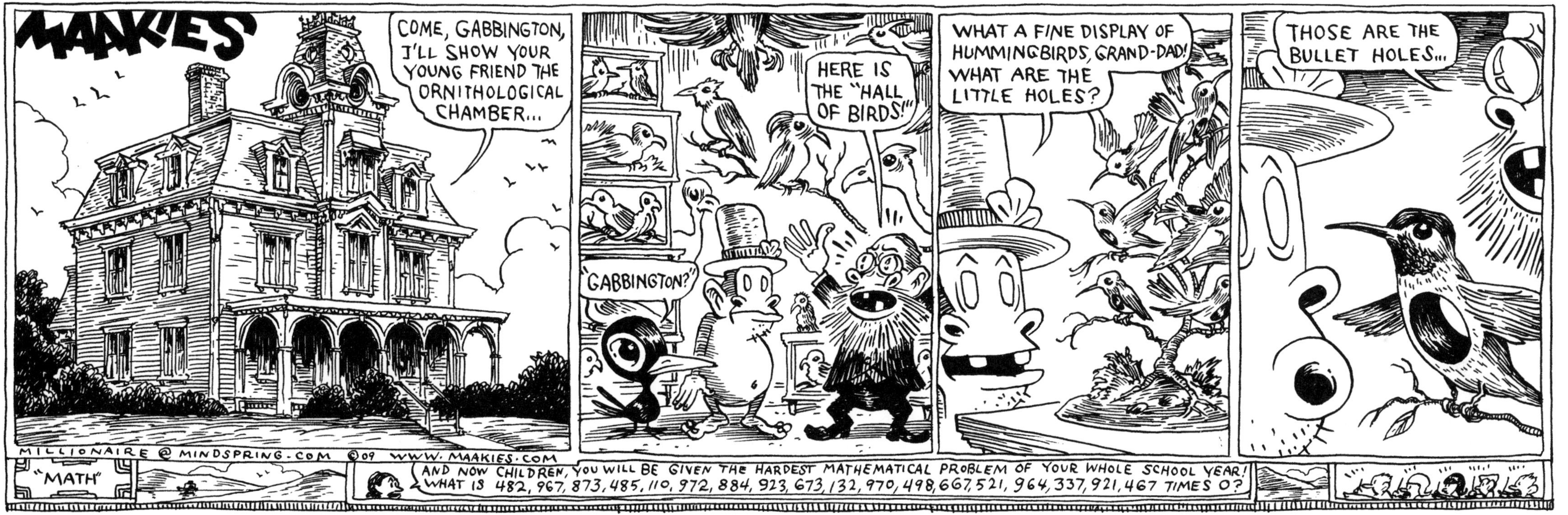
MAAKIES
COME, GABBINGTON, I'LL SHOW YOUR YOUNG FRIEND THE ORNITHOLOGICAL CHAMBER...
HERE IS THE "HALL OF BIRDS!"
"GABBINGTON?"
WHAT A FINE DISPLAY OF HUMMINGBIRDS, GRAND-DAD! WHAT ARE THE LITTLE HOLES?
THOSE ARE THE BULLET HOLES...
MILLIONAIRE@MINDSPRING.COM ©09 WWW.MAAKIES.COM
"MATH"
AND NOW CHILDREN, YOU WILL BE GIVEN THE HARDEST MATHEMATICAL PROBLEM OF YOUR WHOLE SCHOOL YEAR! WHAT IS 482,967,873,485,110,972,884,923,673,132,970,498,667,521,964,337,921,467 TIMES 0?

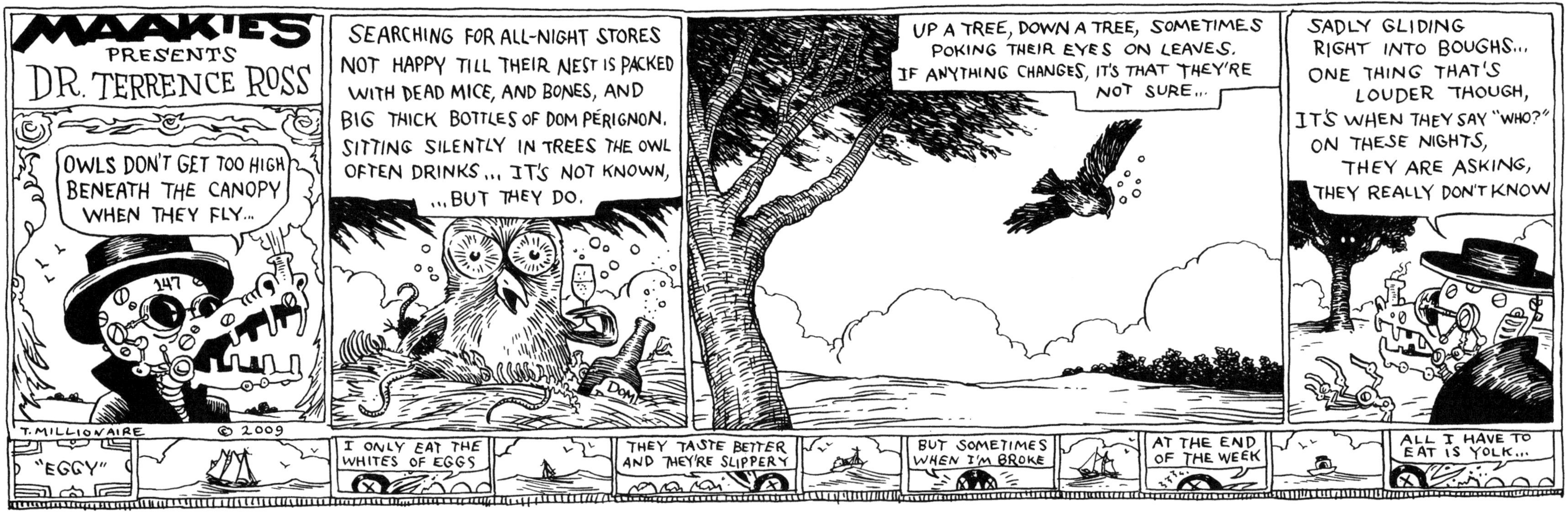

MAAKIES
PRESENTS
DR. TERRENCE ROSS
OWLS DON'T GET TOO HIGH BENEATH THE CANOPY WHEN THEY FLY...
147
T. MILLIONAIRE © 2009
SEARCHING FOR ALL-NIGHT STORES NOT HAPPY TILL THEIR NEST IS PACKED WITH DEAD MICE, AND BONES, AND BIG THICK BOTTLES OF DOM PÉRIGNON. SITTING SILENTLY IN TREES THE OWL OFTEN DRINKS... IT'S NOT KNOWN, ...BUT THEY DO.
DOM
UP A TREE, DOWN A TREE, SOMETIMES POKING THEIR EYES ON LEAVES. IF ANYTHING CHANGES, IT'S THAT THEY'RE NOT SURE...
SADLY GLIDING RIGHT INTO BOUGHS... ONE THING THAT'S LOUDER THOUGH, IT'S WHEN THEY SAY "WHO?" ON THESE NIGHTS, THEY ARE ASKING, THEY REALLY DON'T KNOW
"EGGY"
I ONLY EAT THE WHITES OF EGGS
THEY TASTE BETTER AND THEY'RE SLIPPERY
BUT SOMETIMES WHEN I'M BROKE
AT THE END OF THE WEEK
ALL I HAVE TO EAT IS YOLK...

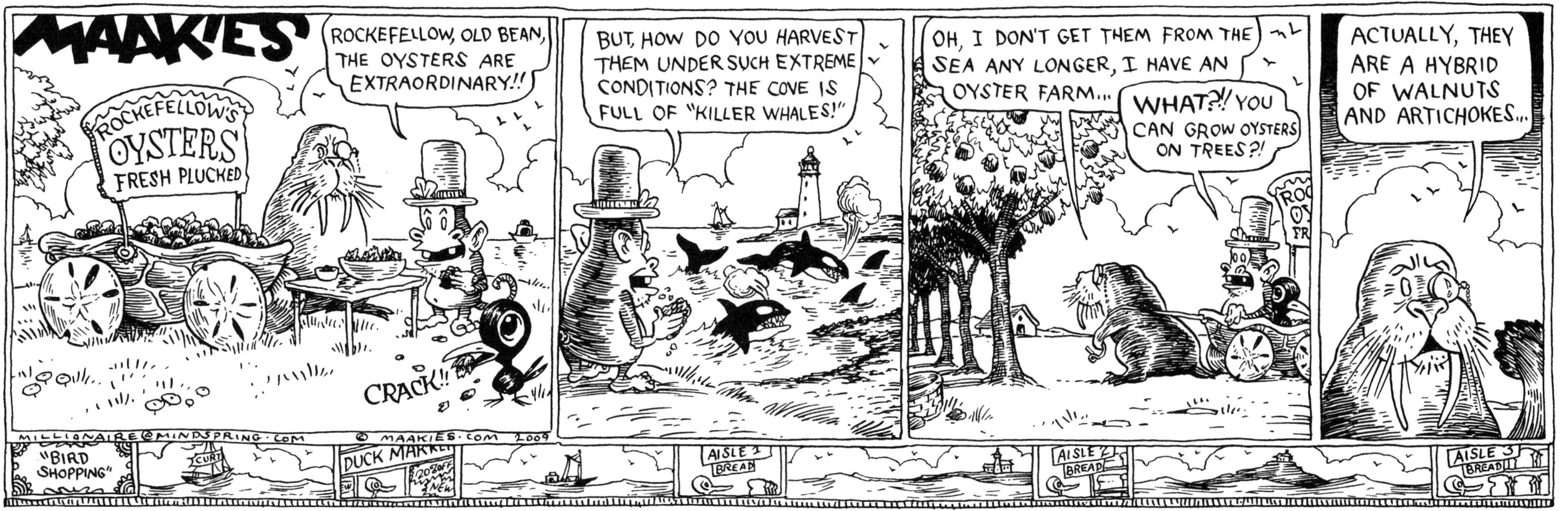
MAAKIES
ROCKEFELLOW, OLD BEAN, THE OYSTERS ARE EXTRAORDINARY!!
ROCKEFELLOW'S OYSTERS FRESH PLUCKED
CRACK!!
MILLIONAIRE@MINDSPRING.COM
© MAAKIES.COM 2009
BUT, HOW DO YOU HARVEST THEM UNDER SUCH EXTREME CONDITIONS? THE COVE IS FULL OF "KILLER WHALES!"
OH, I DON'T GET THEM FROM THE SEA ANY LONGER, I HAVE AN OYSTER FARM...
WHAT?!! YOU CAN GROW OYSTERS ON TREES?!
ACTUALLY, THEY ARE A HYBRID OF WALNUTS AND ARTICHOKES...
"BIRD SHOPPING"
CURT
DUCK MARKET
20% OFF
NEW
AISLE 1 BREAD
AISLE 2 BREAD
AISLE 3 BREAD

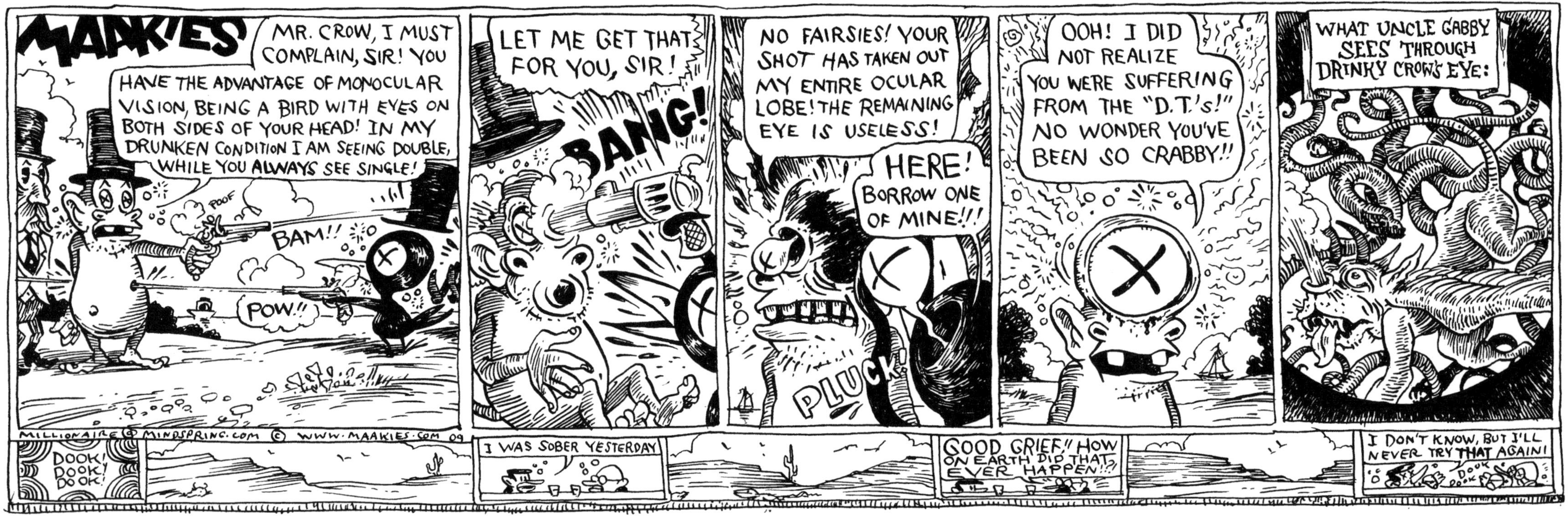
MAAKIES
MR. CROW, I MUST COMPLAIN, SIR! YOU HAVE THE ADVANTAGE OF MONOCULAR VISION, BEING A BIRD WITH EYES ON BOTH SIDES OF YOUR HEAD! IN MY DRUNKEN CONDITION I AM SEEING DOUBLE, WHILE YOU ALWAYS SEE SINGLE!
POOF
BAM!!
POW!!
LET ME GET THAT FOR YOU, SIR!
BANG!
NO FAIRSIES! YOUR SHOT HAS TAKEN OUT MY ENTIRE OCULAR LOBE! THE REMAINING EYE IS USELESS!
HERE! BORROW ONE OF MINE!!!
PLUCK!
OOH! I DID NOT REALIZE YOU WERE SUFFERING FROM THE "D.T.'s!" NO WONDER YOU'VE BEEN SO CRABBY!!
WHAT UNCLE GABBY SEES THROUGH DRINKY CROW'S EYE:
MILLIONAIRE@MINDSPRING.COM © WWW.MAAKIES.COM 09
DOOK! DOOK! DOOK!
I WAS SOBER YESTERDAY
GOOD GRIEF! HOW ON EARTH DID THAT EVER HAPPEN!?
I DON'T KNOW, BUT I'LL NEVER TRY THAT AGAIN!
DOOK DOOK

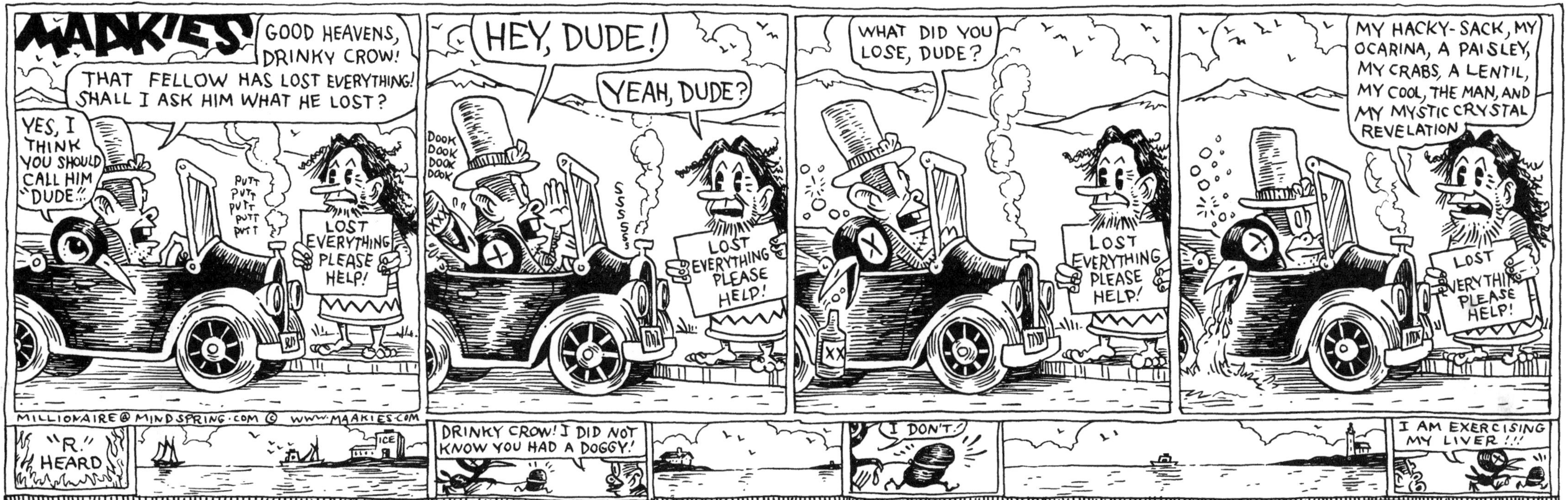
MAAKIES
GOOD HEAVENS, DRINKY CROW!
THAT FELLOW HAS LOST EVERYTHING! SHALL I ASK HIM WHAT HE LOST?
YES, I THINK YOU SHOULD CALL HIM "DUDE."
PUTT PUTT PUTT PUTT PUTT
LOST EVERYTHING PLEASE HELP!
HEY, DUDE!
YEAH, DUDE?
DOOK DOOK DOOK DOOK
SSSSSS
LOST EVERYTHING PLEASE HELP!
WHAT DID YOU LOSE, DUDE?
LOST EVERYTHING PLEASE HELP!
MY HACKY-SACK, MY OCARINA, A PAISLEY, MY CRABS, A LENTIL, MY COOL, THE MAN, AND MY MYSTIC CRYSTAL REVELATION
LOST EVERYTHI PLEASE HELP!
MILLIONAIRE@MINDSPRING.COM © WWW.MAAKIES.COM
"R." HEARD
ICE
DRINKY CROW! I DID NOT KNOW YOU HAD A DOGGY!
I DON'T!
I AM EXERCISING MY LIVER!!!

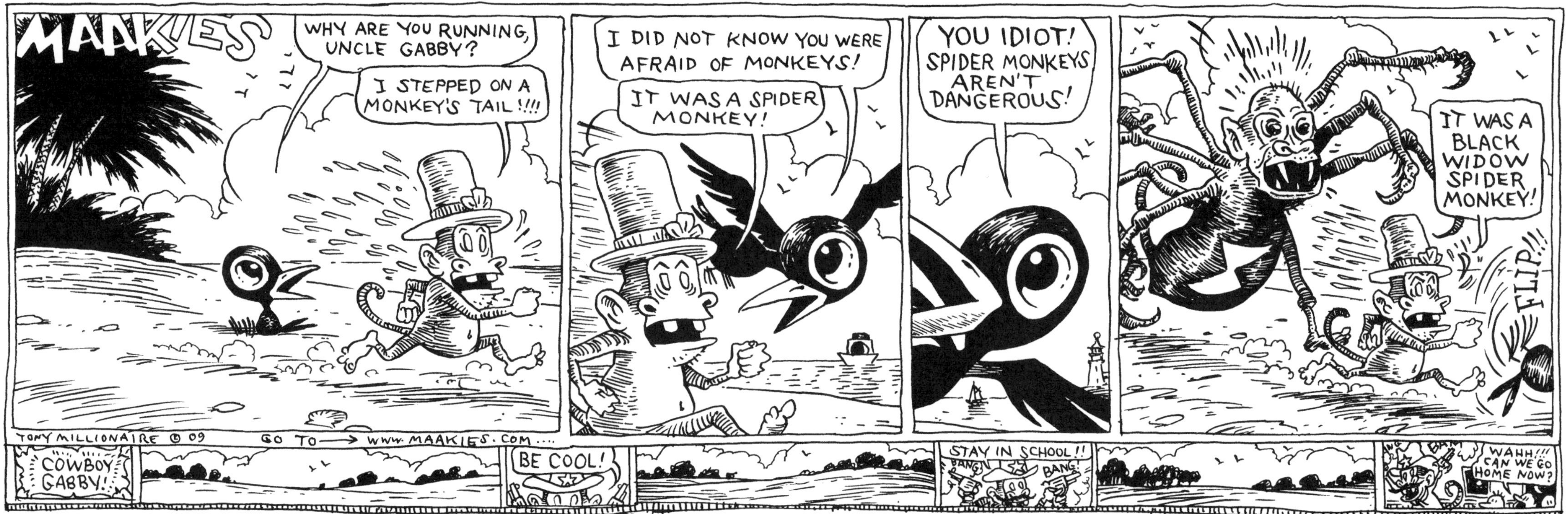
MAAKIES
WHY ARE YOU RUNNING, UNCLE GABBY?
I STEPPED ON A MONKEY'S TAIL!!!!
I DID NOT KNOW YOU WERE AFRAID OF MONKEYS!
IT WAS A SPIDER MONKEY!
YOU IDIOT! SPIDER MONKEYS AREN'T DANGEROUS!
IT WAS A BLACK WIDOW SPIDER MONKEY!
FLIP!!!
TONY MILLIONAIRE © 09
GO TO → WWW.MAAKIES.COM....
COWBOY GABBY!
BE COOL!
STAY IN SCHOOL!!
BANG
BANG
WAHH!!! CAN WE GO HOME NOW?

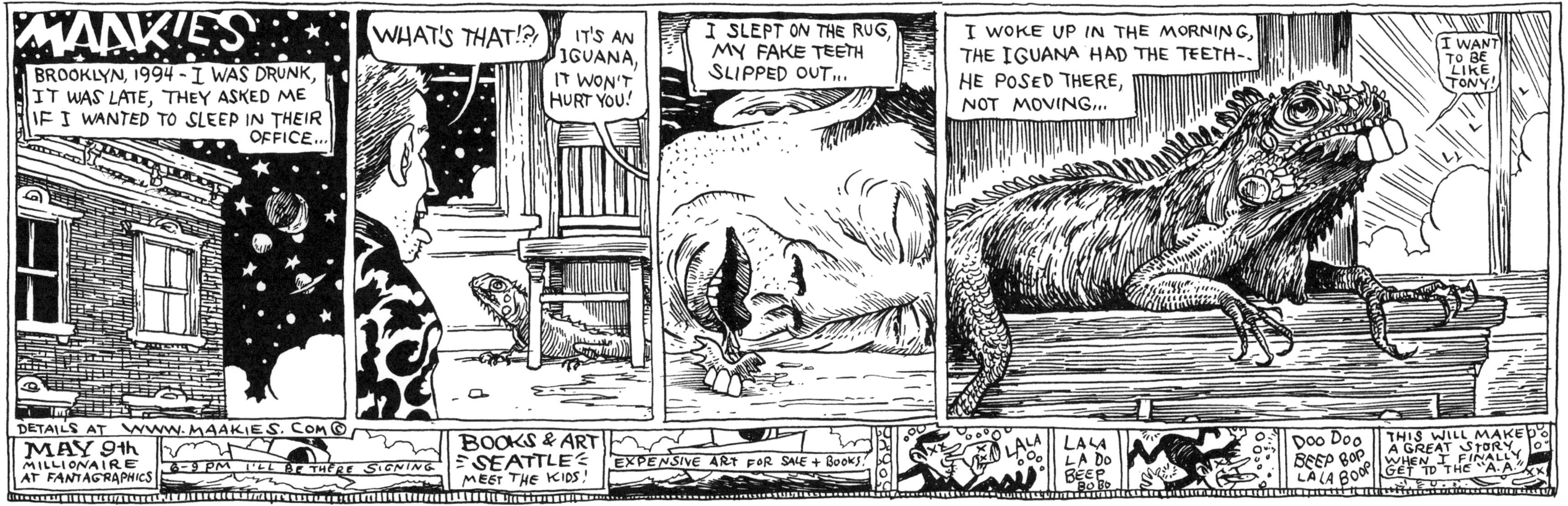
MAAKIES
BROOKLYN, 1994 - I WAS DRUNK, IT WAS LATE, THEY ASKED ME IF I WANTED TO SLEEP IN THEIR OFFICE...
WHAT'S THAT!?!
IT'S AN IGUANA, IT WON'T HURT YOU!
I SLEPT ON THE RUG, MY FAKE TEETH SLIPPED OUT...
I WOKE UP IN THE MORNING, THE IGUANA HAD THE TEETH- HE POSED THERE, NOT MOVING...
I WANT TO BE LIKE TONY!
DETAILS AT WWW.MAAKIES.COM ©
MAY 9th MILLIONAIRE AT FANTAGRAPHICS
6-9 PM I'LL BE THERE SIGNING
BOOKS & ART SEATTLE MEET THE KIDS!
EXPENSIVE ART FOR SALE + BOOKS!
LA LA
LA LA LA DO BEEP BO BO
DOO DOO BEEP BOP LA LA BOOP
THIS WILL MAKE A GREAT STORY WHEN I FINALLY GET TO THE "A.A."

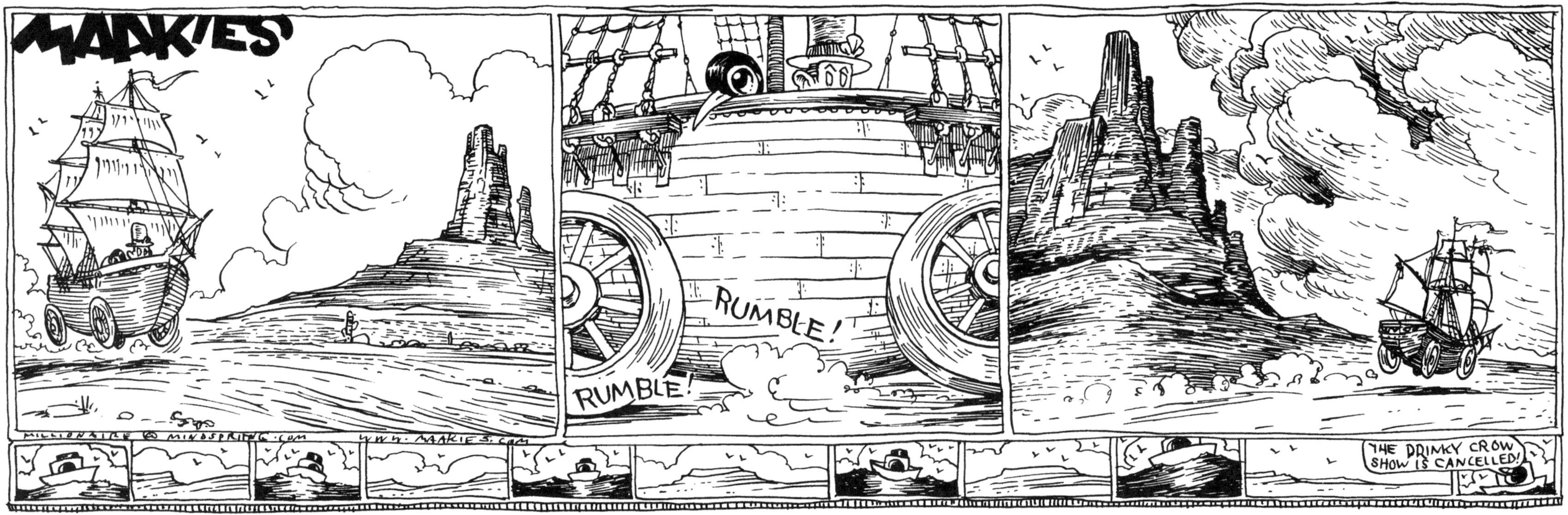
MAAKIES
MILLIONAIRE @ MINDSPRING.COM
WWW.MAAKIES.COM
RUMBLE!
RUMBLE!
THE DRINKY CROW SHOW IS CANCELLED!

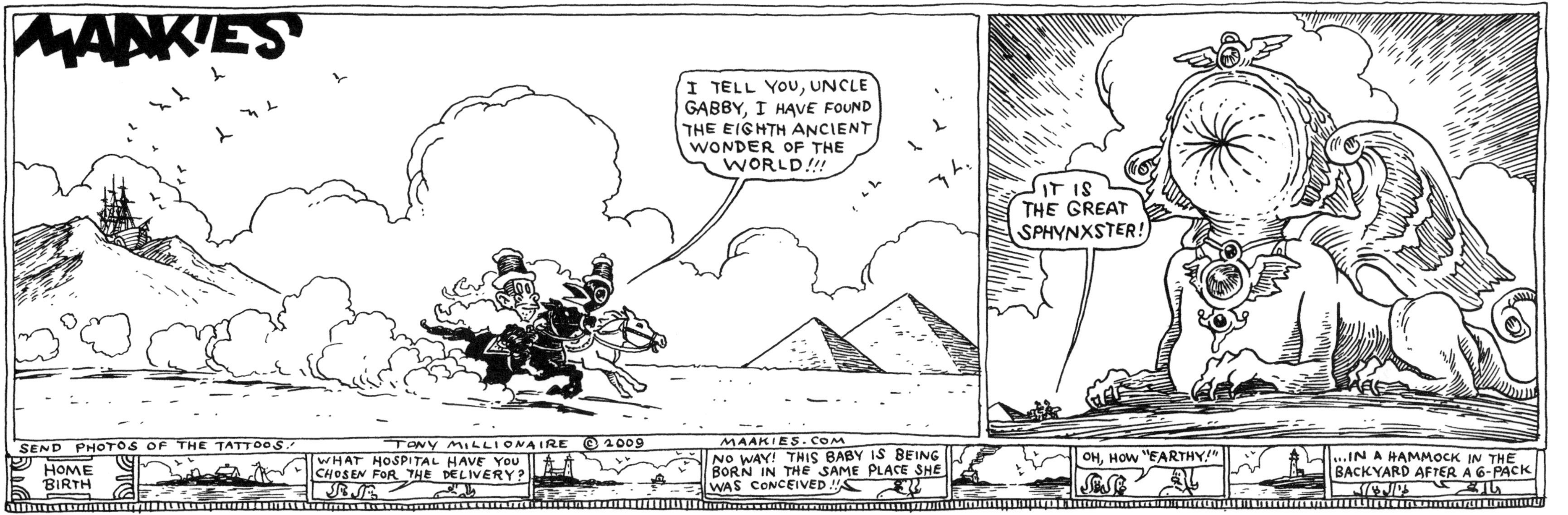
MAAKIES
I TELL YOU, UNCLE GABBY, I HAVE FOUND THE EIGHTH ANCIENT WONDER OF THE WORLD!!!
IT IS THE GREAT SPHYNXSTER!
SEND PHOTOS OF THE TATTOOS!
TONY MILLIONAIRE © 2009
MAAKIES.COM
HOME BIRTH
WHAT HOSPITAL HAVE YOU CHOSEN FOR THE DELIVERY?
NO WAY! THIS BABY IS BEING BORN IN THE SAME PLACE SHE WAS CONCEIVED!!
OH, HOW "EARTHY!"
...IN A HAMMOCK IN THE BACKYARD AFTER A 6-PACK

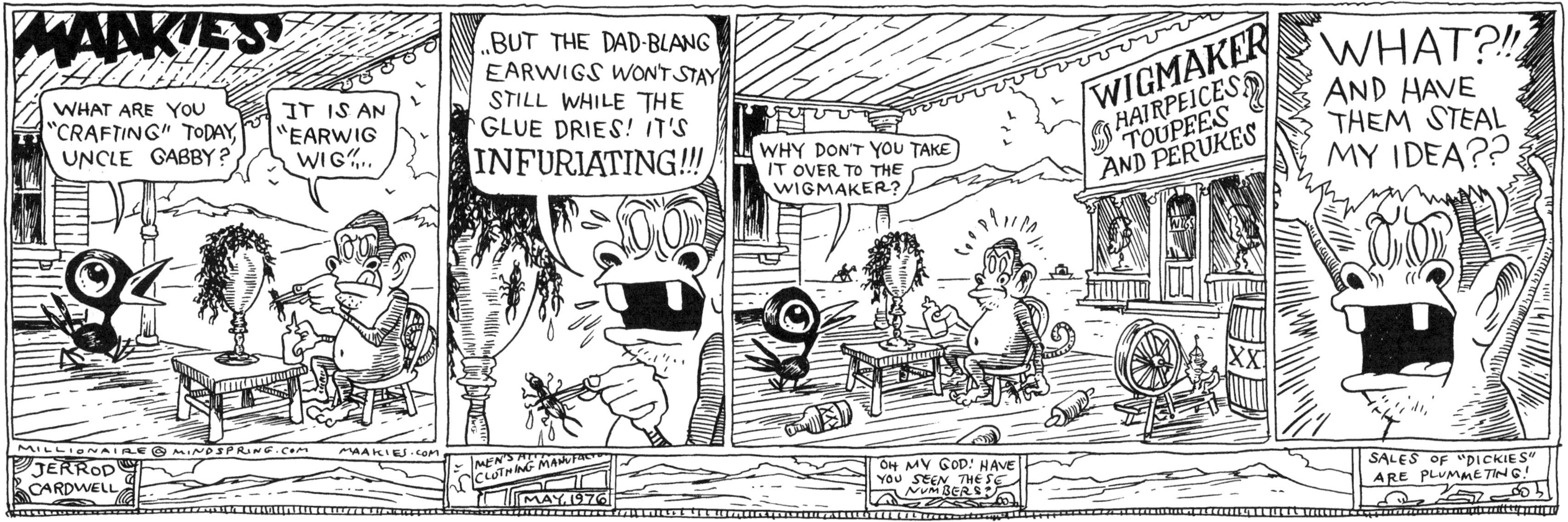
MAAKIES
WHAT ARE YOU "CRAFTING" TODAY, UNCLE GABBY?
IT IS AN "EARWIG WIG"!...
...BUT THE DAD-BLANG EARWIGS WON'T STAY STILL WHILE THE GLUE DRIES! IT'S INFURIATING!!!
WHY DON'T YOU TAKE IT OVER TO THE WIGMAKER?
WIGMAKER
HAIRPEICES TOUPEES AND PERUKES
WIGS
XXX
WHAT?!! AND HAVE THEM STEAL MY IDEA??
MILLIONAIRE@MINDSPRING.COM
MAAKIES.COM
JERROD CARDWELL
MAY, 1976
OH MY GOD! HAVE YOU SEEN THESE NUMBERS?
SALES OF "DICKIES" ARE PLUMMETING!

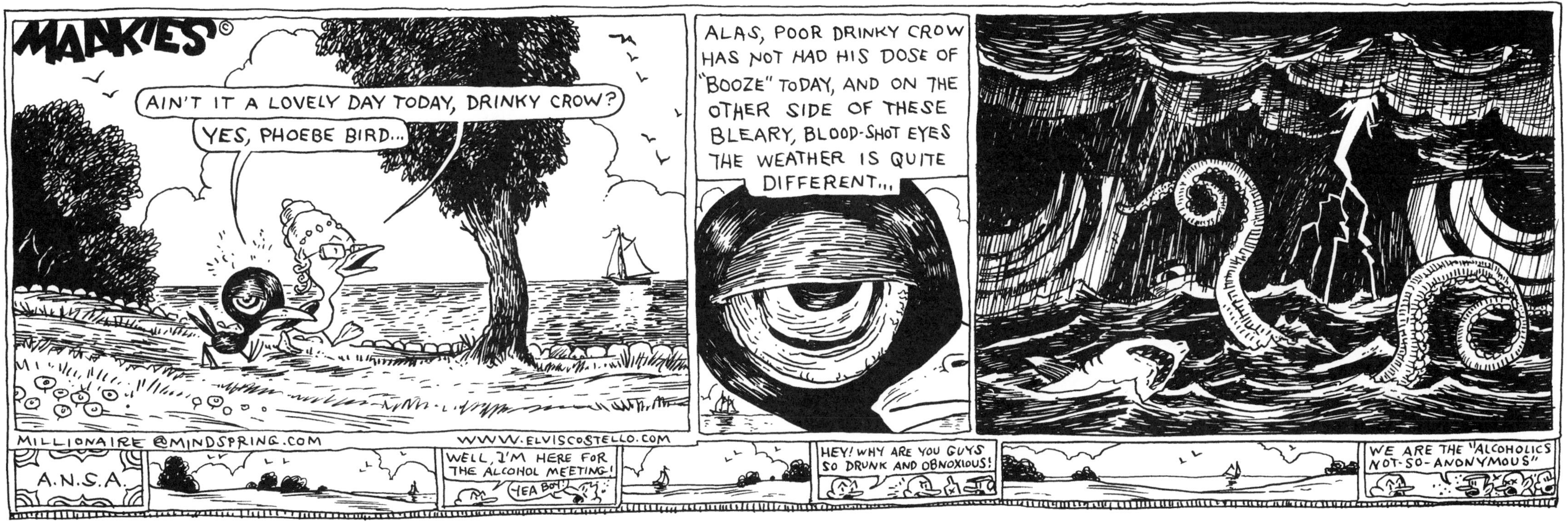
MAAKIES ©
AIN'T IT A LOVELY DAY TODAY, DRINKY CROW?
YES, PHOEBE BIRD...
ALAS, POOR DRINKY CROW HAS NOT HAD HIS DOSE OF "BOOZE" TODAY, AND ON THE OTHER SIDE OF THESE BLEARY, BLOOD-SHOT EYES THE WEATHER IS QUITE DIFFERENT...
MILLIONAIRE @MINDSPRING.COM
WWW.ELVISCOSTELLO.COM
A.N.S.A.
WELL, I'M HERE FOR THE ALCOHOL MEETING!
YEA BOY!
HEY! WHY ARE YOU GUYS SO DRUNK AND OBNOXIOUS!
WE ARE THE "ALCOHOLICS NOT-SO-ANONYMOUS"

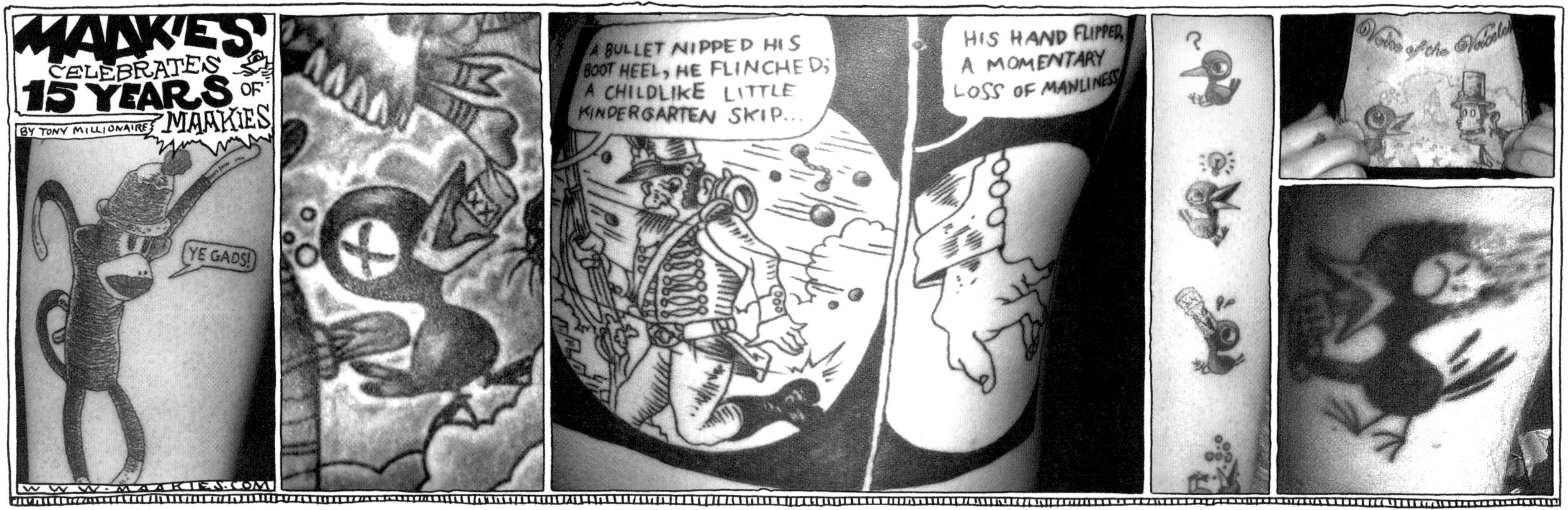
MAAKIES CELEBRATES 15 YEARS OF MAAKIES
BY TONY MILLIONAIRE
YE GADS!
WWW.MAAKIES.COM
A BULLET NIPPED HIS BOOT HEEL, HE FLINCHED; A CHILDLIKE LITTLE KINDERGARTEN SKIP...
HIS HAND FLIPPED, A MOMENTARY LOSS OF MANLINESS
?

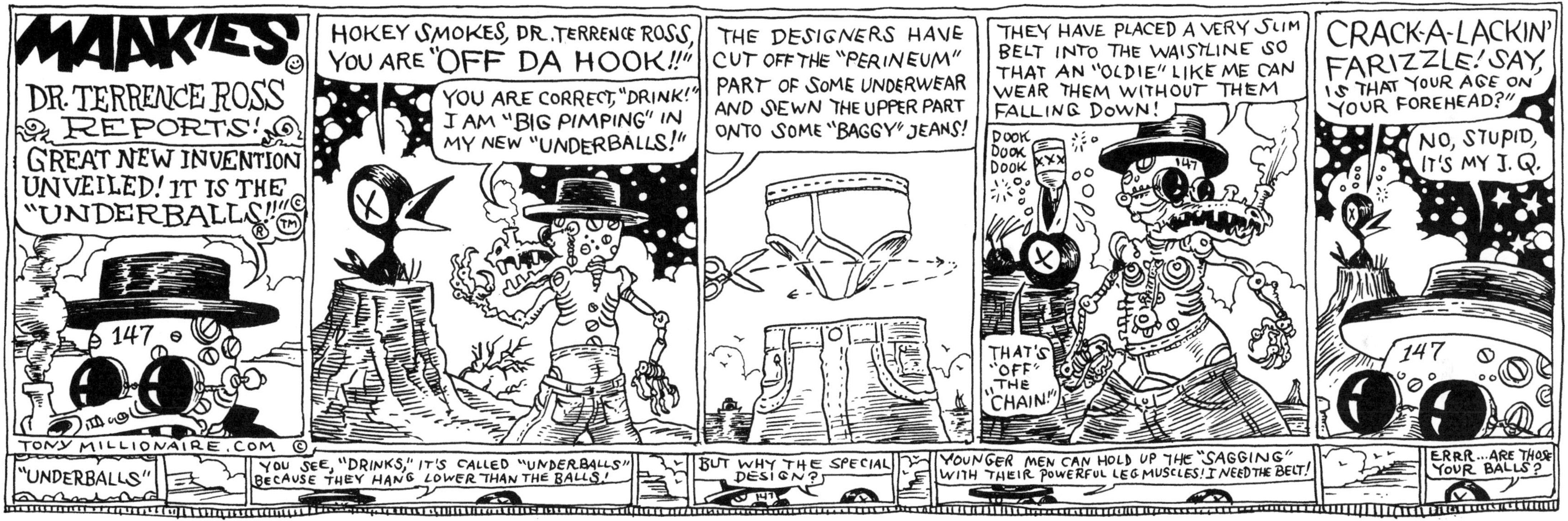
MAAKIES
DR. TERRENCE ROSS REPORTS! GREAT NEW INVENTION UNVEILED! IT IS THE "UNDERBALLS!"
HOKEY SMOKES, DR. TERRENCE ROSS, YOU ARE "OFF DA HOOK!!"
YOU ARE CORRECT, "DRINK!" I AM "BIG PIMPING" IN MY NEW "UNDERBALLS!"
THE DESIGNERS HAVE CUT OFF THE "PERINEUM" PART OF SOME UNDERWEAR AND SEWN THE UPPER PART ONTO SOME "BAGGY" JEANS!
THEY HAVE PLACED A VERY SLIM BELT INTO THE WAISTLINE SO THAT AN "OLDIE" LIKE ME CAN WEAR THEM WITHOUT THEM FALLING DOWN!
DOOK DOOK DOOK
XXX
147
THAT'S "OFF" THE "CHAIN!"
CRACK-A-LACKIN' FARIZZLE! SAY, IS THAT YOUR AGE ON YOUR FOREHEAD?"
NO, STUPID, IT'S MY I. Q.
147
TONY MILLIONAIRE.COM ©
"UNDERBALLS"
YOU SEE, "DRINKS," IT'S CALLED "UNDERBALLS" BECAUSE THEY HANG LOWER THAN THE BALLS!
BUT WHY THE SPECIAL DESIGN?
YOUNGER MEN CAN HOLD UP THE "SAGGING" WITH THEIR POWERFUL LEG MUSCLES! I NEED THE BELT!
ERRR...ARE THOSE YOUR BALLS?

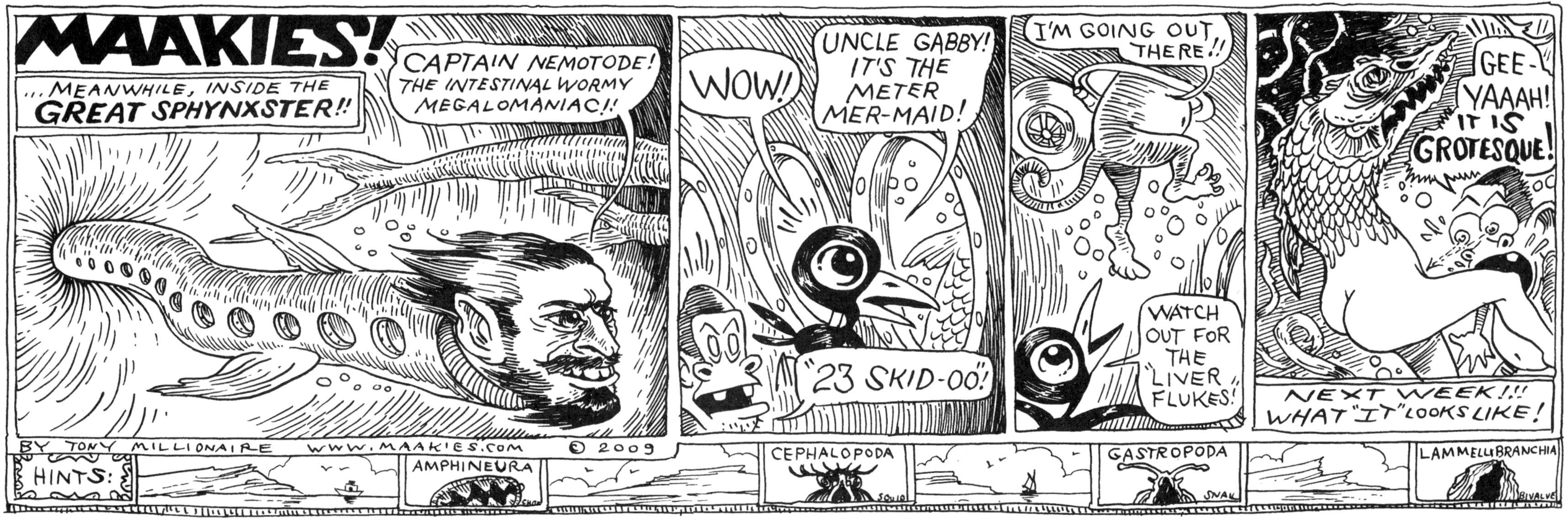
MAAKIES!
...MEANWHILE, INSIDE THE GREAT SPHYNXSTER!!
CAPTAIN NEMOTODE! THE INTESTINAL WORMY MEGALOMANIAC!!
WOW!!
UNCLE GABBY! IT'S THE METER MER-MAID!
"23 SKID-OO"!
I'M GOING OUT THERE!!
WATCH OUT FOR THE "LIVER FLUKES"!
GEE-YAAAH! IT IS GROTESQUE!
NEXT WEEK!!! WHAT "IT" LOOKS LIKE!
BY TONY MILLIONAIRE WWW.MAAKIES.COM © 2009
HINTS:
AMPHINEURA
CEPHALOPODA
SQUID
GASTROPODA
SNAIL
LAMMELLIBRANCHIA
BIVALVE

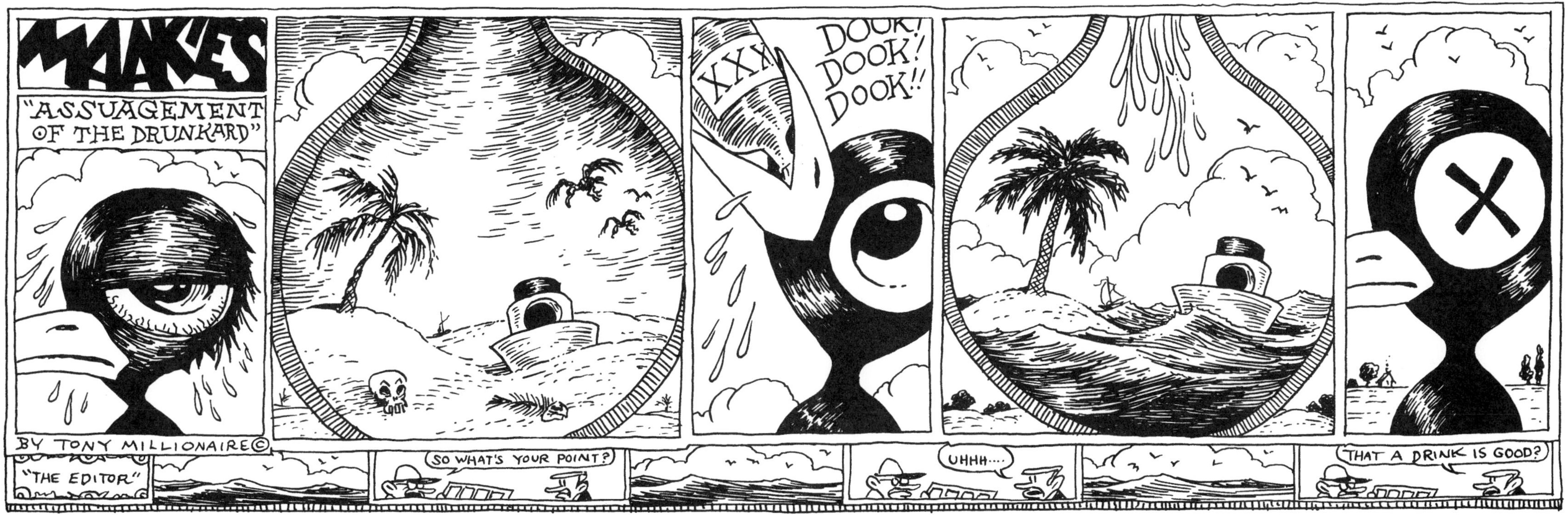
MAAKIES
"ASSUAGEMENT OF THE DRUNKARD"
BY TONY MILLIONAIRE©
XXX
DOOK! DOOK! DOOK!!
"THE EDITOR"
SO WHAT'S YOUR POINT?
UHHH....
THAT A DRINK IS GOOD?

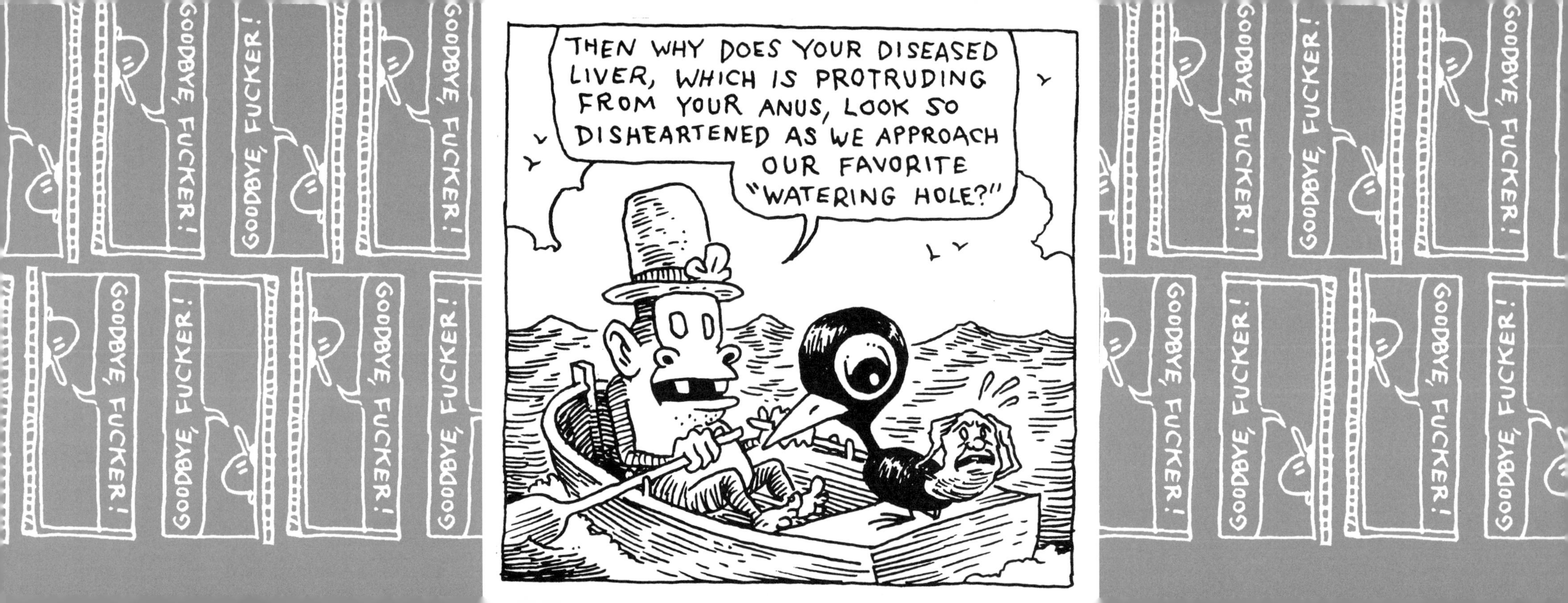
THEN WHY DOES YOUR DISEASED LIVER, WHICH IS PROTRUDING FROM YOUR ANUS, LOOK SO DISHEARTENED AS WE APPROACH OUR FAVORITE "WATERING HOLE?"
GOODBYE, FUCKER!

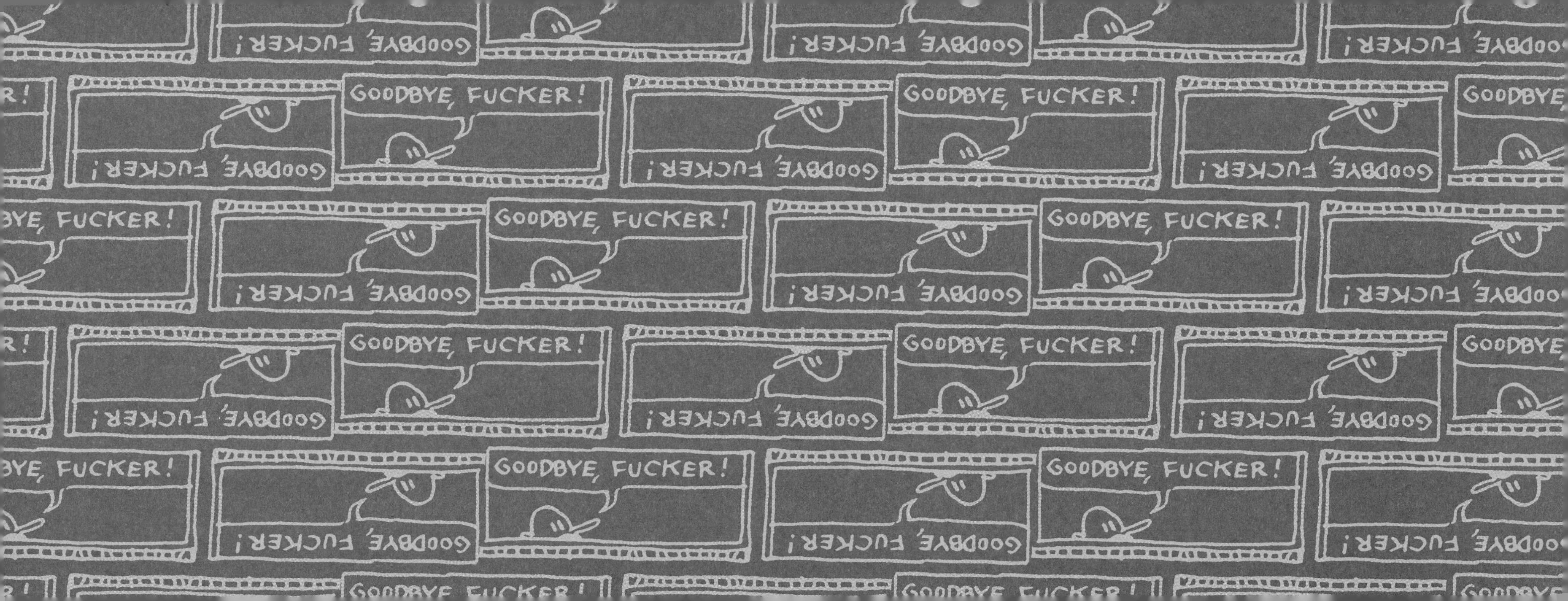
GOODBYE, FUCKER!

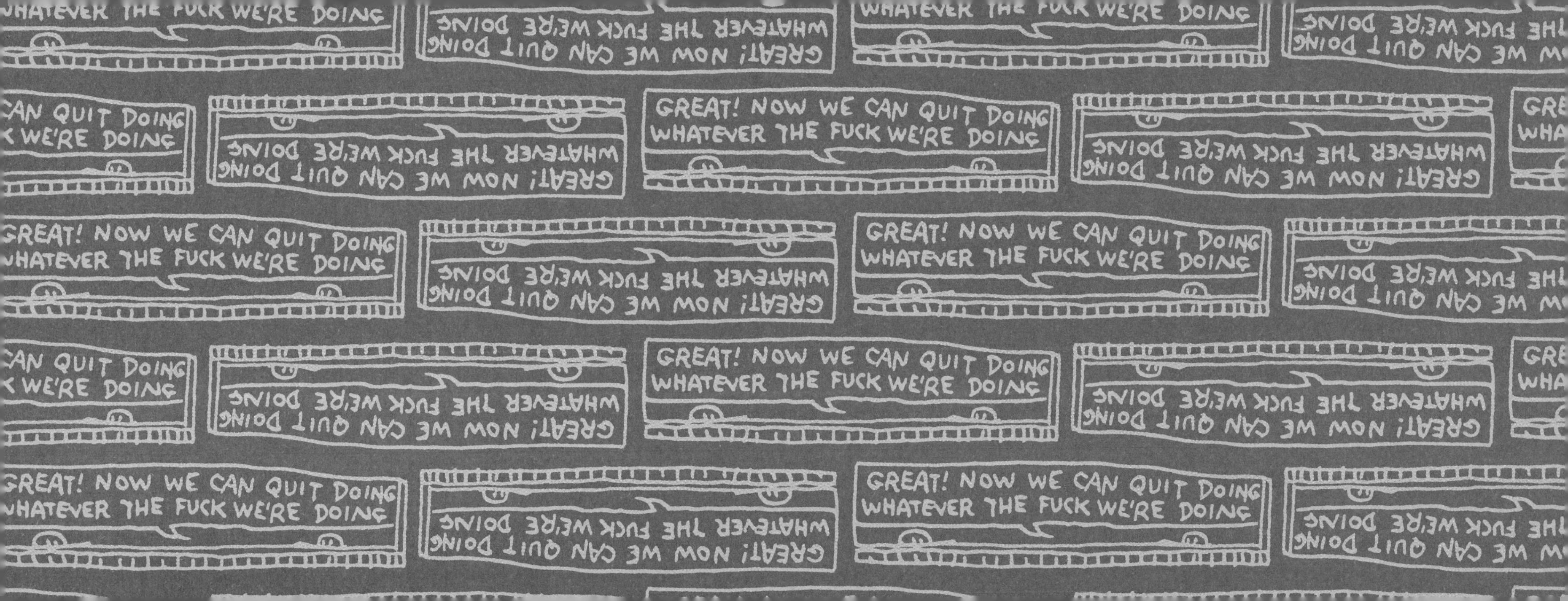
GREAT! NOW WE CAN QUIT DOING WHATEVER THE FUCK WE'RE DOING